Encounters

Encounters

People of Asian Descent in the Americas

edited by
Roshni Rustomji-Kerns

with
Rajini Srikanth
and
Leny Mendoza Strobel

ROWMAN & LITTLEFIELD PUBLISHERS, INC.
Lanham • Boulder • New York • Oxford

ROWMAN & LITTLEFIELD PUBLISHERS, INC.

Published in the United States of America
by Rowman & Littlefield Publishers, Inc.
4720 Boston Way, Lanham, Maryland 20706
http://www.rowmanlittlefield.com

12 Hid's Copse Road
Cumnor Hill, Oxford OX2 9JJ, England

British Library Cataloguing in Publication Information Available

Library of Congress Cataloging-in-Publication Data

Encounters : people of Asian descent in the Americas / edited by
    Roshni Rustomji-Kerns ; with Rajini Srikanth and Leny Mendoza
    Strobel.
        p.   cm.
    Includes bibliographical references.
    ISBN 0-8476-9144-6 (alk. paper). — ISBN 0-8476-9145-4 (pbk. :
alk. paper)
        1. Asians—America—History.   2. Asians—America—Biography.
    3. Asians—America—Race identity.   4. Asian Americans—History.
    5. Asian Americans—Biography.   6. Asian Americans—Race identity.
    7. America—Race relations.   8. United States—Race relations.
    I. Rustomji-Kerns, Roshni.
    E29.06E53   1999
    970'.00495—dc21   99-12191
                                                            CIP

Printed in the United States of America

♾ ™ The paper used in this publication meets the minimum requirements of
American National Standard for Information Sciences—Permanence of Paper for
Printed Library Materials, ANSI Z39.48-1992.

This book is dedicated to

Meera-Catarina de San Juan—India/New Spain (1612–1688)
in gratitude for her courage and her visions

Isabel Gruen de Gual (1969–1998)
in gratitude for her life and her passion for knowledge and justice

and

Casa Bolivar at Stanford University,
where Asia and the Americas continue to meet

Contents

**Part III   Volcán de Izalco, amén—Locating the Body
and the Land**

Foreword

Karen Tei Yamashita

Many years ago when I had to step out to introduce my first novel to the public, I pondered the question I had often seen my more fashion-sophisticated sister ask the mirror: *Is this the look we want to achieve?* What could this mean? It couldn't be answered by my old sewing classes—long lines to effect a slimmer look, horizontal for fullness, darker shades in the fall and winter. There wasn't an answer in *Vogue*. A hairdresser couldn't fix my wild hair. No Shiseido for me; I had abandoned any makeup years before. If readers got a peek at the author behind my work, who would they see? What did my work say about me, and who had I become in the process of writing it?

Sansei was born in California, raised in Los Angeles, educated in Minnesota and Japan, married and had children in Brazil, then immigrated back into the United States and worked in L.A. I had always traveled light, but what I accumulated along the way was significant—local vernaculars and languages, cultural habits, tastes and sensibilities, multiple identities, two kids and a spouse, memories. Things got left behind, shed in many temporary homes across the world. Friends and relatives, social contexts, too, got left behind. For everything left behind, I had accumulated both longing and forgetfulness. How could I wear all these significant trappings from my travels? Drape them over my shoulders? Paint them into my face? Sprinkle their jeweled blessings over my hair? And if I could, would this then be the look I wanted to achieve? I looked in the mirror again. Frankly, I looked naked, even if I could announce the fact in several different languages. Sou pelada. Hadaka da.

I went shopping. Certainly I should be able to buy the look. But what was I looking for? And would I recognize it when I saw it? I thought: distinctive but not snobby, artistic but not artsy fartsy, creative but not cute, unusual but not weird, professional but not bureaucratic, ethnic but not faux or popularly ethnic, alas me! In this sense, shopping was a little like creating an extraterrestrial being. Even if you could imagine it—the look or the extraterrestrial, it would be a re-creation from your experience. Even if the designers had thought of everything, the dress would probably accommodate two arms and one neck, and the alien would probably have one or several eyes. How to clothe me so that the inside and the outside were the same thing. What a ridiculous project! Like clothing an amorphous thing, a monster. Victoria's Secret. Eddie Bauer. Nike. Jessica McClintok. Lands' End. The Gap. The Banana Republic. Guess. Guess who *this* is?

I found some pants. I fell in love with them immediately, if you can fall in love with pants. They were made of hand-woven Indonesian ikat and designed by a Dutch Indonesian woman after the diaper pants of the Buddhist monks. I found them in a boutique in the South Bay Galeria in Redondo Beach. This shop closed its doors a few months after I made my purchase, and when I later inquired about this, I discovered its sister boutique was located on Rodeo Drive. The South Bay must have been too prosaic a place for such offering. Here I had found the character of my look, albeit only the bottom half, and it was housed and appropriated in the most exclusive and expensive sector of Hollywood fashion. What did I expect? After that, even MC Hammer was using my pants. Did Hammer know the reason for the pants? The monks have worn them because it is said the next Buddha will be born to a man; the pants were designed to catch and cradle the baby Buddha. I've been telling my son who sports the oversized pants look that there's a reason, and he should check down there for the Buddha from time to time. Lately, it seems the Buddha could arrive at any moment in places as likely as The Queens, Compton, Magic Mountain, Tokyo, Paris, Rio, or at a South Asian American bhangra techno rap party in New York.

The knees of my pants are fraying in places, but it's always been like that— hand-woven ikat with perceivable fallacies. The weaver made it that way, wove mistakes into the thick cotton thread to dance in archaic patterns, shifting triangles and stripes in shades of browns over black, casting subtle and occasional strands of blue and gold. In her introduction, Roshni Rustomji-Kerns has mentioned other names of woven fabric. Dhoop-chaun. Shot fabric. Tornasolada. Iridescent threads highlighting patterns of bright sunlight and deep shade. To explain the meaning of this project—this book of *Encounters*—Roshni uses the metaphor of fabric and imagines the weave of narratives and concepts, changing patterns, fraying over time, a dynamic movement of overlapping stories, threads encountering and re-encountering. This weaving of encounters of Asians across the Americas throws its fabric over the geography of the broad hemisphere. The warp and woof of diverse narrative genres and visual presentations blur our old ideas of borders as we follow the threads that travel in patterns of diaspora, crisscrossing continents, nations, and cultures in unexpected ways.

With its hand-woven mistakes and its dubious appropriations through Hollywood and the garment industry, this is not a perfect, slick, or neat kind of project. It's rough in places because it is trying to break through, to introduce new voices and to let those voices speak for themselves. But also, like my pants that after all fit my body, clothe my multiple identities, and somehow achieve my *look*, here is a project that gives expression to and represents individuals and communities of Asian descent whose stories are often culturally slippery and complex, overlap, double up, defy, and skirt the old stories as we've known them. In these stories, we travel through the Americas—sometimes defined as nation states such as Canada, Cuba, Bolivia, Brazil, Mexico, Peru, or the United States, but also as geographic regions such as the Caribbean or the American South, urban centers like New York or Mexico City and their ghettoized sites of Chinatowns, and as territorial or imperial constructs such as Hawaii or Puerto Rico. And as we travel, we see these places through the eyes and perceptions and memories of those who claim Asian identities most often in concert with multiple identities. Many of these stories, new to us, have been around a long time, at least several generations; it's time to see the larger world, certainly the rest of the hemisphere. While this project can be the site for theoretical discussions over a variety of issues—diaspora, globalization, postcolonialism, transnationalism—it is also a site for expressions of the everyday. Here then in the pages that follow is the extended fabric of our connecting lives across nations, cultures, and histories, clothing the beds where we dream and make love, the tables where we eat, our bodies as we present ourselves—unfurling passion, shrouding grief, exposing failure, cradling hope—and finally, perhaps, encountering the look we want to achieve.

AUTHOR BIOGRAPHY

Karen Tei Yamashita is a Japanese American writer from California. She lived for nine years in Brazil, the setting for the first two of her novels: *Through the Arc of the Rain Forest,* awarded the 1991 American Book Award and the 1992 Janet Heidinger Kafka Award; and *Brazil-Maru,* named by the *Village Voice* as one of the 25 best books of 1992. A third novel, *Tropic of Orange,* set in Los Angeles and a finalist for the Paterson Fiction Prize, was published in 1997 by Coffee House Press. Currently she teaches creative writing and literature at the University of California at Santa Cruz.

Preface

When Susan McEachern extended her generous invitation to me to submit a proposal for an anthology on any aspect of Asian diasporas, I offered to edit an anthology of works by and about people of Asian descent in the Americas. The selection of the geopolitical area—the Americas—was based on the realization that the existing materials, as well as the scholarship and theoretical frameworks, in the field of Asian American (U.S.) studies have proved inadequate for many of us who are interested in the history of Asia throughout the Americas. The choice was also based on discussions with scholars who study the histories and the geography of Asia in the Americas, on my own research on the history of people from India in Mexico, and on my work with the collection of essays (mainly historical) in *Asiatic Migrations in Latin America* edited by Luz M. Martínez Montiel (1981). The focus of this anthology, the encounters of people of Asian descent with people from other "nondominant" political, economic, and social groups, was selected to explore this issue as it arises in our lives as people of Asian descent constructing and reconstructing our landscapes of space and time in the Americas.

As Rajini Srikanth, Leny Mendoza Strobel, the other members of the contributing editorial board, Susan McEachern, and I worked on this anthology, we knew that we needed to be constantly aware of our own points of view, the terminology, and the different definitions of that terminology we brought to this project. We tried as far as possible not to force our evaluations and selections of the submissions into a pattern set solely by our own work within our academic disciplines of Asian American and transnational studies where America has come to stand only for the United States of America and sometimes includes Canada.[1] We attempted to look at the submissions without trying to fit them into any preconceived theoretical paradigm because we did not wish to present a homogeneous anthology. Such an anthology could have been more accessible for academic discussions and categorization and would have been easier for the organization of the selected works but it would not have reflected the complexities and diversities of the Asian experience in the Americas. We hope our refusal (whenever possible) to use *Asian American* as a generic term for people of Asian descent in the Americas, our decision to include as wide and as disparate a range of voices and experiences as possible, our search for as wide and as disparate a range of genres as possible to present those voices, and our willingness to move away from any rigid definition of nondominant reflect and address the concerns voiced in the conclusion of an essay by the Chinese Caribbeanist scholar, Walton Look Lai.

> There is a new academic tendency in North America which would create a group heading such as "Asian American," and attribute a kind of Hemispheric social identity to these immigrant communities. But the recognition of such an all-embracing Hemispheric consciousness at this point would seem to be more useful as an intellectual notion, rather than as an experienced reality.[2]

When the initial proposal for this anthology was circulated, some of the responses we received pointed out that the anthology would be "chaotic" and "unwieldy." We were told that the works we had selected were too disparate, the genres we were planning to include too wide-ranging and the geographical area we were covering too extensive. Taking for granted that the presence of people from Asia living in the geographical extensions of the Americas was the main reason for this anthology, the disparity of works and genres was deliberate. *Encounters: People of Asian Descent in the Americas* is in many ways a rough-hewn collection. It reflects as much as possible—within the limitation of space and the availability of works—the diversity of the people from Asia who live in the Americas, the diversity of their experiences with other nondominant groups in the Americas, and the diversity of the forms they have selected to express those experiences.

One question asked at the beginning of this project was, Why bring together this complex of diversities—of both Asia and the Americas—into one volume? One answer would point out the political and economic histories many of us as people of Asian descent across much of the Americas share. Another would point out the long and continuing history of our presence in the Americas—starting from the time of the *Manila Galleon* and the other trading ships of the fifteenth and sixteenth centuries and perhaps earlier.[3] Another would discuss the role Asia has played through our presence in the Americas in both the abstract and the tangible construction of what we consider the Americas. Another would try to trace the similarities and lack of similarities in our experiences in the Americas. But to discuss what Wally Look Lai calls "an Hemispheric consciousness . . . as an intellectual notion" and to go beyond this consciousness to what he speaks of as "an experienced reality" one would first need to explore certain questions. These questions include how different people from Asia in the different areas of the Americas (from different classes, genders, generations, length of residence in the Americas, place of birth, and similar factors) define Asia for themselves and for the communities they live in, and how they describe their connections or lack of connections to Asia and recognize their own roles and the role of Asia in the Americas, especially in relation to the roles of others whose participation in the settling or the unsettling of the Americas has been barely acknowledged, denied, relegated to obscurity or denigrated. The answers to these questions will be immensely diverse, but having asked them and received some answers one could try to find patterns of concepts about Asia and Asian Americas that would arise out of the voices and experiences of people from Asia in the Americas. Instead of explicitly asking all of these questions, *Encounters: People of Asian Descent in the Americas* tries to introduce some of these questions by exploring our experiences as people of Asian descent living within the different worlds that make up the Americas.

Roshni Rustomji-Kerns

NOTES

1. We understand the historical and political context of the United States of America within which the term Asian American was used by students in the 1960s and the irony (it is hoped acknowledged in hindsight) of their appropriating the hegemonic use of America. The appropriation barely allowed any recognition of the lives and voices of Asian peoples north, east, or south of the U.S. political borders as also voices of the Americas. Furthermore, as we looked at the submissions from Hawaii, Rajini Srikanth and I were aware that many Hawaiians would not include Hawaii in either the United States or the Americas. We have included works from Hawaii because we feel that the history of Asia in the larger area of the Americas and the Pacific Islands and the focus of this anthology are reflected very strongly in the histories and literatures of Hawaii, especially as they challenge the idea of a homogeneous historical or geographical "America."

2. Walton Look Lai, "Chinese Migration to Latin America and the Caribbean: A Historical Overview" (unpublished paper). See also Wally Look Lai, *Indentured Labor, Caribbean Sugar: Chinese and Indian Migrants to the British West Indies 1838–1918*. (Johns Hopkins University Press, 1993).

3. A number of essays in *México-India: Similitudes y Encuentros a travéz de la Historia*, Eva Alexandra Uchmany ed. (México: ISPAT Mexicana, 1998) discuss the (difficult to prove) possibilities as well as the known histories of the early contacts between Asia and New Spain.

Acknowledgments

This anthology would not have been possible without the support and help of people and institutions across the Americas. I wish to acknowledge with gratitude:

Leny Mendoza Strobel and Rajini Srikanth who worked with me and supported me throughout this project.

The contributing editors who read, evaluated, and helped to select the works included in this anthology: Federico Besserer, Lok C. D. Siu, Rajini Srikanth, Leny Mendoza Strobel, Jeff Tagami, Usha Welaratna, and Karen Yamashita.

Leny Mendoza Strobel, Rajini Srikanth, Lok C. D. Siu, Stephanie Li, and Victoria Bomberry for reading and rereading numerous drafts of the Introduction and for their suggestions; Victoria Bomberry for hours of discussion and debate on critical theories and terminology in the context of the histories and literatures of Indigenous people of the Americas; Ambassador Graciela de la Lama, Professors Maria Elena Ota Mishima, Alfredo Romero and other members of the Department of African and Asian Studies, Colegío de México for their support for this project and their invaluable work on Asians in Latin America.

Isabel Duque-Saberi for her constant help and her pioneering work on the history of people from India in Mexico.

The Center for Latin American Studies (Bolivar House) at Stanford University for believing in this project, for appointing me a visiting scholar, giving me an office and most of all for inspiring me to offer a series of lectures and classes on various aspects of the history, roles, and experiences of people of Asian descent in the Americas. Special thanks to Associate Director Kathleen Morrison, Administrative Assistant Beth Frankland, Professor Fajardo, Visiting Scholar Brasilio Sallum, and my students and assistants Jane Cho, Stephanie Li, Karen Serwer, and Evelyn Castaneda.

Susan McEachern, senior editor, Rowman and Littlefield, who initiated this anthology and without whose constant and generous support this complicated project would not have been completed.

And as always, my gratitude to Charles Kerns who cheered me on when I believed in this project, who assured me that the anthology was important when I decided that it was an impossible project, and who performed mystical, magical feats to keep various computer programs running.

Introduction

Roshni Rustomji-Kerns

The majority of the works in *Encounters: People of Asian Descent in the Americas* are set in the twentieth century. Historical facts and issues are discussed in some of the works, but they are not central to the anthology. Although until recently most of our attempts to describe and analyze our histories in the Americas have focused mainly on our encounters with the dominant economic and political groups in this hemisphere, these attempts have not always reflected the reality of our experiences in the Americas where we live our lives in the context of multiple societies and communities. The framing narrative of this anthology is based on encounters in the Americas between people of Asian descent and people from other nondominant groups. The different definitions of what constitutes a nondominant group take on complex forms as societies change; groups merge or diverge; borders are crossed, recrossed, constructed, or erased; and the centers of power and control shift. This, in turn, complicates most existing theoretical paradigms and frameworks that deal with relationships among different ethnic-cultural-racial-economic groups.

This became clear from the works submitted for this anthology. For example, in Kozy Amemiya's essay, the Okinawan protagonist makes a definite distinction between his encounters with the Bolivians who work with or for him on the land and who lack political dominance (like the immigrants from Asia) and the urbanized, politically powered Bolivians. Furthermore, this collaboration for justice in Bolivia involves two groups of people from Japan—the early immigrants from Okinawa (not recognized as Japanese citizens until recently) and later immigrants from other parts of Japan. When asked about her experiences with other nondominant groups in Mexico, Monica Cinco Basurto, who identifies herself as a Mexican of Chinese descent, writes about being ostracized by some of the Chinese people who have recently migrated to Mexico (with the help of her father) because her mother and paternal

1

grandmother are Mexican. Himani Bannerji expresses outrage and sorrow at
the violence hurled against "minorities" in her poem, "Paki Go Home" by
portraying the physical and verbal violence a South Asian woman experiences
on a street in Canada. Muriel Hasbun from El Salvador explores the history
of her family of displaced Palestinians and displaced European Jews through
her photographs. Lok C. D. Siu, a Chinese American is forced to take refuge
in reluctantly but loudly yelling "yo soy gringa" when faced with a traffic
policeman's harassment in Panama. Kathryne Jeun Cho's father, who is from
Korea, was respected when he appeared in his dentist's coat in Brazil, but in
the United States of America he is regarded as a janitor going to work in his
white coat. Phuri Sherpa from Nepal, married to an Anglo-American woman
and working with Mexican and Mexican American men, speaks of the work
ethic of nondominant groups while he shares the process of learning both
English and Spanish with his young son in a small town in northern California. Rienzi Crusz, a Sri Lankan who immigrated to Canada, addresses the
focus of this anthology through poems on the people and landscape of the
Caribbean.

In her essay, "Lebanese Immigration to Mexico," Luz María Martínez
Montiel writes, "Many itinerant [Lebanese] merchants [in Mexico] learned
Indian languages first because before settling down in a big city, they trav-
elled throughout regions with large indigenous populations."[1] Federico Besserer, an anthropologist who does fieldwork in Oaxaca told me about a Zapo-
tec elder's encounter with an Indian—or at least the idea of an Indian—from
India in the old Mexican comic books and radio series, *Kaliman*. The elder
was quite impressed by the marvelous feats of this hero from Asia (who has
blue eyes because his father was from Europe!) in Mexico. "But tell me," he
said to Federico Besserer, "even this man from so far away as India walks our
land as a God. When will it be our turn to walk as Gods on this land?" In
Milton Hatoum's novel, *The Tree of the Seventh Heaven*, the disputes between
a Lebanese Christian wife and her Lebanese Muslim husband in a remote
village in Brazil are observed and sometimes commented on by their Brazilian maid who acts as a link between the members of the family.

Scholarly works such as In-Jin Yoon's *On My Own: Korean Businesses and
Race Relations in America* describe and analyze encounters between Asians and
people from other nondominant political groups in the United States of
America. In-Jin Yoon points out correctly that "despite the growing importance of relations between minority groups . . . theories and empirical research on this subject are still scarce. Conventional theories have limitations
in explaining such relations because they tend to focus on the majority-mi-
nority relations, particularly those between whites and blacks."[2] Karen Isaksen Leonard's *Making Ethnic Choices: California's Punjabi Mexican Americans*
(1992) and the "no passing zone" 1997 special issue of the *Amerasia Journal*
(vol. 23, no. 1), also explore the area of cross-cultural and interethnic rela-

tionships between people of Asian descent and other communities in the Americas. Steven Masami Ropp's graduate work at the University of California, Los Angeles (unpublished) is based on interviews with high school students of Asian descent from Latin America now living in the multiethnic city of Los Angeles.

Current discussions of Asian histories and experiences in the Americas as they revolve around conceptual theories such as diaspora studies, globalization, the Pacific Rim, postcolonialism, postmodernism, and transnationalism remain incomplete without the presence of the larger—and definitely more complex—picture of people of Asian descent throughout the Americas regardless of their similarities and lack of similarities, connections and lack of connections. And they remain incomplete when based only on selected concepts that have been accepted as worthy of discussion by us as scholars while other concepts (usually non-European or non-Euro-United Statesian in origin) are rejected because of disinterest or ignorance. The works in this anthology are not presented within any specific frameworks of discourse on diasporas, immigrations, identity formations, or multiculturalism. Instead of constructing yet another codified, theoretical paradigm, we found ourselves formulating questions about existing paradigms. We realized that in many ways this is an introductory anthology. It introduces primary materials for further investigation in the field of Asian American studies and for conceptualizations and dissemination of scholarly theories within the field. By not selecting to present the works in a recognizable or an explicit contemporary academic theoretical framework; by raising questions regarding the probabilities or the difficulties of using different theories; by crossing disciplinary, geographical, and historical boundaries; and by including different genres of narrative, the anthology itself (as well as many of the people portrayed in it), is on precarious ground. Instead of a hypothetical cutting edge, some of us find ourselves more on the cut and raw edge of explorations in the field of Asia in the Americas. To extend Gloria Anzaldúa's phrase, we are faced with "una heria abierta." Where the reality of our lives and their absence in academic explorations of Asian Americas collide, there is an open wound that needs to be acknowledged, discussed, and—one hopes—healed.

This does not mean that the works in this volume—separately or as a collection—cannot be discussed within existing frameworks of academic theories and terminologies, but it does mean that none of the theories as traditionally expressed feel adequate or comfortable for an extensive discussion of our experiences as people from Asia in the Americas. For example, for the purposes of an anthology such as this, discussions of postcoloniality and transnationalism demand knowledge of the different types, patterns, and linguistic constructs of colonialisms and of the histories, time frames, and constant metamorphoses of internal and external colonialism in the different areas of Asia and the Americas. Where, for example, do the experiences, stories, art, and primary voices of the Chinese in Mexico deported to China at the beginning of the twentieth century and later (some of them) allowed to return to Mexico or those of the people of Japanese descent from Peru interned in the United States for "illegal entry" during World War II and then forced to go to Japan or those of Phuri Sherpa from Nepal working in a restaurant owned by a Greek family fit historically into the contemporary debates on postcolonialism and postmodernism that use mainly European and Euro-United Statesian philosophical, political, and psychological concepts? And how do the contexts of economic class, the importance or lack thereof of religious beliefs and practices—public and private, and the different configurations of ethnicities, races, languages, and art as lived by individuals from Asia in the different areas of the Americas from post-Colombian times to the present fit into scholarly explorations of diasporas and migrations without being treated as a passive historical backdrop for contemporary "Asian American" studies?

Interestingly, anthologies such as this one also bring up issues about the geography and the concept of "Asia." These issues are usually ignored or barely addressed until questions are raised regarding the selection of works that will represent Asia or people from Asia in any given project. The diversity of Asia and of the people of Asia is stressed in these instances and we have attempted to do the same through our selections. But in our discussions of diversity and who from Asia? where from Asia? and when from Asia? we tend to forget or to underestimate the importance of the constant attempts at "reforming" Asia as a historical and a geopolitical construct in many parts of the Americas—specifically the United States of America. Asia in the Americas (and in other parts of the world, including within Asia itself) has been and continues to be defined and described according to the external and internal cultural-economic-political agendas of the dominant econo-political powers. And very often, many people of Asian descent in the Americas take these politically manipulated ideas of Asia as the definitive (if fluid) perimeters of Asia in their discussions of what is Asia or who is Asian. The situation becomes even more difficult when the complicated geographical, historical, and cultural concepts and realities of Asia are extended into the diverse areas of the Americas. One notes that this difficulty seldom arises in discussions about Europe—also a diverse and complicated concept and reality—in the Americas.

An anthology such as this may benefit most from a framework that not only challenges and expands the current theoretical paradigms and terminology but that also tries to look at the works in this collection through the eyes and the voices, the important images and symbols of the people of Asian descent portrayed here. In "The Fiction of Asian American Literature,"[3] Susan Koshy states that a "theoretical weakness" exists in the field of Asian American Literature Studies. She sees a need to "generate new conceptual frames that work in the interests of social change." She is also aware of the "risk of unwittingly annexing newer literary productions within older paradigms . . . [that may perpetuate] hierarchies within the field." Susan Koshy's comments are made within the field of Asian United States of American literature and literary theories, but they also reflect many of the concerns that arise when we face the interdisciplinary and complex field of studies in Asian Americas. To try to answer her challenge, I suggest that instead of arguing over "newer" or "older" paradigms we begin to carefully explore and actively include relevant images and language from the analytical traditions from Asia, Asian Americas, and other nondominant cultural and political groups in the Americas in the paradigms we create or recreate in studying Asian Americas.[4] I suggest this not through any romantic notion of the past or of root cultures—in time or place—or of what should be considered "authentic," "non-Orientalizing" ideas about Asia and Asians (in Asia or in the Americas). I suggest this through a need to include and hear ideas and theories that are not firmly entrenched in or dependent on European and Euro-United Statesian scholarship but are a vital part of many of our lives as Asians in the Americas. This process would reflect the experiences of much of our public and private lives in the Americas as people of Asian descent living in societies that may claim to be dominated by European ideas and traditions but that in reality have a much more complex texture of cultures. For example, how does one conceptualize being Asian in terms of religious and philosophical belief systems in a Latin American country if one's family publicly participates in the rituals of the Catholic Church (including baptizing all family members as Catholics and giving names that are considered Christian or western) but at home follows the rituals and tenets of Buddhism the family had practiced in Asia?

The changing codes of behavior that define or describe one's constant movement from being Okinawan, Bolivian, or Okinawan Bolivian are questioned in Kozy Amemiya's essay by the father from Okinawa speaking of his son who grew up in Bolivia. Women and men from South Asia in the United States will often speak of their public personae as defined by the "American" clothes they wear and the American English they speak when they leave their homes to participate in "American" life. When they return home or participate in South Asian activities they change into clothes they consider their own, such as saris or kurtas or dhotis and speak their mother language, another South Asian language, or English with a South Asian voice and terminology shared within the particular South Asian group. But when Tomoyo Hiroishi, who grew up Japanese in Mexico, came to the United States, she realized that Mexico was really her home and painted a portrait of herself dressed in the clothes of an indigenous woman from Mexico. The complex of cultures—private, public, academically acknowledged or ignored—brought from Asia and then stressed, manipulated, or denied as part of our texts as people from Asia in the Americas informs the way we perceive ourselves and our cultures of mono, dual, or multiple homes. The complex language of these cultures needs to be included in our academic theorizing to a much greater extent as we describe and analyze our lives in the Americas.

The concept of a palimpsest has been suggested as an image for this anthology.[5] The multiplicity and diversity of voices, the presence of different histories, and the range of definitions of nondominant could be set within the pattern of a palimpsest. But a palimpsest is also a paradigm of domination that works on erasures, and the process of layering. The erasures and layerings can set up hierarchies of voices and experiences that would defeat the purpose of this anthology. Instead of a palimpsest, I suggest a different process and imagery, a metaphor borrowed from the kind of weaving that produces a fabric known in South Asia as dhoop-chaun,—the combination of bright sunlight and deep shade—in English termed as "shot" fabric and in Spanish as tornasolada. It is an iridescent fabric (often silk) of changeable and variegated colors because of the different colored warp and weft used in the weaving. Different colors come into prominence according to the way light falls on the fabric and the way it is moved for different viewings of it.

A weaving of different and disparate narratives and theories into a larger fabric that would allow a number of theoretical frameworks and languages to explore rather than erase one another (for some notion of academic dominance and legitimacy), an attempt to find and include concepts from the traditions of analyses in Asia and Asian Americas would reflect the complexities and complications behind the realities of our lives in the Americas. The process of selection would still exist, but whatever is selected and the languages used for the discussion would inform one another—possibly even stand out against one another—without erasing or dominating. The result may lead us to the different views on Asia and on being Asian in the Americas presented by different generations of immigrants, exiles, and residents and it may even allow us to experience individual works of literature and art as creations of the writer's or artist's personal, unique vision rather than as "factual" social documentaries for entire communities. The realization that we needed to expand our definition of nondominant for this anthology and include a range of voices and genres without emphasizing one kind of encounter or voice over another could be seen as our attempt to work within this idea of a fabric of interwoven narratives and concepts.

The works presented in this anthology may be from "nondominant" groups, but they are not voiced from marginal or from helplessly in limbo, hyphenated spaces. Trinh T. Minh-ha's perceptive statement that to use "marginality as a starting point rather than an ending point is also to cross beyond it towards other affirmations and negations"[6] echoes the point of view (explicitly or implicitly) of most of the works in this anthology. It is the centrality of the experiences that stands out. Margins and centers depend on where one stands and from where one decides to view oneself. Histories and experiences that may be perceived as on the margins of a larger society are central to the lives of the people involved with the encounters and to the societies and communities—politically, economically, socially empowered or not—within which they take place. And they challenge the conflation of race, ethnicity, and nation in which, for example, people of Asian descent in the Americas are seen as always being (or often forced into becoming) distinct and separate from their place in Asia, denying their constantly shifting roles in the histories and cultures of both Asia and the Americas. Rey Chow's discussion of borders, intellectual issues, and the creation of new fields of study and her conclusion that "we think *primarily* in terms of borders—as *para-sites* that never take over a field in its entirety but erode it slowly and *tactically* "[7] can refer not only to a project such as this anthology but to the issue of centrality of the voices of people of Asian descent and their experiences. The experiences and voices in this anthology are an intrinsic part of the structure of overlapping and flexible centers around which cultures, societies, economics, and politics revolve in the Americas.

Although questions regarding migrations, diasporas and exiles—multiple or otherwise—do emerge in some of the works in this anthology, they are not the main concerns presented in the narratives. The main concerns involve the negotiating and renegotiating of relationships, spaces, and places.[8] These concerns are presented within the context of the affirmation of assigned identities, the re-fusing of identities, and the formation of roles and spaces in the everyday business of homemaking in the Americas. The stories, poetry, artworks, and scholarly essays in this anthology can also be seen as constituting a dialogue—or at least a possible starting point for such a dialogue—between people of Asian descent in the Americas. And as with all narratives, factual or fictionalized, it is the locations in time and space—be they physical, abstract, or conceptualized—of these experiences which form the sites for the action and the amplification of the encounters, the collaborations, and the conflicts.

The anthology is not organized according to the larger and more specific geographic locations in Asia and America; it is organized instead by the public and private (separate or overlapping) theaters, the more general, the imagined, or the everyday familiar sites in which these encounters take place. The multiple, often fluid and overlapping locations that appear in these works involve families, communities, countries, and the imagination. The constant and complicated structuring of identities and relationships—assigned, declined, selected, asserted, public, private—reflects the locations—homes, schools, workplaces, streets, shops, vacation places, political headquarters, parties, the mind, or the heart—where the encounters are played out. And in the end, as in Part III of this volume, these encounters and their sites are recreated in the landscapes of art and sometimes even onto the physical bodies of the protagonists themselves.

NOTES

1. Luz M. Martínez Montiel, "Lebanese Immigration to Mexico." In *Asiatic Migrations in Latin America*, Luz M. Martínez Montiel, ed. (México: Colegío de México, 1981), 151.

2. In-Jin Yoon, *On My Own: Korean Businesses and Race Relations in America* (Chicago: University of Chicago Press, 1997), 175.

3. Susan Koshy, "The Fiction of Asian American Literature," *The Yale Journal of Criticism* 9, 2 (1996): 315–346.

4. A colleague in Mexico who is a scholar of Asian philosophical systems, the women's movement in India, and the history of people from Asia in Mexico pointed out that seldom are Buddhist ideas on the nature of time or Indian theories on the complicated nature of language included in scholarly discussions of "Asian American" literatures and theories. "After all," she said,"you are trying to analyze the works of artists who may be influenced more by Buddhism or Hinduism or other Asian or indigenous beliefs than by Freud, Judeo-Christianity, or Euro-American transnational systems." Luis Nishizawa, the son of a Japanese father and a Mexican mother, speaks of his works as arising from the art of discipline he learned from one grandfather and the discipline of art he learned from the other. It would be interesting to include an exploration of "discipline" and "art" as defined by Nishizawa's Asia and Mexico within a theoretical framework that discusses Asian art in the Americas. Observing and connecting our histories through very personal comments such as those by Phuri Sherpa on the work ethic of different ethnic groups in the United States, through events such as the informal coalitions in Bolivia formed among the Okinawans, Bolivian workers in the rural areas, and the Japanese Embassy; and through literature such as the poem by a Chinese father in Nicaragua on his daughter's political murder may bring us closer to forming more flexible and interacting frameworks of theories. And these in turn might help us to meet Susan Koshy's important demand that we generate new conceptual frames that "work in the interests of social change."

5. It is interesting to use the idea of a palimpsest as the central image in the ongoing "postcolonial," "neocolonial," "who-added-the post-to-the-colonial?" "colonial" debate. In-Jin Yoon examines his data on the relations between Korean Americans and African Americans within a framework of four dimensions of the conflict: structural, psychological, situational, and political. See Yoon, *On My Own* (1997), 176.

6. Trinh T. Minh-Ha, "Cotton and Iron." In *Out There: Marginalization and Contemporary Cultures*, Russell Ferguson, Martha Gever, Trinh T. Minh-Ha, and Cornel West, eds. (Cambridge: MIT Press, 1990), 331.

7. Rey Chow, *Writing Diasporas: Tactics of Intervention in Contemporary Cultural Studies* (Bloomington: Indiana University Press, 1993), 16.

8. Arif Dirlik in an unpublished paper, "Place-Based Imagination: Globalism and the Politics of Place" (Duke University, 1998), analyzes some of the definitions and discussions of place, space, and location in contemporary postcolonial and feminist literature. His discussion of Asians in the United States being identified as "bridges" between Asia and the United States is thought provoking and needs to be added to discussions regarding the conceptualizing of Asia by Asians in the Americas. The issue of the immigration-residential time framework of individual Asians in the Americas

in the process of conceptualizing Asia and the acceptance (or nonacceptance) of the idea of being a "bridge" also needs to be studied at greater length.

REFERENCES

Chow, Rey. *Writing Diasporas: Tactics of Intervention in Contemporary Cultural Studies.* Bloomington: Indiana University Press, 1993.

Dirlik, Arif. "Place-Based Imagination: Globalism and the Politics of Place." Unpublished paper, Duke University, 1998.

Ferguson, Russell, Martha Gever, Trinh T. Minh-Ha, and Cornel West, eds. *Out There: Marginalization and Contemporary Cultures.* Cambridge: MIT Press, 1990.

Koshy, Susan. "The Fiction of Asian American Literature." *Yale Journal of Criticism* 9(1996): 2.

Leon, Lamgen. *Asians in Latin America and the Caribbean: A Bibliography.* Asian/American Center Working Papers. New York: Queens College Asian/American Center, 1990.

Martínez Montiel, Luz M., ed., *Asiatic Migrations in Latin America.* Thirtieth International Congress of Human Sciences in Asia and North Africa. México: Colegío de México, 1981.

Yoon, In-Jin. *On My Own: Korean Businesses and Race Relations in America.* Chicago: University of Chicago Press, 1997.

Part I

In Search of My
Ombligo—Locating the Family

1

China in Mexico: Yesterday's Encounter and Today's Discovery

Monica Cinco Basurto

This is a narrative about myself—the daughter of a Mexican mother and a Chinese father. It is also about my father—the son of a Mexican mother and a Chinese father. It is a narrative about what it means for me to be a Mexican descended from China and what it meant for my father to rediscover his two countries, China and Mexico.

My paternal great-grandfather came to Mexico at the beginning of the twentieth century. He set up a shop that sold fabric, and his son, my grandfather, followed him to Mexico and opened a store that sold leather. Both stores were in Sinaloa. My grandfather married a Mexican woman, and my father was born in Mexico. My Chinese grandfather, my Mexican grandmother, and my father and his brothers and sisters went to China when Mexico's anti-Chinese policies forced much of the Chinese population to leave Mexico. My father eventually returned to Mexico and married a Mexican. I was born in Mexico.

When I was a girl, it gave me great pain that in school my classmates called me and my father Chinese. It was not only our last name that caused us to be a novelty; our daily life was quite different from my friends' lives. For example, our house was always filled with people whom my father had helped to come to Mexico from China. They stayed with us because they were afraid to stay in a hotel. When I invited my school friends to my house, they were surprised to see so many people staying in my home. They also found our food extremely strange and considered it quite unconventional that it was my father rather than my mother who always cooked in our house.

My father looks as Mexican as my mother. Physically he resembles his Mexican mother, and he has few Asian features. However, his contact with Chinese culture from a young age, and the fact that he lived in China for

13

more than thirty years make him seem more Chinese than Mexican. He reveals this unconsciously every day. Even though he returned from China to Mexico—the country of his birth—as a young man and although he married a Mexican, he still practices many Chinese customs such as celebrating the Chinese New Year, cooking Chinese food, and speaking Cantonese and Mandarin with me and his Chinese friends.

Many details of my father's life and habits are different from those of the people around him, which to some degree has made me different as well. For one thing, he works long hours at his business, so part of our family time takes place in the restaurant he owns. The restaurant is not only a meeting point for other members of the Chinese community in Mexico but is also a place of encounter with the many peoples represented in the mosaic that is Mexico City.

Work is very important to Chinese people, and it is the same for my father. Some of my father's friends go home just to sleep and come back to work early in the morning. Others even live in the same building as their business. If people want to talk to my father, they come to the restaurant, as that is the most likely place to find him. My father never charges for the food he serves his friends and relatives, and he is always very generous. That is the way Chinese people are.

My father also likes to talk to his Mexican customers and friends in the restaurant. People are always very curious and ask about the Chinese things on display in the restaurant, such as pictures made of shells or woven from the feathers of hundreds of birds. Mexicans ask my father about his life and how he came to Mexico. They also often ask my father to write their names in Chinese characters. Unfortunately, most of them know little about China or about the Chinese in Mexico. If they see a person with slanted eyes they immediately say "this is a Chinese person," even if he or she is Japanese or Korean or of another Asian nationality.

When we are at the restaurant my father talks to me in Mandarin because he likes people to hear us talk in his father's language. I like to talk to him, too, and that is why I am taking classes and learning Mandarin. But I do not understand most of our relatives because they speak Cantonese.

My father speaks both Mandarin and Cantonese, which is why the Chinese Embassy in Mexico often calls him to translate those languages into Spanish. Most of the people at the embassy are Pekinese and speak Mandarin. Pekinese people in Mexico are often highly educated and view those who speak Cantonese mostly as peasants. I have noticed that if the Chinese Embassy gives a party it is usually the Pekinese community that is invited. My father does not feel comfortable with such discrimination. I have also noticed that when we are invited to a Cantonese party usually by someone whom my father has helped to come to Mexico, we are seated at a table with Mexican guests rather than with the other Cantonese.

Between these two worlds that meet in my father's restaurant, at our house, and at social events, I have learned to mobilize and enact my Chineseness. But at the same time I am constantly reminded of how Mexican I am. For example, when I invite friends to our house, they see my family as a Chinese family, and I am reminded about how Chinese I am. I eat like a Chinese, I look like a Chinese and I understand other Chinese people and Chinese culture. But then again, when I am with my father's Chinese friends and family I am perceived as a Mexican because I do not speak the language accurately, I look different, I dress differently, and I think differently.

To have a Chinese father means many things to me. It is more than other people's curiosity about the things we eat daily or the Cantonese my father sometimes speaks to me. Having a Chinese father and grandfather has made me aware that I am a fusion of two distinct worlds. Having a Chinese father and a Mexican mother has meant I have had to constantly learn two systems of values and meanings. These two universes, very separate from one another, find a point of encounter in my siblings and me. I see us as the border where these two worlds converge.

For the generation of my siblings and myself, to be a descendant from China offers us an opportunity to try to become a part of the already existing, established world of China in Mexico. But because my father has helped so many relatives leave China and come to Mexico, I also feel I am a part of the lives of those Chinese who have arrived more recently. I have shared the experiences of my Mexican childhood with cousins and other relatives who are undergoing many transformations and difficulties as they begin their lives in this country.

I feel I am in a privileged position to try to understand the new Chinese immigrants because my father has told me about the experiences of the older generation of immigrants. But I have realized that what my father experienced in Mexico two or three decades ago is not similar to what my cousins who have just arrived in Mexico are experiencing now. My father and his generation's conception of what it means to be Chinese has changed because even though many of them were born here, they were forced to leave Mexico and spend many years of their lives in China before they could return to Mexico. This not only altered their lives but also created my perception of China and Mexico. I must confess that it is sometimes very difficult for me and my generation to penetrate the minds and feelings of my father and his generation of Chinese in Mexico because of their experiences of dislocations.

To be Mexican moves me deeply, but the nostalgia my father feels for China has been transmitted to me as well. I cannot avoid feeling Chinese, yet I may never feel completely Chinese. I experience constant rejection from those Chinese who, like my cousins, have arrived in Mexico recently. They reject me because I am not from China and because my mother is not Chinese. These relatives, who are my age, see my father and myself as not completely Chinese. They stay among themselves. I also feel these young people do not have the same love my father and his friends have for China. China gave my father and his family refuge, and my father is grateful for this. But the young people leaving China now do not look back; they only look ahead to Mexico where they come to join their families and to work and make money.

The following is my father's story in his own words.

I was born in Sinaloa on July 4, 1930. My father was Chinese, and my mother was from the town of Guamuchil, Sinaloa. He spoke perfect Spanish and English. My mother and father met here in Mexico City but moved back to Sinaloa. My father had a leather factory and a fabric shop in Sinaloa.

I remember very little of the five years I lived in Mexico, but from what my mother used to say it appears my father was not treated well by most people because he was Chinese. She said that they did not like strangers. They treated her badly, too, because she had married a Chinese. Her family accepted my father, but the others did not. Mexicans who had married strangers were looked down upon. When they were in the streets, people threw stones at them.

In the decade of my birth, my father and mother were expelled to China as part of a policy enforced by Mexican President Plutarco Elias Calles, who deported all of the Chinese in Sinaloa and Sonora arguing that they controlled too many of the businesses in those places. My father lived for many years in Mexico, but I do not remember how many. When they expelled my father from the country, I had to go with him. I was taken to China when I was five. Two of my older brothers had left earlier to study in China.

When my father was ordered to leave the country, everything we had was left in the care of a man. My father left him in charge of the factory and the store with the agreement that each month he would send us the money from the things sold in the store. But the man only sent us something when the war with the Japanese began. When my father was killed in Manila during World War II, my mother hoped I could return to Mexico and collect the money. And that is one of the reasons why I later returned to Mexico. But I was unable to collect the promised money.

After we left Mexico we went to Hong Kong and later to Canton. During this time my father did not work. Later he went to Manila in the Philippines, taking two of my brothers, Jesus and Alfonso, and they started a restaurant. During those years, I lived with my mother—who did not speak Chinese—in China while my father lived in Manila. He would send us money and would come to China each year to visit us.

My father and brothers died during the invasion of the Philippines when the Japanese bombarded Manila. We stayed in China suffering the consequences. I was only fifteen or sixteen years old, but I had to begin to work. Fortunately, we had bought a house in China. It was a very big house with two floors and my mother and three of my brothers lived in that house. There were seven siblings. All of us were born in Mexico, and all of us were taken to China at a young age. When my father and two of my brothers died, my mother was left alone in the house for long periods because I had to leave her and go to work, my sister Maria Luisa had died, and my sisters Dora and Lupe had left to live with their husbands. Since my mother spoke no Chinese, she was very lonely. She had only one friend, a Guatemalan woman who had married a rich Chinese man. This woman helped us a lot during the war. My mother loved her very much.

When the Communists entered our city we lost everything. My sister Dora's first husband was very good to us, and he—like the woman from Guatemala—helped us a lot during our difficulties. He had contacts with the Catholic Church in China and also in the United States. It was through him that I became a spy in Formosa against the Communists. But a girlfriend betrayed me, and I had to escape.

I left China in 1956 and arrived in Hong Kong with 50 centavos and a shoe. Since I was carrying my birth certificate, which said I was born in Mexico, I was considered a Mexican. I was asked to call the consul general of Panama who was in charge of the affairs of the Mexicans in China. I wanted to leave China, so I wrote to him.

In 1959 I became a member of an association of Mexicans supporting the Catholic Church in China and Hong Kong. We wrote a letter to President Lopez Mateos asking for his help in repatriating Mexicans of Chinese descent. In 1960 Mexico allowed the repatriation of 365 Mexicans of Chinese descent.

I returned to Mexico in 1960 as part of this group of repatriates. I tried to bring my mother and my brother over, but they were unable to arrange their papers in time and could not leave. Some time later my mother was given an exit card, but I had no money to bring her over. She had to stay in Macao for more than thirteen years under the care of Mexican nuns who gave her asylum until she could return to Mexico.

I was able to bring my mother, my sister, and my sister's sons to Mexico. Now everyone in the family is fine. Some are in the United States, one is in Guadalajara, and the rest of us are in Mexico City. Twenty-one members of our family are here. I brought them all to Mexico.

I have worked at many things, but now I own a restaurant. I love China very much. I was raised there. I lived more than half of my life there. But I would no longer go back to live in Canton. I have spent the other half of my life here in Mexico. My wife is Mexican, and I have Mexican children. There is no reason for me to go back to live in China.

I enjoy talking to Mexicans more than to Chinese. Many Chinese here are very jealous among themselves and do not like to live with Mexicans. We speak the same language, but often they do not like to talk with me because

I am a mestizo or mixed blood. I do have more Mexican than Chinese friends, and we get along very well. People see me as Chinese, and I like to be seen that way. But I am Mexican.

It is no longer as it was before in the time of President Calles. Now many people like me to talk to them about China, and I like to do so. It is no longer like the time when my father lived here. Now we Chinese are treated well and are accepted as both Chinese and Mexican.

Translated and edited by Federico Besserer and Roshni Rustomji-Kerns

AUTHOR BIOGRAPHY

Monica Cinco Basurto is a student in the Department of Anthropology at the Universidad Autonoma Metropolitana. She is doing her field research on the Chinese community in Mexico City. She plans to study the Chinese community in San Francisco for her graduate work, compiling a transnational ethnography of Chinese diasporic communities in metropolitan areas of the Pacific Rim.

Federico Besserer teaches in the Department of Anthropology at the Universidad Autonoma Metropolitana in Mexico City. His early work and publications focused on working-class cultures (including the cultures of Japanese workers) in the transnational mining enclaves in northern Mexico. Since 1988 his research has focused on migrant workers and the construction of their de-territorialized communities. Born and educated in Mexico, Federico Besserer has also studied at the University of California, Riverside. He is a Ph.D. candidate at Stanford University.

2

Con Tacto
touch/contact/connection

Kay Reiko Torres

ARTIST'S STATEMENT

My photographic work is about making connections: recalling a dream / realizing a fantasy / travelling to someone faraway / overcoming hurt / appreciating a friend / valuing family / savoring a fleeting moment / laughing at myself / visualizing music / responding to dance / heeding forces / envisioning a sensible world / seeking responsibility and unity in my world community.

Diptychs, triptychs, collage, and images with text have been my preferred forms of presentation. These formats define my personal connection with a situation, an idea, a person, or an experience.

*   *   *

CON TACTO is an ongoing body of work inspired by people who have made impressions on me through shared experiences or through events from their lives they have related to me. I have photographed one hand (the back and the palm) of the subject's choosing—the hand because it reveals the subject's unique experience and history and represents a physical means of communication. The middle image of the triptych recalls a personal memory/ association with that person. Some involve text of a recounted moment others a visual detail that provokes thoughts of a special connection I have with the subject.

At present, this body of work includes eleven two-dimensional triptychs (16″ × 20″) and five three-dimensional works.

Gracias a N. G. La Banda por la inspiración musical.

19

CON TACTO—MA & GA. Mixed media collage. Reprinted courtesy of Kay Reiko Torres.

This collage of my mother ("Ma") and my daughter, Gabriela ("Ga"), is part of a three-dimensional piece of the *CON TACTO* project. The repeated images in the background are of my sister and me dancing for my dad's camera. My mother and my daughter are extremely close, particularly in their love of music and expression through dance: my mother through tap dancing, Gabriela through hip-hop, and Afro-Cuban folkloric and popular dance.

CON TACTO—MOM. Silver gelatin prints and text. Reprinted courtesy of Kay Reiko Torres.

When I asked my mother what was the proudest moment of her life she immediately responded, "It was when I toured as a tap dancer on the Orpheum Circuit. Imagine! Getting paid to travel and do what I love most: DANCE!" Who inspired this daughter of Japanese immigrants to pursue a very American art form? The legendary African American tap dancer Bill Robinson. Her mother took her to see him perform live in Los Angeles, and it was a day that changed my mother's life.

CON TACTO—GA & PA (GT & CT). Silver gelatin prints. Reprinted courtesy of Kay Reiko Torres.

This piece includes the hand of my daughter, Gabriela ("Ga"), and that of her father ("Pa"), César Torres. The connections are apparent: the ponytail, the earring, the love shared between the two. Gabriela's father was a musician who was born in Colima, Mexico. He joyfully shared his love of music and of his culture with his daughter before dying of cancer at the age of forty-two.

CONEXIONES. Mixed media, 8″ × 10″. Reprinted courtesy of Kay Reiko Torres.

This collage includes two old family photographs. One documents a friend, accompanied by his brother and sister, at his elementary school graduation in Cuba. The other is a photograph of my older sister and me taken in the United States. The connections? The old photographs, the directness of the children's looks into the camera, the "dressed alikeness" of the siblings. The background colors represent the Americas and the colors of of the flags of the two nations in which the two families live. The photos brought me to consider the stories of our ancestors coming to this continent so we could meet and relate today. One family is mixed descendants of Middle Eastern, African, and European peoples who came to the Americas; my sister and I are descendants of Asians in the Americas.

AUTHOR BIOGRAPHY

Kay Reiko Torres is a third-generation Japanese American, born and raised in Los Angeles. She grew up under the influence of a professional tap dancing mother who shared with her daughters her love of dance and the music of a variety of cultures. Her father imparted to his children a love of community, travel, and photography. Kay became involved with photography, producing Spanish-language photo stories on immigrant rights, union organizing, and rape awareness with a collective of Latin American artists and immigrants. Her interest in experimental photography developed later. Through studies and travels in Latin America—especially Mexico, Brazil, and Cuba—and her work in Los Angeles with immigrant teenagers, Kay has come to see and appreciate the diversity, commonalities, and intersections of various cultural communities.

3

Sophie's Conflicts

Usha Welaratna

When Sophie's family fled from Cambodia to the United States in 1982 after surviving the horrors of Pol Pot's "killing fields," Sophie (not her real name) was just five years old. The family began their new life in Massachusetts, but like many other immigrants and refugees before them Sophie's family soon migrated to other places that offered better work. Their first city of hope was Chicago, and the next was Long Beach, the second-largest city in Los Angeles County. I met Sophie in 1994 when I was conducting anthropological fieldwork for my doctoral degree, looking at factors contributing to conflict and accommodation among blacks, Hispanics, and Khmer or Cambodians living in Long Beach.

I first interviewed Sophie's older sister about her experiences growing up as a Cambodian in the United States. When she discovered that I was particularly interested in encounters between Cambodians and their ethnic neighbors, she said her younger sister would have a lot to tell me because whereas she herself had moved to the area recently after a divorce, her sister had lived there since 1989 and had confronted interracial issues at school. I arranged to meet Sophie the following week.

I am a Sri Lankan immigrant, and my association with Cambodian refugees began in 1987 when I studied their adjustments to the United States. The results of that work, which was conducted in northern California, appear in my book, *Beyond the Killing Fields: Voices of Nine Cambodian Survivors in America*. My present work, which is conducted in southern California, naturally grew out of my previous research. But although my previous research site was also in a depressed area of the city, it was not half as troubled as the ethnically diverse inner-city neighborhood in which Sophie lives. Therefore her experiences (as well as those of other Cambodians who live there) reveal important dimensions of the Cambodian odyssey I had not encountered before.

24

When I first saw Sophie, who was a sophomore in high school, she struck me as one of the most beautiful Cambodian women I had ever met. At seventeen she was shapely and slender, with an abundance of long wavy hair and a husky voice. When I asked if she would tell me about her experiences with blacks and Hispanics, she began her narrative without hesitation. I present Sophie's voice, along with some of my observations and findings, here.

TRADITION AND CHANGE

"I've encountered a lot of prejudice because when I was, like, thirteen or fourteen years old I was dating a black guy," Sophie said, surprising me with her opening words because "dating" is not part of traditional Cambodian culture and is still not accepted by most parents as proper behavior, particularly for girls. Cambodians come from a culture in which arranging suitable marriages for children has been considered a parental duty, although final approval has rested with the prospective partners. Even when two people met and fell in love, as sometimes happened, it was customary to obtain parents' permission and blessings before marriage. Until children reached marriageable age, whether they lived in the city or in villages they were expected to go to school for as long as the parents could afford to send them.

Although in America many teenage romances begin in school, in Cambodia schools were typically not places for romantic liaisons. They were institutions that were respected as places where children were taught not only to read and write but also to learn culturally appropriate behaviors that would make them good parents and citizens in the future. Most Cambodian adults continue to uphold these values in the United States, and in fact, some parents view the United States school culture as detrimental to the welfare of their children because of its permissiveness. Sophie, however, appeared to have a problem in addition to that of having violated a cultural norm by having a boyfriend at a young age.

"I was called names by my own race," she said. "They called me a traitor and stuff like that."

"Because your boyfriend was black?" I asked.

"Uh-huh. They called me a Negro. I was like, I don't care, you know. And some people, they dislike me because of that. 'Oh her? She's always with black people!' That's how they categorize me—like black people. Not true. I have a lot of Asian friends and friends of different races."

"Who called you names?"

"My peers in school. But it didn't bother me because when I date I look at people for who they are not their color, you know. But as time went by and by, they just kind of accepted it because I was still seeing him. I guess, like, they can't break it up, so they might as well accept me."

I asked Sophie what attracted her to her boyfriend.

"See, I was the new girl, and he was in my classes," she replied. "When I came to school I didn't know anybody, and he was my first friend. He was the first person in that school to accept me for what I was, and I felt at ease with him. He saw the real me. He introduced me to his family at their house, and they also were real nice. One time he wasn't going to school because he was sick, but his mom picked me up from my house and she gave me a ride. So first of all it was friendship, and then we got to like one another and got closer. He's a very nice, outgoing person. That's what I like about him.

"At the beginning, when my friends would say 'ugh, I can't believe an Asian girl is going out with a black guy,' he basically stood up for me, and I feel good about that. He was always there for me."

"Who discriminated against you? Was it Cambodians?" I inquired.

"It was everybody. Whites, blacks, Asians—like, Chinese, Vietnamese, and also my own people. But now I have been accepted by blacks, and it's, like, cool, you know. Actually, I think the Cambodians are the most prejudiced, but then I'm around them more, and I hear all this 'oh, why are you friends with this and that?' I hear this from my people in stores, conventions, parties. Let's say you go to a party, and your date is from another race. (Looking at me) Now you'll be okay, you look Asian, you know. But if you have blonde hair or you are an African guy or something, they go, 'Gosh, why is she bringing him? He's not Asian, why is she bringing him?' Stupid remarks like that. I don't hear much of that from black or Hispanic people. But again, the people I hang around are like me. They see the inside—not outside—of people."

Are Cambodians more prejudiced than other ethnic groups, as Sophie claims? In my own research I have not found them to be collectively any more prejudiced than other groups. Rather, as with other groups, the nature of prejudice among Cambodians varies depending on their individual beliefs and experiences, as well as on environmental factors. Then why would many of Sophie's peers not accept her black boyfriend and other non-Asians based on *race*? After all, it is widely accepted by scholars that the human species is not (contrary to what the concept *race* implies) divided into exclusive, genetically distinct, homogeneous groupings similar to subspecies. We know that it is a social construct based on misconceived and ethnocentric notions of biological superiority and inferiority of peoples and one that is used to privilege one group over another. In fact, as Michael Omi and Howard Winant (1986) remind us, "race" is a historically specific ideological imposition upon peoples previously unclassified as such. Whereas scholars acquainted with Khmer note that an aesthetic preference for light skin existed among Khmer peasants even before European contact, they also believe that this preference was based not on modern notions of racializing groups but rather on the *economic* success of the light-skinned Chinese migrants who had resettled in Cambodia through the years (Becker 1986; Criddle and Mam 1987; Smith 1994).

Even if the Khmer favor lighter skins as a marker of ethnic "success"—a description that does not generally fit the blacks or African Americans in the vicinity I studied—this historically determined attitude does not fully explain the discrimination against Sophie's boyfriend displayed by her peers. What is surprising about their discrimination is that Cambodian youth are now aligned with darker-skinned black youth in the gang war against lighter-skinned Hispanics. Therefore, other factors need to be considered to understand the behavior of Sophie's friends and family. Some of these are rooted in the particular immigrant history of Cambodians and the place and space they now occupy in the U.S. social structure. Others stem from the general immigrant history and culture of the United States. Together they have created an environment that has heightened the sense of ethnic solidarity among Cambodians and produced an environment promoting ethnic stereotyping, hatred, and mistrust.

CAMBODIAN REFUGEES IN THE UNITED STATES

When Cambodian refugees began arriving in the United States in the 1980s, they entered a world that was vastly different from the one they had known— racially, culturally, and structurally. To begin with, unlike the United States, which is no longer occupied and ruled mainly by its native peoples, the land we now call Cambodia has been continuously occupied by ethnic Cambodians since prehistoric times. Furthermore, although they lost political powers and territories to Thai and Vietnamese invaders at various periods of their long history and beginning in 1863 the French ruled Cambodia for almost a century, ethnic Khmer continuously remained by far the numerical majority and regained the independence of at least some of their territories. As a rule, the Khmer also remained the main culture-producing and culture-bearing unit of the country even when it was under foreign occupation.

The most glorious period in Cambodia's history is that between the ninth and fifteenth centuries, known as the Angkor period, when Khmer kings ruled over parts of Thailand, Vietnam, and Laos. During this era a new social hierarchy and cultural system modeled on Indian culture, structure, and religion gradually replaced the country's tribal egalitarian system. By the end of the Angkor period a distinct Indianized Khmer identity unified the people; Theravada Buddhism had evolved, and the values and beliefs—such as those pertaining to parenting, education, and marriage still upheld by most adult refugees were firmly established. As recounted by narrators in my earlier work, other features of this largely non-Western worldview include cooperative social norms, consideration of the welfare of family and community over that of the individual, and respect for elders, monks, teachers, and each other through word and action, nonaggression, nonviolence, honesty, generosity, and devotion to family.

Until they arrived in America's urban ghettos, Cambodians had experienced little cross-cultural interaction with groups not of Asian descent. When European traders first arrived in Southeast Asia, the Cambodian capital of Phnom Penh was under Vietnamese occupation, and the Vietnamese had closed the Cambodian ports to foreigners. The only group allowed to enter the country was Christian missionaries, whose efforts to convert the Theravada Buddhist masses to Christianity did not succeed. Even though the country became a French colony in 1863, only the urban elite (about 15 percent of the total population) was exposed to the colonial masters. Of these, a considerable number were Cambodians of Chinese and Vietnamese origins.

Cambodia's two largest minority groups were the Chinese Cambodians and Vietnamese Cambodians, and they and the nearby countries represented the "global network" to many rural villagers. In many cases the ancestors of these minorities had migrated to Cambodia from China and Vietnam several centuries earlier; thus even though members of both groups maintained some continuity of their linguistic and cultural heritages, most Vietnamese and Chinese Cambodians also spoke Khmer, and the Chinese were willingly assimilated into ethnic Cambodian society through intermarriage.

The Vietnamese, on the other hand, even when fair skinned, were traditionally disliked and mistrusted by Cambodians as historical enemies who invaded their land. Their hegemony was particularly resented because when the Vietnamese conquered Cambodia they attempted to impose not only political but also cultural control over Cambodians. As mentioned, Cambodian cultural and religious systems are rooted in India, whereas Vietnam was influenced by China. So as David Chandler (1983) asserts, the two peoples were separated by a deep cultural divide, and during their occupation the Vietnamese aggressively attempted to eradicate Cambodian culture in every possible way because they viewed their own traditions and customs as far superior to those of their subjects. The Cambodians greatly resisted these efforts, and stories of Vietnamese atrocities have been transmitted from one generation to the next.

Since independence, however, the Khmer have been politically and culturally dominant, and it is they who excluded the Vietnamese from integrating into mainstream society. But even in the case of the Vietnamese, Khmer discrimination is based not on biology but on cultural and behavioral differences. This is confirmed by the fact that although Thai also invaded and occupied Cambodia, much less animosity exists toward the Thai because as a group that was also Indianized the Thai made no attempt to eradicate Cambodian culture.

African Americans, however, have not had historical links to Cambodian people, and most Cambodians encountered blacks only after they arrived in the United States. Even though at times individuals from the two groups engage in fights and verbal altercations, their youth are allies in the ongoing gang war. It should be noted that Cambodian-Hispanic animosities are also not rooted in "racial" animosities per se. Instead, they are rooted in events that began with the Mexican-American War, when Mexico lost half its territory to European invaders, and the original inhabitants of the land were uprooted and displaced by the emerging capitalist economy and social system.

When blacks started to immigrate to Long Beach in the 1940s, they encountered little resistance from Hispanics whose numbers in the area had greatly diminished as a result of restrictive immigration laws. But when the 1965 Immigration Act enabled large numbers of Hispanics to enter the United States, thousands resettled in Los Angeles County. Over time, conflicts between blacks and Hispanics over various issues began to unfold. Ethnic conflict in Long Beach increased dramatically with the resettlement of thousands of Cambodians in the 1980s. Some Hispanics who viewed the refugees as the latest invaders coming to take over their land began to beat Cambodian youngsters with the intention of driving them away from the area. Instead, the Cambodians formed their own gangs, and today they are allied with black youth in retaliation against Hispanics.

So why should Sophie's peers object so vehemently to her black boyfriend? I believe that a closer look at the way race, class, and ethnicity intersect in the Unites States will provide some answers.

RACE, CLASS, AND ETHNICITY IN THE UNITED STATES

Because most of the educated urban elite had been killed or had died from illness or starvation under the Khmer Rouge, the vast majority of Khmer refugees who arrived in the United States were people with rural origins. Of these, most were women who had survived horrendous traumas and whose husbands, fathers, mothers, children, and other loved ones had perished under the most horrible circumstances.

In Cambodia many village women operated small businesses selling produce or homemade sweetmeats, but they were mainly responsible for running their households. When they arrived in the United States neither they nor the men, who had worked as farmers, artisans, pottery makers, and the like, had job skills that enabled them to enter industrial America. Even the few professionals who had miraculously survived the killing fields were compelled to enter the bottom rung of the U.S. working class as janitors and assembly line workers because they lacked English-language skills and their knowledge of French served no purpose in their new setting. The group as a whole lacked economic capital because the Khmer Rouge had confiscated their personal assets, and those who had managed to save some of their valuables either by hiding them from the regime or by earning them after independence lost most of their possessions either to bandits who attacked them as they escaped from their country or in the refugee camps.

Unlike people from other Asian nations such as China, Japan, Korea, the Philippines, and even India, Cambodians had not migrated west in search of new opportunities. So when the refugees fled their country with no preparation or even knowledge of their ultimate destination, they had no core group in the Unite States to assist them in the resettlement process or to help service providers become acquainted with the newcomers. Therefore, in contrast to some post-1965 Asian immigrant groups that entered middle-class America because they originated from middle-class professional backgrounds in their native lands, this group, as refugees with rural backgrounds, lacked much of the social and economic capital that would have enabled them to do so. Consequently, the refugees had little choice but to resettle among America's urban "underclass," made up mainly of poor blacks and Latinos.

In the field of race relations in the United States, the most widely addressed issues are those pertaining to black-white relations. The history of African Americans began with racially determined views that stated that Africans represented the lowest level of human evolution and were inherently incapable of full assimilation into the European system—explanations that were used to justify the bondage of Africans as chattel slaves in southern plantations. But slavery officially ended in 1863, and a black middle class was born following the Civil Rights Movement during the 1960s. So why have some blacks remained at the bottom of the U.S. social hierarchy? William Wilson (1987) argues that the black "underclass" emerged because of continued structural inequality and oppression, loss of jobs in inner cities due to relocation of industrial plants to other areas, and the abandonment of poor blacks by their more well-to-do members. Wilson defines this group as a class with high rates of joblessness, teenage pregnancies, out-of-wedlock births, female-headed households, welfare dependency, and serious crime.

A single social fact such as the disproportionately high numbers of blacks in America's prisons is sufficient to demonstrate to any observer of the U.S. society that African Americans, more than any other group, symbolize ethnic "failures" in this country. What the statistics do not explain, however, is that—as widely demonstrated by research and scholarship—this situation is the result of structural oppression rather than of ethnic-specific factors. Any incoming group is quickly informed both through environmental factors and through media representations that African Americans are not a desirable group for association and emulation. I believe these macrostructural representations greatly influenced Sophie's peers in Long Beach in their attitudes toward her and her boyfriend.

On the experiential level Cambodians—like members of other groups living in Sophie's neighborhood—are victimized on a daily basis by robbers, gang members, and drug traffickers. Not all inner-city dwellers engage in these behaviors, and most are law-abiding citizens. But some residents do commit crimes and resort to violence, and many Cambodians fear blacks as the main perpetrators of robberies, thefts, and drug trafficking. So even though some Cambodian youths also now participate in urban violence, many in the group continue to idealize and uphold their traditional beliefs and values—which, as shown earlier, run counter to "underclass" behaviors—and thus tend to be critical of blacks.

Although some may argue that blacks, through their own behavior, create and perpetuate such perceptions, Wilson and numerous scholars have demonstrated conclusively that the "underclass" phenomenon cannot be separated from the macrosocial history of the United States. My own research confirms this view. But victims of crime are seldom concerned about such explanations; instead, their particular experiences inform their perceptions of others. So although not all African Americans are criminals, their criminalization as a group—even by other minorities—continues.

Sophie, however, clearly does not stigmatize blacks, and I asked her what led to her outlook. She replied, "I don't like to categorize people by race. I basically want to get to know the person inside. That's what counts most. Even though some people say 'oh you know, he's black, he's Mexican, you can't be friends with him,' I say I don't care as long as the person inside counts. I like to get to know the real person."

Sophie's response reveals an outlook that is commendable not only because of its maturity in attempting to understand both herself and others but also because of the strength and determination she must possess to sustain her convictions. I was curious to discover who or what factors influenced her outlook.

A MODEL FOR CONFLICT RESOLUTION

"My mom and dad taught me that," said Sophie. "I remember when I'd say 'oh god, I can't stand her. She's Mexican or she's black.' My mom would say, 'Don't say that about people. Not all blacks or not all Mexicans are bad.' I listened to that and kind of took that in. It *is* true, you know. Not all people are bad no matter what race they are. Some are bad and some are good. You have to accept people for who they are. Now I say that to my friends, but . . . sometimes when I walk with a Mexican girl some Asians would stare me up and down. I just tell them 'don't look at me that way,' you know? I just say that straight out. And they say, 'oh, she's talking to a Mexican girl' or 'oh, she's talking to a black girl!' But I don't care. I will be friends with whom I want to be friends with. First get to know them, then accept them for what they are—that's my model.

"So I don't let other people influence me at all. I can be easy to talk to, be outgoing. But if you get to know me and didn't accept me for what I am, I don't worry about you. I stay away from you. Some people accuse me of being stuck up just because I don't talk much. I don't think that's fair. I know the person I am, and if they can't see that, that's too bad for them. You have to understand, I can also be cruel. If I'm very nice to you and you still talk stuff, accuse me of something, I tend to see the person you are and I stay away from you."

Although I am tempted to theorize that Sophie's parents' perspectives are rooted in Buddhist teachings, which promote habits and values such as tolerance and nonviolence, I realize that few Cambodians, although they practice or have been exposed to these same ideals, appear to display the same openness to ethnically diverse peoples. So we need to look at ways in which Sophie's parents may differ from others of their group who live in the same neighborhood.

Both of Sophie's parents grew up in the Cambodian capital and have college degrees. Thus they would have been exposed to ethnically diverse groups far more than individuals who grew up in villages and interacted primarily with family and members of their own community. This urban, college-educated background conceivably contributes to an ability to be more open to culturally diverse peoples. Furthermore, unlike most Cambodians who are unemployed and are generally committed to living out their days in the crime-ridden urban ghettos because they lack resources to move into better neighborhoods, Sophie's father is employed, and the family can at least hope to move into a safer neighborhood. Such hope, I was told by another Cambodian adult in similar circumstances, gives them the strength to be more tolerant of others who are less fortunate and to cope with daily problems.

Finally, in conversations with her, I discovered that Sophie's mother is more knowledgeable about U.S. history than refugees who are illiterate and that she therefore has a better understanding of her ethnic neighbors. But had Sophie's mother known that she was dating an African American—a practice that I stated earlier, is not a part of Cambodian traditions—I wonder if she would have reacted with less understanding. I asked Sophie, "Did your parents know you were dating him?"

"My mom kind of knew because he kept calling me all the time, but not my dad. Basically my mom is real easy, but she never asked me about it. And it wasn't serious dating—it was just on and off, you know, we just went out. But my parents really don't let me go out much—they don't think it's proper for a girl to go out too much. But when we went we always had to go out in a group because my mom doesn't allow me to go out alone."

"Why is that?"

"My mom is basically scared I might get pregnant. I told her no, even if I am young I know better than to jump into bed with someone. But I guess it's just that my two best friends at school are pregnant now. They are Cambodians. So I understand how she feels, though I do not agree with my mom that I should always stay at home."

CONCLUSION

This narrative demonstrates that education to enhance interethnic awareness, and understanding and increased opportunities for the socioeconomic advancement of inner-city dwellers, are essential to bring about progressive social change. Education in ethnically diverse settings—particularly when newly arrived migrants resettle there—should include information that will provide an understanding of the process whereby particular groups came to be situated in specific niches of the U.S. social structure, a knowledge of how the status of these groups may influence their behaviors, and a tracing of how those behaviors lead to negative stereotypical perceptions of others that do not reflect the environmental factors that produced the behaviors. Similarly, older groups should be informed about their new neighbors.

But education by itself is not sufficient to resolve ethnic conflicts. As shown in numerous studies, most such conflicts are generated by poverty and by competition for increasingly limited resources—whether for housing, education, or jobs. These deprivations need to be addressed if we are to begin to heal some of the fractures that are currently disrupting families and communities in urban America.

REFERENCES

Becker, Elizabeth. *When the War Was Over: The Voices of Cambodia's Revolution and Its People*. New York: Simon and Schuster, 1986.

Chandler, David. *A History of Cambodia*. Boulder: Westview, 1983.

Criddle, Joan, and Teeda Butt, Mam. *To Destroy You Is No Loss: The Odyssey of a Cambodian Family*. New York: Atlantic Monthly Press, 1987.

Ngor, Haing S. *A Cambodian Odyssey*. New York: Macmillan, 1987.

Omi, Michael, and Howard, Winanat. *Racial Formation in the US: From the 1960s to 1980s*. New York: Routledge and Kegan Paul, 1986.

Smith, Frank. *Interpretive Accounts of the Khmer Rouge Years: Personal Experience in Cambodian Peasant World View*. Madison: Wisconsin Papers on Southeast Asia, Occasional Paper no. 18, 1994.

Welaratna, Usha. *Beyond the Killing Fields: Voices of Nine Cambodian Survivors in America*. Stanford, Calif.: Stanford University Press, 1993.

Wilson, William Julius. *The Truly Disadvantaged: The Inner City, the Underclass, and Public Policy*. Chicago: University of Chicago Press, 1987.

AUTHOR BIOGRAPHY

Usha Welaratna is originally from Sri Lanka. She is the author of Beyond the Killing Fields: Voices of Nine Cambodian Survivors in America. *She is a lecturer and consultant on intercultural relations and is currently working on her second book,* The Presence of the Past in Conflicts and Coalitions Among Cambodians, Blacks, and Hispanics in Long Beach.

4

The Boy under the Bridge

Kathryne Jeun Cho

Crouched under the bridge, he cried silently. Wrapping his arms tightly around his legs, the child stared blankly at the unsold stack of newspapers. The day was almost over, and sadly, the rain had kept him from selling that day's edition. At the tender age of nine his head should have been filled with careless and childish thoughts, but all the boy could do was worry about that pile of newspapers. Afraid to go home empty-handed, he prayed for a miracle.

"Young man, I'll take that stack," stated an elderly gentleman who had appeared before him. Baffled, puzzled, and excited, the child simply handed the man the soon-to-be-outdated wet pile of newspapers. The child never saw the man again, but he never forgot his kindness and vowed to express his gratitude somehow, somewhere, and to someone.

That nine-year-old boy was my father, Dr. Jung Hyun Cho. Born during the Japanese occupation of Korea, on the thirtieth of April 1938, my father grew up in a small farming village south of Seoul called Jungnam Mokpo. Like many other Koreans raised under colonial rule, my father envisioned a better life elsewhere. Although his start in life may not seem unique, his accomplishments make him very special. As his story will reveal, even in the darkest hours dreams can come true. As a colony Korea was stripped of power, honor, and dignity. Many of its citizens lived internally and were forever colonized. But "America," they were told, "is the land of freedom." As a believer in miracles, my father became a special Post-65 Korean American Immigrant.

As a result of the Japanese surrender to the World War II Allies on August 15, 1945, Korea was liberated from thirty-six years of Japanese domination. As told by my father, "Japan's defeat in the world war meant Korea's freedom from Japanese rule. To us children, though, it meant food for our stomachs. At times we would starve for four, sometimes five days! Those were hard

35

times. Our diets consisted mainly of barley gruel, if at least that. But we remained hopeful that things would soon get better."

From newspaper deliveries, shoeshines, shoemaker, and dressmaker to
fountain pen repair, my father did whatever he could to help sustain his family. As fate would have it, by the time he entered the twelfth grade in 1950
the Korean War had broken out. Colonization occurred once more, and liberation from war was to be delayed for another three years. It was then that
he first saw an American. "I was fascinated!" he said. "The way they looked
and spoke seemed so foreign. I wondered what species of people they were.
They were so different from us! I knew, however, that they were far more
advanced than we were. Their products were much better than ours." Educated by U.S. missionaries, my father learned at an early age that America
was not only spiritually but also culturally superior to Korea: "At school we
were heavily influenced by things American. We learned about American culture, history, language, literature, songs, and dance. Even instructions at the
University were given in English!" For many Koreans going to America was
indeed like a dream.

After graduating from Seoul National University with a B.A. and an M.S.
in dentistry, my father worked as an assistant professor. My father was very
popular. He would often find flowers on his desk. Of all the women he met,
he was struck the most by Hee Sub Shim who was introduced to him by a
mutual friend. At five feet eleven inches in height, Hee Sub, like himself, was
very tall for a Korean. The wedding took place in 1966, a year after the 1965
Immigration Act which nullified the national origin quotas. As a result, many
Koreans took the opportunity to leave the country for the United States. But
for my father, life in the United States was a distant dream.

My father heard many wonderful stories about America, especially from
classmates who were privileged enough to have studied overseas. To my
father, the foreign exchange students seemed special, more cultured. It was
hard for him not to envy them. Not only was my father financially unprepared, but because of the draft he could not leave Korea. He secretly har-
bored a desire to be a student in America. Clearly, like the writer Carlos Bu-
losan and many other Asian immigrants, my father carried idealized visions
of America.

Despite his own aspirations, my father quickly asserts that my mother was
very influential in his decision to leave Korea. Contrary to statements by
many scholars, many Post-65 Immigrants' decision to come to the United
States was not solely based on the "whim of the male." Wives often persuaded their husbands to immigrate. As stated by Eui-Young Yu, "[a] distinct
characteristic of the Korean population in the United States is an unusually
high representation of females. The overall sex ratio of the Korean population at the time of the 1970 Census was 68 males per 100 females." (41) As

this study indicates, women also displayed a great desire to go to the United States.

My father was sure that he wanted to see America someday, but he had to take care of my grandmother, so he felt obligated to stay in Korea. With his dental practice thriving in Yeoni Dong, his plan was to remain and fulfill his duties as a son. But because my mother and grandmother did not get along, my father decided to leave sooner than expected. He told me, "Your mother would pester me about leaving as soon as possible."

When my mother's older sister left for Brazil, my mother pressured my father to emigrate. Although Brazil was not the country he had chosen, my father sold all we had and prepared to emigrate. In summer 1974 my family left with $30,000 U.S. in cash along with thousands of other Korean immigrants we left our homeland for the American continent.

The U.S. involvement in Asia led to a new political, economic, and military alliance between Asia and America. By using the threat of communism, military dictators came into power in many parts of Asia. At times, such authoritarian rule made economic development in Asia possible; however, it also generated dislocations, causing many Asians to leave their country. In Korea the (U.S.-backed) dictatorship of Chung Hee Park (1961–1979) forced economic modernization and industrial growth, causing Seoul to grow at a tremendous pace. To compete in the world market, Korea also began to develop an export-oriented economy. Striving to keep prices of goods competitive in the international market, government-backed industries secured low-wage labor by prohibiting strikes and creating a surplus of workers. Furthermore, government anti-inflation policies kept rice prices so low that an agricultural crisis was precipitated.

Unable to survive in farm communities, millions of Koreans moved to the cities. Unfortunately, urbanization collided with an unexpected population explosion that raised the number of Koreans from "25 million in 1960 to 35 million in 1975" (Takaki: 438). Following this sudden outburst of the urban population, employment shortages and overcrowding led many Koreans to seek opportunities elsewhere. Meanwhile, the United States was suffering a shortage of people in medical and other professional fields. Since Korea had such professionals in abundance, many of them left the country in search of a better life. Others left for political reasons.

With U.S. support, Chung Hee Park established the Korean Center Intelligence Agency which was used liberally by the president to harass people. As my father described, "Secret service men even infiltrated campuses, and many students were tortured and killed." But unlike the majority my father did not leave because of economic struggle or political oppression. He left, in his own words, "Because of a dream. I say I left because of the war, but I left because I wanted to see America."

Many Koreans did not qualify to enter the United States directly, so they ventured to South America. Hoping to better their chances for entry to the United States, many went to Brazil, Argentina, Peru, and other South American countries as stopovers. Because of his status my father could have easily entered the United States of America under the professional category, but because of my mother his dream of seeing America had to wait. In Brazil, after receiving another degree from São Paulo University, my father resumed his position as a doctor, establishing a successful practice in Aclimacao. In reflecting on his life in Brazil compared with his experiences in the United States, he says, "Because of my white uniform Brazilians showed respect even on the streets. But here [in the United States], if I step out in my dental gown they mistake me for a janitor." Most of my father's professional friends were in the United States, however, and visions of that country kept haunting him.

Finally, in 1979 my father persuaded my mother to migrate a second time, this time to the United States. With U.S. $50,000 in cash, our family left Brazil. In 1976, because the shortage of professionals had been alleviated and the U.S. economy was not doing as well as it had been a decade earlier, the U.S. Congress decided to restrict the number of professionals and other workers allowed into the country (Chan: 147-8). Circumventing limitations placed by the Eilberg Act of 1977, which further constrained the immigration of professionals, my father somehow attained visas for America.

Already in his forties, my father once again assumed the role of a student. For two years my father did not come out of his room. I'd catch glimpses of him on his way to the bathroom, and I barely recognized him. His hair was disheveled, his face was unshaven, and his eyes were bloodshot. For many other Koreans time to study was a luxury they could not afford. Forced to get jobs right away, many immigrants faced occupational downgrading. Doctors, lawyers, professionals, and pharmacists became grocers and store owners. Like the experience of earlier immigrants, the irony within the great American dream proved harsh enough to have awakened them from that dream.

As part of downgrade mobility, many immigrants ventured into small businesses. Since most Koreans lacked prior entrepreneurial experience, they learned this skill in the United States. At their arrival many started work in maintenance companies, in sewing factories, as janitors, or as laborers in other menial jobs. Consequently, many scrounged and saved enough to buy a store.

Usually, as my father did, Koreans participated in *kyes*, or a rotating credit system. As my father explained, "It's like a bank but a little different. We pool together a certain amount of capital each month, and whoever needs it most that month takes the pot home. Everyone is allotted a turn in receiving the money, so everyone benefits. One time I had twenty-seven different *kyes* going at the same time. But a word of caution," he added. "You have to know the people you give your money to. There are many instances when people default on their payment and run away with the money, thousands of dollars are lost that way!"

After accumulating enough starting capital, the immigrants start small businesses for various reasons. Language inadequacy and a desire for autonomy are the primary forces moving them to start small businesses in Black ghettos, barrios, and racially mixed areas. Here they do not need to speak English, they can profit from a minority clientele, and if they have no family support they can take advantage of cheap labor.

My father was fortunate enough to pass the dental board examinations. As a certified dentist, he is presently practicing in Reseda. He told me, "Many times your mother nagged me about buying a store. But how could I? I've never been a merchant before. I knew I could pass the exams, so I just asked her to be patient." Like many other Korean immigrants, my father suffered from language anxieties. However, having lived in Brazil and having learned Portuguese, he easily mastered Spanish. As he explained, "I learned Spanish not from books, but from my nurse. I had to—more than 50 percent of my patients are Hispanic. Because I lived in Brazil, I feel more comfortable with them. When I first came to the U.S. I worked as a managing doctor for an American Caucasian dentist. However, solely based on my race, certain clients who were Caucasian refused to be treated by me. I was very shocked and hurt. But I've never had this problem with my Hispanic clients. Rather, they trust me, not only because I speak their language but because I, too, am an immigrant. I think they can tell that I understand their daily immigrant struggles . . . I know that my Hispanic clients trust and like me . . . especially those who bring me tamales!"

Today when he speaks about his "days under the bridge," my father's story seems more fiction than reality. But the boy under the bridge did grow up, and as he had promised himself, he made something of himself. Like so many people who grew up in a war-torn, hungry land, my father came to America in search of a better life. Here, as an established, prominent doctor, he fulfilled his promise to repay his debt. As a dentist he is well-known for his service to people in need. He visits Mexico every year with a team of volunteer doctors and nurses and treats as many people as he can. In addition, with the help of Oriental Mission Church, he takes donated clothes, food, and school supplies to churches in Tijuana to be distributed to the many families in need. He explained to me, "I wanted to repay that gentleman's grace with kindness to others, and I have the opportunity to do that now. Whenever I go to Mexico I'm reminded of my own childhood . . . How hungry and cold it was growing up! There are so many children in need . . . so many helpless mothers unable to provide simply because of the poverty surrounding them. I'm glad that I can at least help alleviate some of their physical pain."

As in the days when U.S. soldiers distributed food and clothing to Koreans, my father feels compelled to do what he can. He says, "In America I've been able to repay some of that generosity by helping others in need. Since as an immigrant, I'm culturally and linguistically familiar with those from the Hispanic community, I feel that I can make the greatest impact here."

Many Koreans shared my father's dream. Some have fulfilled that dream here in America, but many have not. To legitimize Korean experiences in America, all of the struggles, defeats, and victories need to be revealed. Until then, Koreans will continue to remain in the U.S. mainstream as political, cultural, and social mutes—always as the "colonized." Yet as my father's story illustrates, even as immigrants, Koreans are most assuredly making an impact, especially on the lives of others like themselves, regardless of their ethnic or racial background.

REFERENCES

Chan, Sucheng. *Asian Americans: An Interpretive History*. Boston: Twayne Publishers, 1991.

Takaki, Ronald. *Strangers From a Different Shore: A History of Asian Americans*. New York: Penguin Books, 1989.

Yu, Eui-Young, Earl H. Philips, and Eun Shik Yang, ed. *Koreans in Los Angeles*. Los Angeles: California State University, Los Angeles, 1982.

AUTHOR BIOGRAPHY

Kathryne Jeun Cho was born April 13, 1968, in Seoul, Korea. She immigrated to São Paulo, Brazil, in 1974, and in 1979 she moved to the United States. She resides in California and is a graduate student in comparative literature at UCLA. She is working interdepartmentally with the Asian American Studies Center and the Department of Spanish and Portuguese.

5

In Search of My Ombligo

Stephanie Li

My maternal grandmother once told me that when a baby is born you have to bury the ombligo, or umbilical cord, in a safe place. That way the child will always know where she is from and will not be fated to wander the earth looking for her place and her home. My grandmother told me this in reference to my father who is always looking for a better job opportunity and taking the family with him. We have lived in many parts of the United States, and I think my parents will move a few times more. My grandmother says that my father is looking for his ombligo. I wonder if someone forgot to bury it for him. It is not a Chinese tradition and is certainly not a casual practice in New York City where he was born. I wonder what has become of it.

My grandmother buried the seven ombligos of her children in the yard behind the house she has lived in for almost eighty years. It is an old house with wrought iron bars on the windows and a tiled courtyard in the middle. I remember as a child running over the faded yellow tiles in sandals, the white Mexico sun above and the sound of a language I understood by tone, not by word. I return there, to Monterrey, almost every year, although the place I leave from in the United States changes.

Although I first learned my grandmother's meaning of the word ombligo last year, the search it implies has been with me for a long time. Her concern for my father's ombligo gave a name to my nostalgia, and the sense of belonging and community in the sound of her voice impressed me. Whereas both of my father's parents were Chinese mine are of entirely different cultures. I know that, like my father, my ombligo was not buried beside a familiar tree or in a green yard. I was born in the Midwest of the United States, apart from all of my extended family and missing not only them but the place they had disappeared to. Nostalgia seems to always coincide with the awareness of difference, and so it was with me. In discovering my heritage and ethnicity as a child, I came to recognize myself as alien from others. It was a startling real-

41

ization to learn that my mother spoke with an accent, that other children did not know Spanish nursery rhymes, and that they did not sleep with a panda like my paternal cousins. I wondered why chopsticks were not available in the school cafeteria and why neither of my grandmothers made apple pie.

Only rarely have I experienced overt racism; mostly I am the recipient of polite mistakes and inquisitive ignorance—like the misread sign of my name, Stephanie. "But what is your real name?" people have asked, smiling with earnest curiosity. "Stephanie," I reply. "No, what is your real name, your Chinese name?" I satisfy them by telling them my middle name, Sheu-Jing, which was given to me by my grandfather. It means "petite virtue." Almost inevitably the response is "oh, that is so beautiful." And I wonder if that means Stephanie is not—not beautiful and not quite real—and I wonder if I should smile at the compliment.

I decided to spend last summer in San Luis Potosi studying literature and exploring areas of Mexico I had never seen before. It was the first time I had been there without my mother to translate everything into English and explain our eccentric relatives within an American framework. I wanted to discover Mexico myself, to know my family members as individuals rather than as characters in stories told by my mother, and to wonder at my own reflection among the people and the movement of Mexico. I was looking for my own ombligo. My identity in the United States seemed more about mistakes and casually adopted roles than the nearly tangible ombligo I imagined I might find in Mexico.

Before I left, my father reminded me that the first Mexicans were Chinese people who had migrated across the continents millions of years ago when Asia was attached to the Americas. Would Mexico then be a new part of an old self? Could all my difference, of China and of Mexico, reside in the same country? Was my nostalgia geographic as much as it was a part of my own self? Had once united land separated, only to leave me stranded alone in the ocean between? I went to Mexico to search not restless water but land and the places and people marked by memory. The story I heard, the one that has first risen to cross that distant sea, is that of my mother and father.

My mother is proof that you don't have to live in the place where your ombligo is buried. She has lived in the United States for over twenty-five years, and it is here that she raised my brother and me. My parents met in graduate school in New York. They studied pharmacology and spent many afternoons talking and going to the movies. They fell in love, and when my mother went back home to Mexico my father decided to visit her. From the start it was an encounter of discovery. He was met at the airport and bombarded with cheeks to kiss. Hola, kiss, hola, kiss, and the ritual was repeated with every new relative. The touch was as new as the dozens of faces that swept past him, and there, finally, was my mother among a family much larger than any he had ever known. At the time of his visit, they had known each other for a few years. But in Mexico they recognized one another anew within the movement and customs of my mother's homeland, a world entirely foreign to my father. He suddenly became attuned to different social norms and expectations as when, like a liberal American, he thought he would be staying at my mother's house. He quickly caught on to a more conservative sense of propriety and made arrangements at a nearby hotel. It was a short, surprising visit that determined the fate of their relationship.

Now my parents laugh at the awkward and unexpected situations during that momentous visit. Even separately they tell the same stories, as if their love has unified memory as well as two separate cultures. To my father's surprise, all of their dates in Mexico were chaperoned by one of my mother's brothers or a giggling group of her nieces. With my uncles, my father—the "chino americano"—was playfully warned to take care of my mother. "Do you know Smith and Wesson?" one asked "They are our other brothers." Knowing my father, I am sure he smiled at the American reference brought to a Mexican reality, and I imagine that he was extra careful that evening as he thought of guns that my laughing uncle has never owned. My cousins, then bright young girls, proved more inquisitive. They had never seen an Asian person and stared with curious disbelief at my father's slanted eyes and broad nose. "Pero puede ver con ojos tan chiqitos?" (but can he see with such small eyes) one asked. My father opened his eyes wide for them and tried to see as much of Mexico as he could.

What did he see? What did Mexico look like to him then? Was it the same as what I saw as a child and what I remember now that I am so far away from there? Bright colors and laughing, familiar faces seated around a wide kitchen table, hot pavements and sticky popsicles, the call of street vendors and the clanging of church bells, curious fruits revealing new colors beneath their rinds. I think it must have filled him with some kind of promise—the faces of children he would later see to maturity, the sound of laughter he would come to share, and my mother, the woman he loved.

My father arrived home from Mexico, and forgetting the reserved nature of Chinese custom, he enthusiastically embraced both of his parents. "Johnny, what is this?" my grandfather immediately asked, taken aback by his son's spontaneous display of affection. They were a family that rarely touched one another. For them, love was displayed through respect, hard work, and dedication to the family. But my father had just returned from a world where, as he jokingly says, "it takes half an hour to just say hello or goodbye," where touch was freely exchanged between family and friends. He brought home pieces of Mexico with him that day, and later he would bring his wife.

I think of my father returning to the United States and throwing himself on the stiff and surprised bodies of my grandparents, and I smile. I think of it as the first embrace of a new freedom and of another culture brought back to his own family. It was as if he communicated with his parents in a language newly learned from Mexico and my mother's family.

But of even greater surprise to my Chinese grandparents than their son's sudden embrace was the announcement of his engagement to my mother. My father has two sisters, but he is the only son, the only child capable of passing on the Li name. As in many Chinese families it was expected that he would marry a Chinese woman, and the pressure to do so was especially strong since he was the only male child. My father was determined, however, and when my mother voiced her concern to him about his parents' response to their engagement he replied, "Well, they will have to learn to live with it." He expressed a freedom and resolve that surprised my mother. To begin their own family, they would have to transgress familial obligation and cultural expectation. Although both families were apprehensive, my parents were in love and decided to get married.

I wish I could have seen their wedding. It was the first and only time my Chinese grandparents went to Mexico. My mother, the youngest of seven children, was the last of her siblings to marry. It was a celebration of so much—the end of her childhood and that of her brothers and sisters, the promise of a new life in the United States, the union of two people in love, the union of two cultures.

My father arrived with his parents, his two sisters, one brother-in-law, and four nephews and nieces. Everything was ecstatic and new. They were rushed to a party where the children broke a piñata and conversations among my four grandparents were translated. It was a huge sharing and celebration of a world broadening before them, the union of Mexicans and Chinese and the infinite possibilities of a life ahead in the United States. My uncles from both sides of the family discussed potential business deals, the nieces and nephews gathered candy from the exploded piñata, my grandparents absorbed all of the activity in their separate languages, and in the center of it all were my parents.

The night before the wedding one of my uncles picked my father up from his hotel and announced that it was time for the mariachi band. My father knew nothing of the Mexican tradition of serenading the bride on the eve of the wedding, but encouraged by my uncle's enthusiasm and the group of men with guitars and *vestidos de charro*, he went along. He didn't know any of the songs but he danced to the music and shouted my mother's name from the street and into the night's darkness. He must have been relieved to see her, to know that the madness and noise were more than another of my uncle's crazy antics. It was as though he was flying blind through so many unfamiliar customs and faces but every awkward moment and surprise led him back to my mother and her smile.

The wedding was held on a warm August evening in a small chapel close to my grandparents' house. All of my mother's nieces—including the two daughters of my father's sister—were dressed in pale yellow gowns, nine flower girls in all because my mother refused to choose only one or two. The entire wedding was a celebration of inclusion—every word was spoken in both English and Spanish, including a speech my paternal grandfather delivered that emphasized the wonder and promise of the occasion. One of my uncles read from First Corinthians, chapter 13, my favorite passage in the Bible: "If I speak in the tongues of men and of angels, but have not love, I am a noisy gong or a clanging cymbal . . . For now we see in a mirror dimly but then face to face. Now I know in part; then I shall understand fully, even as I have been fully understood. So faith, hope, love abide, these three; but the greatest of these is love."

After the priest's homily, my parents faced one another and spoke their vows. I wonder if understanding flooded both of them at that moment. I think of those vows as the culmination of all that had been done to bring them to that point because in the ultimate moment of their wedding it was not the union of two cultures or the comparison of differences and similarities between Mexicans and Chinese that mattered most but the simple expression of love and the courage of their union.

They left the chapel amid the heavenly voices of a children's choir singing "Ave Maria." I so wish I could have been there and joined my voice with the choir. The wedding ended to the sound of children, who sang in neither Spanish nor English but communicated a beauty that both transcended and belonged to all languages and cultures.

The wedding reception was held at one of the few Chinese restaurants in Monterrey, and the entire banquet was overseen by my paternal grandfather. It was the first time that most of my mother's family had eaten Chinese food and the last time that relatives from both sides of my family would be together. The days of celebration must have seemed very brief then, with the moments of ecstatic cultural union and discovery ending with my parents' lone departure to the United States. The next day they flew to Jamaica for their honeymoon, my father's family returned to New York and Maryland, and the others scattered to their homes in Mexico.

When I imagine the evening of my parents' wedding I am sure my ombligo was there somewhere in the chapel, the reception room, amid the happy union of my grandparents, parents, uncles, aunts, and cousins. Maybe it left with my parents and traveled back to the United States with them. Or did it stay in Mexico where I discovered the memory of their initial union? Part of my ombligo seems to be buried among all of those memories and in their wedding—the only meeting of the two sides of my family. I see now how my experiences and my self are reflected in that past. My father's return embrace of his parents is the embrace I extend to all aspects of my family and its history, the determination of his freedom to marry my mother is a strength I seek as I claim my unique ancestry, the celebration and courage of their marriage is what I hope for my own future, and their love—which has grown through over twenty-five years of marriage, is the foundation of my own being and understanding of the world. From both sides of my heritage I have learned to value my family and to seek my freedom, and it is there that I find the union of my cultural identity.

Perhaps my grandmother was wrong and my father really does know where his ombligo is. Like his grandfather who left China for the United States, my father seeks a new life, and so we have settled in many parts of the United States. When I see him with my mother, I know that together they carry and hold his ombligo. When I am with my parents I think mine is there, too, for awhile at least. But I must always leave—for school, for Mexico, for what will soon be the beginning of my professional life. I know I will never find my ombligo; rather, my inheritance demands that I create it over and over again through memory and faith. Like my parents, I will probably move many times. Amid the movement I am learning that memories are inevitably elusive, a slippery foundation for something as important as an ombligo. I choose, then, to write as well as to remember—like now, as I write of memories and of the future my family and I will create within the broad landscape of the Americas.

AUTHOR BIOGRAPHY

Stephanie Li graduated from Stanford University in 1998. She was the coordinator for the Stanford Working Group on People of Asian Descent in Latin America and edited the 1998 spring edition of Americas and Latinas: A Journal of Women and Gender *which included a special section on the experience of Asians in Latin America. At Stanford she majored in comparative literature and focused her studies on texts from the United States, Latin America, and Russia. Her senior thesis examines issues of invisibility and consciousness in the works of Fyodor Dostoevsky and Ralph Ellison. Currently, she is a high school English teacher in the San Francisco Bay Area and plans to attend graduate school in the near future.*

6

We Sail across Memories

Aly Remtulla

for Bruce, Karen, Kartar, and especially Nand

We sail across memories
to the New World,
enacting Columbus's journey
but coming across
another sea.

Eager husbands greet
us at port—we have come
here to live with strangers.
I expect to be alone,
to be surrounded by
whites, so I am surprised
to find others
living in my skin.

Pati does not want me
to mix with these women
with thick braids.
He calls them uncivilized
and their husbands weak.

But we bridge the
distance. Our skins
close the gap of
centuries. We tie
our blood-tipped hair
into knots, and wear
each others' tongues.

These are my sisters,
with obsidian eyes
and desert breath.
We share a history
of empire, and of
displacement.

We are reunited in
this foreign home—
my sisters and I,
all Indians.

Note: *Pati* means husband.

AUTHOR BIOGRAPHY

Aly Remtulla is a South Asian Muslim born in Kenya and raised in Canada. He was an honors graduate of Stanford University where he majored in anthropology and minored in Asian American Studies and biological sciences. His poetry has appeared in Trikone Magazine, Weber Studies, *and* Contours of the Heart: South Asians Map North America. *He has several academic essays and book projects forthcoming. He has been awarded a Rhodes Scholarship (1999) for graduate work at Oxford.*

7

Lessons from the Field: Being Chinese American in Panama

Lok C. D. Siu

"My friend, wat you lookin' fo?" There was something in those words, maybe the intonation, the accent, the rhythm in which they were spoken. It was as if I was awakened from a dream I did not know I was dreaming. The man simply asked in his matter-of-fact Caribbean smoothness, "My friend, wat you lookin' fo?" And all I could do was stand there, silent, flushed with memories that had escaped me a long time ago.

In those few seconds nineteen years of unconscious questioning suddenly erupted like a volcano, shaking the very foundations of what I thought I knew. It was the way in which those words were spoken or heard that embodied the spirit of my father and all his peculiarities. In that moment of revelation everything fell into place. It finally made sense to me why my father used to address strangers on the street as "my friend." I used to think it was purely his naïveté, his lack of city sophistication that made him think everyone was his friend. And there was also his peculiar accent, one that I couldn't place until now. It wasn't exactly Chinese or completely Spanish but a combination of both with a heavy Caribbean influence.

In those few words, "My Friend, wat you lookin' fo?" I rediscovered a history, a place, a cultural context through which memories of my father gained new depth and meaning. Until then, I had not realized how much Bluefields had shaped my father. But being there, hearing the layers and mixture of voices in the open market, feeling the unbearable humidity, and seeing the Afro-Caribbean presence, I recognized elements of him all around me. Bluefields was so clearly a part of him. It saturated his speech, his gestures, his sense of humor. It even revealed itself in the way he moved and walked, ever so slowly and patiently. Nicaragua. Nicaraguita. So this is the place my father once called home, the place where all his stories begin and end.

That visit to Bluefields, Nicaragua took place almost nine years ago, but I remember it like it was just yesterday. It took twelve hours by bus, a night stayover in Rama, and an hour by speedboat to reach Bluefields from Managua. The difficulty in reaching the Atlantic Coast, where Bluefields is located, reflects the historical and sociocultural separation between the two regions. And unlike the people of the Pacific Coast who speak mostly Spanish, people on the Caribbean side speak English as much as Spanish. The constituency of Bluefields is almost all Miskitu Indians now, although according to my father and his friends there was once a sizable Chinese population of at least a few hundred people. In 1990, however, I could locate only one family whose surname was Chinese. Most of them had fled before the Sandinista Revolution in 1979, seeking political asylum in Miami, Los Angeles, San Francisco, or other parts of Central America.

Since that fateful journey I've made a special effort to return to Nicaragua and to explore other parts of Central America. And with every visit I learn a little more about the place and come a little closer to sharing my father's love and compassion for the land and people there.

It was during one of those summers of traveling in Central America that I came across Panama. From the outset, Panama captured my imagination. I was shocked and excited to see the incredible presence of the Chinese there. With two "Chinatowns," a Chinese school, a Chinese Cultural Center, at least twenty Chinese restaurants in the heart of the city, Chinese bakeries, Chinese video rental stores, and Chinese people everywhere, Panama has one of the largest, oldest, and most vibrant Chinese communities in Central America. I knew then that I wanted to learn more about the Chinese in Panama—how had this community become so different from the other communities in Central America?

So it's not all that surprising that I decided to undertake graduate research on the Chinese in Panama, and when the time came for me to conduct fieldwork research off I went to Panama City. For thirteen months I tried to gain some tangible knowledge about the workings of this Chinese community in Panama. And although thirteen months of cultural immersion cannot be fairly or easily summarized in the next few pages, I share glimpses of my personal experience in Panama. The first scenario deals with my trials in looking for an affordable apartment in Panama City, and the second describes one of my encounters with Panamanian traffic police.

*   *   *

These apartments once housed U.S. military personnel. Like matchboxes they line up in neat rows along the block. Functional and uniform, they represent U.S. military expansionism all over the world. They are the same kind of bungalows you'd find on old U.S. military bases everywhere, although these have outlived their function and are now occupied by Panamanian families. Entire families would fit into a small one-bedroom apartment, which made me feel a little guilty for taking up so much room by myself.

I was assigned to one of these prisonlike apartments. I never liked the place much. It was dark, lifeless and eerie, and it was located across the railroad tracks from the Curundú projects, right in the heart of the red light district. Few taxis would go by there after dark; the ones that did were carrying customers for the prostitutes. Several times I tried to hail a taxi at night from outside my apartment; the ones that stopped had mistaken me for a prostitute and quickly shot off, leaving me momentarily confused and later (when I realized what was happening) furious.

Soon I began my mission of apartment hunting. I grabbed the newspaper and looked at the classified section. Day after day I worked with real estate agents and looked at dozens of apartments. It was interesting how they recognized my American-accented Spanish almost immediately. As soon as I opened my mouth they would reply in Spanish-accented English, "Oh. You are looking for an apartment." I tried all kinds of contortions with my mouth to distort or hide my accent, but nothing worked. Next came setting up appointments and describing myself to them. "Yes, I'll be wearing jeans and a white shirt. I'm Chinese American." They would reply, "I thought you were American."

"Well yes, I am American, I am Chinese American. I am Chinese but have lived in the United States most of my life."

"Oh, so you are Chinese."

"Yes, I am Chinese. Chinese American."

It usually took a few tries before we ended this exchange; they usually resigned out of courtesy and I out of frustration. I always found it rather puzzling that despite the 100,000 ethnic Chinese living in Panama, Panamanians still had difficulty understanding that there may be Chinese in the United States as well. But then again, that was the reaction my friends in the United States had when I told them I was doing research on the Chinese in Panama. They would say: "Chinese in Panama? Wow. I didn't even know there were Chinese there." But if there were Chinese in Chillicothe, Ohio, why wouldn't there be Chinese in Panama City, Panama? Let's face it, the Chinese are everywhere.

My search continued, and I became more and more discouraged by the expensive housing costs. One day a Panamanian friend asked me, "Is someone calling for you? You know that owners and real estate agents ask a higher price when they know you are American. And clearly, your accent would give it away immediately." So began the second phase of my apartment search. My friend conscientiously called apartments for me, and sure enough, the rates were lower.

I finally saw a place I liked in El Cangrejo, but the asking price was still too high for what my fellowship allowed. As I thanked the real estate agent and apologized for wasting her time, I handed her my Stanford business card and wrote down my local phone number in case she came across something in my price range. She called that evening, proposing that I meet with the landlord of the apartment and explaining that maybe he would lower the price for a "respectable *paisana*"[1] such as myself. "Not everyone can get a Ph.D. from Stanford, you know," she assured me. "Someone of your talent may appeal to the compassion of this landlord who, by the way, is also *Chinese*." Perhaps she knew something I didn't, so I went along. What's to lose? At the very least, I could meet a possible interviewee.

His condo had "Chinese" written all over it. I noticed the emblematic red square with the Chinese character meaning *prosperity* hung upside down on the front door, the shoes and house slippers lying to the side of the entrance, glimpses of red-and-gold color combinations throughout the house. Almost instantly I felt at ease at the sight of these familiar things. The maid showed us to the landlord's office. As we entered he turned around, smiled and respectfully shook our hands. His short hair was neatly parted, combed, and gelled to a gleaming black glow. His short-sleeved shirt was beyond clean. It was crisply ironed, as were his dress pants, and their modest colors matched perfectly. Everything was neat, simple, practical—a typical Chinese Latin American male aesthetic. I recognize it in varying degrees in Chinese men throughout Central America. His mannerisms and gestures suggested a rather elegant, aristocratic sensibility. And his smooth, nicely bronzed skin reflected years of lounging, not working, under the tropical sun. His reserved, suave, understated qualities translated to being smart, confident, yet approachable and friendly—traits unmistakably befitting an accomplished businessman.

At first I was quite amused that two Chinese people were being introduced by a Jewish Panamanian woman. The usual formalities were conducted in Spanish, with his slightly Chinese accented and mine recognizably American. But as soon as he realized I spoke Cantonese his expression changed as if his facial muscles had finally relaxed, and we slipped comfortably into our native tongue. We spoke on our own terms, at our own pace, covering personal questions of who I was, where my parents lived, what they did for a living, how I had come here, and what I (a single young woman) was doing alone in Panama. Along the way, we discovered some coincidences: Our families were from the same region of China. We had mutual Chinese friends in Panama. His son had lived in San Francisco and loved California.

As we continued our conversation I grew more and more amazed by the multiplying intersections at our lives. Within minutes our relationship had taken on new depth. Returning to the issue at hand, he asked how much I was currently paying in rent. It was $200 less than the advertised price of his apartment. Without hesitation he responded, "Take my apartment. Pay me what you are paying now; $200 is just a drop in the bucket for me. It's better that you are safe and that I know you'll be a good tenant." With that, he invited me to Dim Sum with his family and friends.

Although it seemed that I obtained this apartment by pure luck, I knew that his act of altruism was made possible by several factors—some of which had to do with our ethnic and linguistic ties and some with my social class background as suggested by my status as a graduate student from the United States. The credibility of my story was further enhanced by the fact that the landlord's children had gone through a similar process while studying abroad in California. My foreignness, hence, was mediated and undermined by these factors.

*   *   *

Encounters with the traffic police in Panama are infamous. They've become a necessary rite of passage. You haven't lived in Panama until you've had some sort of dealing with the police.

Hearing myself screaming at the top of my lungs "*Yo soy gringa! Yo soy gringa!*"[2] was the last thing I expected. I'd like to think of it as a momentary lapse of reason, an instinctive survival tactic that took hold immediately after I was paralyzed by fear. Yes, I admit it. That was my response to the traffic policeman who noted, in his wise and knowing way, that the Smithsonian driver's license I was carrying is issued only to Americans. He told me this assuming that I was not American.

I grew angry, but could I blame him? How could I expect Panamanians to accept without scrutiny the fact that I'm American? Even Americans are unconvinced that Asian Americans are American. In Panama as well as in the rest of the world, the stereotypical American is white, male, big, and wealthy. As a small, Chinese woman driving a 1976 Toyota Corolla, I couldn't be farther from that image. How do I begin to explain to these Panamanian police that not all Americans are big white men, that there are Chinese living in the United States, just as there are Chinese in Panama? I became flustered and upset as the officer glared at me in disbelief with a smirk on his face that not only reflected his amusement at my frustration but also triggered my realization that this was an absurd but very real cross-cultural encounter. Patriotism aside, I thought my claiming gringohood was the only leverage I had in these types of legal-political negotiations in Panama.

The officer carefully inspected both my California and Smithsonian driver's licenses. He wasn't interested in matching my face to the photos; he was looking for legitimacy in those cards. When he pulled me over he had expected to find a recent Chinese immigrant from China (who would have been more willing to give him "coffee money" than I was). When I spoke in Spanish claiming I was American, he undoubtedly became a little confused. Where was my gringo accent when I needed it? Or was it just not registering with him? He looked at me some more. I simply did not fit his projected image of a Chinese immigrant.

With one last examination of my face and my various identification cards, the officer turned to his partner and remarked, "Ella habla español." The subtext was "she's not one of those recent Chinese immigrants. She's not bribable." Having said that, the officers quickly changed their tone of voice. Rather than scrutinize me further one of them asked if I was related to Director Siu, the supervisor of the Police Academy. Since my last name is also Siu and Panama City is a small city, he automatically assumed there would be a familial connection. In Panama, it seems, everyone is related by less than three degrees of separation. Without hesitation I assured him that all Siu's are related and that I, as a Siu, am related to this Director Siu of the Police Academy. And in case that wasn't enough to convince them of my innocence, I added in my most arrogant tone of voice, "In fact, he's my father's first cousin." It worked like magic. With that additional piece of information the two police officers nodded approvingly, smiled, then waved me off. This was my first, if not also my most valuable, lesson in Panamanian politics.

*   *   *

After thirteen months of research in Panama I returned with boxes of notes, documents, tapes, maps, and anything else that might be even slightly related to my work. I learned in the process of unpacking, however, that the most difficult things to sort through aren't necessarily the material data I systematically collected; rather, they are the incidental, everyday experiences of adjusting to life in Panama that keep resurfacing, begging for deeper analysis. What my personal interactions revealed are just as telling of what it means to be Chinese in Panama as the rest of my data. In fact, it was in my daily practices of negotiating life in Panama that I confronted the limits of my assumptions of what it means to be Chinese: how being Chinese in the United States is quite different from being Chinese in Panama and, more precisely, how my being Chinese American gave me access to certain insights while simultaneously providing a critical distance for interpretation. Certainly, similarities can be drawn from our common experiences as part of the Chinese diaspora in the Americas. But there is still much to learn about the ways in which local and national historical developments shape our understandings of ethnicity and belonging, as well as the differential strategies and tactics we adopt in order to operate in different contexts.

NOTES

1. *Paisana/paisano* literally means countrywoman and countryman. In Panama as other parts of Latin America, the term is used to describe or address a Chinese person in a respectable way. Most commonly, it is used by Chinese people to address or refer to one another.
2. *"Yo soy gringa, yo soy gringa"* translates to "I am American, I am American."

Gringa/gringo refers to foreigners, usually those who are racially white. In Panama, because of the widespread presence of the U.S. military, gringa/gringo is most often used to refer to American woman/American man. Again the terms maintain a connotation of whiteness.

AUTHOR BIOGRAPHY

Lok C. D. Siu is a doctoral student in the Department of Social and Cultural Anthropology at Stanford University. Her Ph.D. dissertation concerns the ethnic Chinese in Panama and examines their different imaginings and practices of "community." Upon completing her dissertation, she intends to continue research on the Chinese in Latin America as well as to explore the effects of media and technology on Asian America.

8

La Búsquedad de la Identidad— In Search of My Identity

Tomoyo Hiroishi

This woodblock was created in April 1997 when I finally started feeling comfortable about my identity. The different masks in the shelf represent the two cultures I grew up in simultaneously: Japanese and Mexican. My hands, which are reaching toward the shelf, suggest the choice I might have to make between two identities: Am I a Japanese or a Mexican? After seeking my identity for awhile, I realized I did not need to choose either after all. My longtime confusion was no longer negative; it became a positive aspect in my life. I have created my own distinct culture by combining the most intriguing and amazing elements of my two origins.

I think I am going to let the masks stay where they are.

AUTHOR BIOGRAPHY

Tomoyo Hiroishi was born in Mexico City in 1974. Her parents are from Japan. She was educated at the Japanese School and the American High School in Mexico City. She graduated summa cum laude in graphic design from Boston University in 1997 and is currently the art director for the World Paper, *an international publication based in Boston. One of her prints was selected for an exhibition in Japan while she was a student at Boston University.*

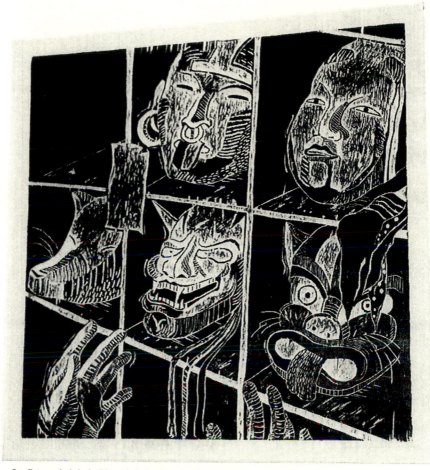

La Búsquedad de la Identidad (In Search of My Identity). Woodblock, Black and White, 26″ × 26″. Reprinted courtesy of Tomoyo Hiroishi.

9

American Dreams
An Original Play

Velina Hasu Houston

> *This is for my father, the late Lemo Houston, who returned from World War II and the Korean conflict forever changed by the travesties of war, and by the American racism that placed him at the front line of combat.*

American Dreams had its world premiere Off-Broadway at the Negro Ensemble Company in 1984.

An excerpt from
ACT ONE
SCENE ONE

(Afternoon. Lights fade in to reveal MANFRED BANKS. Standing on a chair, he uses hammer and nails to hang a *noren* [a Japanese door hanging] in the kitchen archway that leads offstage. He hangs it upside down. An upbeat love song from the swing era plays loudly on the radio, and MANFRED sings along. He's a tall, handsome man. His attitude is jazzy, leisurely; he's the eternal good-time man. He wears casual slacks, a white tank-top T-shirt, and slippers. He smokes a cigar and occasionally snaps his fingers to the music. Phone rings. MANFRED answers it.)

58

MANFRED

Yo.
(a pause)
Why hello Alexis darling!
(mood darkening)
No, he ain't here yet, so keep your skirt down.

(He hangs up the phone in anger. Suddenly, a mass of womanhood darkens the archway from the other side and yanks the *noren* down, causing MANFRED to stumble and fall off of the chair. The woman, FREDDIE BANKS, enters. She is an obese, very dark-skinned woman stuffed into an undersized, brightly colored housedress and wearing scuff house slippers. She has a strong, striking face. She trudges, every step seeming to leave her out of breath.)

MANFRED

(in reaction to his fall)
Gotdamn it, Freddie. You're like a buffalo sometimes, you know?

FREDDIE

Don't want that damn Jap flag hangin' in my house. Why'd he send us that thing anyway? What's he want from us?

MANFRED

We gotta make 'em feel at home, Freddie. Times is hard enough on people like them.

FREDDIE

Ain't gotta do nothin' but tell that high-falutin' brother of yours that he can take his Tokeeyo tart right on out of here. Tell him there ain't no house, no—

MANFRED

Now Freddie.

FREDDIE

Ain't no family, no party, ain't nothin'. And if you don't want to tell him, I'll tell him myself.

MANFRED

I reckon we gotta get him a house somehow.

FREDDIE

Now, Mannie, you had a right to that money. He raised that brown-nosin' sister of yours and sent you off to live with some aunt after your mother died. I figure it's comp money.
    (laughs, pleased with herself)

MANFRED

She was a good aunt.

FREDDIE

An Indian squaw? Please. That's why you eat so funny.

MANFRED

You forget. My mother's name was Running Deer.

FREDDIE

Wish I could forget it. All I know is, this is the first time in years Negroes ain't been at the bottom of the heap. Let them Japs slide on over to the U.S. of A. Yeah, let 'em. 'Bout time we had somebody to walk on.

> (MANFRED tries to put the *noren* back up, but FREDDIE grabs it and rips it into shreds, tossing the pieces onto the dining table.)

MANFRED

Aw, baby, come on. Tell me what's really bothering you today.

FREDDIE

Don't be trying to get on my sweet side now.

MANFRED

Baby, all sides of you are sweet.

FREDDIE

You really have grown to love me, haven't you, Mannie?

MANFRED

Yeah, you're my special woman.

FREDDIE

Not that special.

MANFRED

Don't worry. It'll happen again.

FREDDIE

Lord knows, I got enough room to carry five children.

MANFRED

Yeah. Lord knows.

FREDDIE

(pops her fingers to the music)
I been readin' 'bout a new diet, but I think I just got large glands, you know?
Like Mrs. Robinson.

MANFRED

Yeah, large glands, honey.

FREDDIE

Yeah, large glands.
(a pause)
Manfred. Who was that on the phone earlier?

MANFRED

Somebody for Creed.

FREDDIE

He don't have no friends left here. Except for one.
(a pause)
Was it her?

MANFRED

I swear women got an antenna in the middle of one of their breasts or somethin'. Yeah, it was her.

FREDDIE

Why didn't you just say so, then? Your tongue get tied up when you gotta
say her name? Say it.

MANFRED

Oh, Freddie, that girl don't mean a thing to nobody. You're worth ten of her.

FREDDIE

Say her name then. Look me in the eye and say it. Ten times.

MANFRED

A-A-A-Alexis.

FREDDIE

Uh-huh.

MANFRED

Alexis.

FREDDIE

Case is closed, Manfred Banks.

>(A faint knock on the door grows louder until MANFRED and FRED-DIE finally hear it over the din of the music.)

CREED

(offstage)

Hey, Manfred. Mannie, are you home?

>(At the sound of CREED'S voice, FREDDIE frowns and MANFRED turns down the music. FREDDIE squashes herself into the easy chair and reclines. MANFRED opens the door. Enter CREED BANKS and SETSUKO BANKS. CREED is tall and as handsome as MANFRED, but they differ considerably in attitude. CREED is serious, pensive, and exudes a gentle warmth. He wears a khaki Army dress uniform with cap. He grins at his brother who pinches his jaw affectionately. SETSUKO is a delicate, petite, attractive woman. Timid and nervous, she wears a stylish outfit of the times—a full skirt, an angora sweater, a jacket, and low-heeled pumps.)

CREED

What's the word, Mannie?

MANFRED

Yo, Creed! Long time no see, brother.

CREED

Hi, Freddie.

FREDDIE

Fredella, please.

CREED

(finding her amusing)
Fredella? Since when did anybody call you anything but Fred or Freddie?

FREDDIE

Been a lot of changes 'round here.
(a look at MANFRED)
Amen.

(SETSUKO stretches to remove CREED'S cap for him. Realizing his forgetfulness, he grins. She smiles and holds onto his cap.)

CREED

Well . . . this is my wife, Setsuko.

FREDDIE

Say what?

CREED

(slow articulation)
Se—tsu—ko.

MANFRED

Can we call you Sue or Koko or somethin'? Ain't no easy name you got there.

SETSUKO

Setsuko.

CREED

Yes. Se—tsu—ko. Try it. It's phonetic.

MANFRED

Set—soo—ko.

SETSUKO

Setsuko.

FREDDIE

(swings around and takes a look at her)
Yeah, yeah. We got it.
(points at herself)
Fredella. Fruh—del—la.

(CREED steps out of the door and
brings in their luggage. MANFRED is
quick to assist.)

SETSUKO

(to Freddie, in accented English)
May I sit, please? I tired.

FREDDIE

Don't want the fabric wearin' down. Can't afford to buy a new sofa 'till a year
or two, so sit light.

SETSUKO

(sits carefully)
Hai.

FREDDIE

Hi? Child, we finished with the hellos and how-are-yous five minutes ago.

CREED

"*Hai*" means yes in Japanese, Freddie.

FREDDIE

Christ.

MANFRED

Freddie, calm down now. She's had a bad morning. Woke up early.

FREDDIE

I've been having a great morning. Slept late, listened to my programs—

MANFRED

Radio makes her evil.

SETSUKO

I am sorry. I keep mixing up English and Japanese.

FREDDIE

Uh-huh.

MANFRED
(searching for an excuse, any excuse)
Uh, foreign languages wear on Freddie, what with all the Puerto Ricans in the City.

SETSUKO

Ah, my father same way when Americans came to Japan.

FREDDIE

Uh-uh. Ain't the same 'cause the Americans will sooner or later leave Java.

MANFRED

Not Java, Freddie. Japan.

FREDDIE

Yeah. Lots of Javanese comin' over here now.

SETSUKO

Japanese.

FREDDIE

That's what I said.

CREED

Of course, Freddie. I mean, Fredella.

MANFRED
(tempering)
Well, I must say, it's good to have you back, brother. I was gettin' tired of bein' the only man in the family.

CREED

Yeah, we got the telegram from Blue River. Is everything set for Saturday night?

MANFRED

Saturday?

FREDDIE

(laughs, turns away her gaze, and relaxes)
Yeah, Saturday.

CREED

Boy, it's been a long time since I've seen an American party.

FREDDIE

Well, don't hold it over our heads.

CREED

Fredella. Has my brother not been the good husband you deserve lately?

MANFRED

What? I been on my best behavior.

FREDDIE

(cuts a glance at MANFRED and then at CREED)
Nobody told you to volunteer for the Korean War, too, and then go right back to Java. We all know you didn't do it for the good of your country—or the good of this family either.

SETSUKO

No other way to stay together. My mother sick. I stay in Japan to take care of her.
(with difficulty)
She . . . die in my arm.

FREDDIE

What scratch is she talkin'?

SETSUKO

(holds up her arms as a gesture)
My mother. She die in my arm.

MANFRED

I understand. You speak good English.
(imitating her movement)
She die in your arm. Right, Suko?

CREED

Setsuko.

MANFRED

Man, ain't no big deal.

FREDDIE
(stands, unable to contain her pleasure)
Ain't no homecomin' party either.

CREED

What? But Blue's telegram said all my old friends were—

MANFRED
(covering)
Yeah, bad times. People workin' extra jobs and stuff. Been hard on Negroes.

FREDDIE

The Negroes who came home after the war, who gave two cents about the wives and girlfriends they left behind. Ain't none of them gonna come celebrate your homecomin', Mr. Creed Banks.

CREED

My friends are Negro, white, brown, yellow, and red.

FREDDIE

Christ. Here we go again with your crayon box. Thought nine years would rid you of that philosophy crap.

SETSUKO

Kureyon box?

FREDDIE

Yeah, Tokeeyo. You in there, too.

CREED

Freddie. Setsuko's been looking forward to meeting you.

SETSUKO

I never before met an American girlfriend.

FREDDIE

Jesus.
(a pause)

She ain't been here but two minutes and she got me using the Lord's name in vain. Some kind of devil work coming down here.

MANFRED

Got to keep Freddie away from that radio.

FREDDIE

(to CREED)

You want to know the truth, you teepee-head Negro? Ain't nobody comin' to see you and your—her—'cause last thing Negroes need is to be seen favorin' a Jap.

SETSUKO

No call me "Jap."

MANFRED

Yeah, Freddie, that's enough.

FREDDIE

(to CREED)

You always talking about your mother and that tasteless flat bread she used to make. Boy, you a colored man living in the U.S. of A. You can forget about your mother, forget you got all that mixed blood because nobody gives a darn about it. This country's colored and white, and ain't no room for anybody else, thank you very much.

CREED

Regardless of the race situation in this country, Setsuko isn't a Jap. She's a Japanese and, if we're going to be a family, you'd better learn that.

FREDDIE

Oh, I'm scared.

(a quick pause)

Don't threaten me, Mr. Creed Banks.

CREED

I think my very presence threatens you, and that's no fault of mine.

MANFRED

Go along in the kitchen and get us some drinks, Freddie.

(to Setsuko)

Want a beer, Princess?

CREED

She'll have some milk.

SETSUKO

Hai. Milk would be good.

FREDDIE

You just gonna let them come in here and act like I'm their slave or something?

SETSUKO

I get drinks. Just tell me where—

CREED

You sit still and make yourself at home.

MANFRED

It's called hospitality, Freddie. You know it and you usually do it better than anybody I know.

FREDDIE

Well, let me go find my lace apron and silver tray. I'll be serving you out on the veranda.
    (storms out to the kitchen)

CREED

How's her blood pressure, Mannie?

MANFRED

High. And her mouth gets fatter every day.

SETSUKO

I think she no like Japanese. Hard to forget war. My sister same way.

MANFRED

Princess, she
    (imitating her accent)
"no like" pretty woman, especially thin ones.

CREED

Come on, Mannie. Don't be hard on Freddie. She's just suffering from a little culture shock. Setsuko's cousin fainted the first time she saw me.

MANFRED

What? Freddie ain't sufferin' from nothing. She's just had a checkup. She's just—
    (searches for excuse)

SETSUKO

    (brushes off the hem of her skirt)
Dirty, *ne?*

MANFRED

    (taken aback)
Why that ain't nice to say!

CREED

She means New York's dirty, Mannie, not Freddie.

SETSUKO

Ah! *Gomen nasai.* I mean city dirty. Not like my home. Before American bombs come, everywhere buildings and streets clean.

CREED

In the country where Setsuko's father had a farm, everything looked like a picture. I wish you could see it, Mannie.

MANFRED

Her father's a farmer.

CREED

Well, more accurately, it was an estate. He had tenant farmers who managed the land for him.

MANFRED

You mean like slaves? Her daddy had slaves?

SETSUKO

He was large landowner. Americans take away his land, give to tenants. They call it "democracy." My father . . . take his own life after war. He was ashamed about losing family land.

MANFRED

Must not been too happy about gettin' a colored son-in-law either.

SETSUKO

    (firmly)

He was unhappy about Creed because he was a Yankee and M.P.
   (a pause)
War hard, but, still, I miss home.

MANFRED

Well, this is your home now. Ain't nothin' like a free country.

CREED

Since when has it been free?

MANFRED

Well, you're an American. At least you're free.

CREED

My wife's an American now, too.
   (an uncomfortable pause)
Maybe we should head out to our new house. When did you see it last?

MANFRED

The house? Oh, guess it was last month.

CREED

Were they surprised when a colored man made the down payment in cash?

MANFRED

Yeah. Thought I was a pimp.

SETSUKO

Pimple?

CREED

Like *yakuza*, like a gangster.

SETSUKO

Ah, *wakarimashita*.
   (on MANFRED'S stare)
See? Sometimes I mix up words and speak half-half, new language—Japanese English. We become Japanese and American family, *ne*.

MANFRED

Something tells me that won't sit quite right with Freddie. Not right now, anyway. Yeah, well, uh, ain't you goin' to spend no time with me before you move on into your own little house, Creed?

CREED

What with Freddie so upset, it would be better for us to go. The house has been our dream, Mannie, you know that. We saved that money for a long time.

SETSUKO

(proudly)
Creed saved so we can have our own house.

MANFRED

But what about your orders? Have you checked with the Army brass?

CREED

I'm sure I'll be stationed somewhere around here. Even the Army knows better than to send an interracial couple to some southern fort. I talked to the major last week and he said everything would be fine.

MANFRED

Yeah, but we need some time, brother. I seen you once after World War II and once during that Korean stuff. Man, we got nine years to catch up on. Let's get out the bourbon and some cigars. Freddie? Freddie, where's the drinks? Yeah, we'll do this welcome home stuff right. Gotta catch you up on Blue River, too. Our sister's one great woman. Freddie?

FREDDIE

(comes out with a large bowl full of heaps of ice cream) Ain't no milk. I gotta send for groceries later.

MANFRED

But, Freddie, Creed's—

FREDDIE

Fredella's tired, honey.

(FREDDIE exits to bedroom.)

MANFRED

Well, we can party by our own selves. How does that bourbon sound?

SETSUKO

What does he mean, Creed?

CREED

Whiskey and *hamaki*.

SETSUKO

Ah, *so desu.*

MANFRED

They really do say "ah so," huh?

CREED

(explaining to her, "one drink")
Ippai-no nomimono.

SETSUKO

Hai, dake desu, ne.

MANFRED

Boy, you talk that Jap stuff good, brother!

CREED

Mannie, you shouldn't use the word "jap."

SETSUKO

Please no use that word.

MANFRED

What? Come on, man. Don't mean no harm. Ain't it just short for Japanese?
Like an abbreviation?

CREED

Yeah, like "nigger" is short for "Negro." Apology accepted.

MANFRED

Oh, I see. Okay. Sorry.

SETSUKO

We have lot to learn about each other. Do not worry. I sure I will make mistakes, too.

MANFRED

Well, let me go get the elixir. Y'all just make yourselves comfortable. My house is your house is my house.
(winks at CREED and exits to kitchen)

AUTHOR BIOGRAPHY

An award-winning multigenre author, Velina Hasu Houston writes plays, film and television, cultural criticism, poetry, and prose. Her acclaimed, internationally pro-

duced plays include her signature play, Tea. *Plays have been commissioned by the Mark Taper Forum (two), Manhattan Theatre Club, Asia Society, Honolulu Theatre for Youth, the Lila Wallace—Readers' Digest Foundation New Generations Play Project, and others. For film, she has written for Columbia Pictures, Sidney Poitier, PBS, Lancit Media, and others. She has edited two drama anthologies for Temple University Press. Her plays appear in anthologies published by Vintage Books—Random House, Applause Books, Smith and Kraus Books, University of Massachusetts Press, and University of Texas Press. Her many awards include the Remy Martin New Vision Award in screenwriting from Sidney Poitier and two Rockefeller Foundation fellowships. A Phi Beta Kappa, she is an associate professor, resident playwright, and director of the playwriting program at the University of Southern California School of Theatre and a member of the Writers Guild of America, west. In Japan, five documentary films about her work and family have been produced by Nippon Hoso Kai, Mainichi Hoso, and Television Tokyo Channel 12.*

10

A Portrait of the Poet: Small-kid Time

R. Zamora Linmark

I.

When I was in fifth grade,
Miss K. made us write a poem
for the State Annual Poetry
Contest, Division III.

. . . if you're chosen, $100.00. . . .
Our eyes went bonkers. Our faces
wore hundred-dollar smiles. Even
"Twinkles" Batongbacal's packed-on
makeup and "Honeygirl" Perez'
scotch-taped eyelids were peeled
off by the crisp Ben Franklin.

. . . read your poem out loud . . . top three . . .
We all gave the evileye
to each other, thinking,
Eh, wot? You tink you one poet?
No way, Jose. I get da last word.
We walked around with an I-spit-
on-your-poem-attitude, except
to Jennifer Stewart cuz
she was the only one who could
speak, read, write English right.

II.

I told Miss K. I did not
know what to write
           so
she popped a quarter out.

75

"Here, catch the 52 Circle Island. Write
          'bout the people on the bus,
                study their faces,
                     and write.
                          If
                        you're
                      still stuck,
                 ask for a transfer
          and keep riding the pen."

III.

For one week, we were frustrated.
Line breaks, metaphors, similes,
Haole-write English. But when sixth-
period PE came, we spilled out
our insecurities with sham battle,
German dodgeball, flag football,
and every ball imaginable.

IV.

When time came,
everyone went up:

> Jr. Santiago, the only Filipino who had enough courage to
> admit he ate black dogs, wrote 'bout his first time at a cockfight
> in Waipahu.

> Edward Caraang, III, wrote 'bout coming to America and shop-
> ping at Gem's.

> Lisa Ann "Honeygirl" Perez wrote 'bout her third time with
> her babe Darren.

> Frank Concepcion wrote 'bout being an altar boy in the Philip-
> pines and the fun he had with the priests who played with him
> and let him sleep over.

> Cary Kaneshiro wrote 'bout winning the Chinese Jacks compe-
> tition.

> Randall Keola Lim wrote 'bout his first time with "Honeygirl"
> Perez inside the big cannon in front of Fort Derussy.

Swee Ming "Suzanne" Low wrote 'bout Dim Sum.

Darren Sipili wrote 'bout beefing Randall after school.

Kalani "Babes" Aiu, my best friend, wrote 'bout surfing at the North Shore with the tsunami waves breaking the bones.

Pedro "Boo" Arucan wrote 'bout his rose-tattooed chest.

Domingo Bocalbos wrote 'bout the uninvited bees who wrecked his birthday picnic, grinding all the lumpias, pansit, and pig's blood.

Jennifer Stewart wrote 'bout the military importance in Hawaii.

Mary Ann Fujimoto wrote 'bout spending X-mas at Hale Kipa cuz her mother lost it after her "other half" croaked from crystal meth.

Tyrone "Foots" White wrote 'bout being Popolo in Kalihi.

Joey "Boogaloo" Silva wrote 'bout winning the 1st Annual Breakdancing Competition held at the State Capitol.

Mataele Mataele wrote 'bout this road in the deep end of the valley diverging and he could not figure out which one to take, so he took the path that was less familiar, that had lesser footprints, and he ended up in Kahuku.

Purificacion "Twinkles" Batongbacal wrote 'bout her sixth time.

V.

I wrote 'bout:

Hungry bees eating space, black dogs losing it first time

America raiding scotch-taped Kalihi while Pedros drowned in Franco's German-spit second time

Dim in the Philippines, P.I. Joes missing in Fort Derussy's dead-end pockets third time

Immigrants coming to Kalihi twinkling with their American crystal meth dream fourth time

Smiles that can break evil bones after school, culture breakdancing beef in front of Gem's fifth time

Uninvited priests with their rose tattoos, grinding fighting cocks and preaching last words on a hundred dollar altar sixth time

(And I wrote 'bout a pig cap pen bleeding a hundred dollar poem.)

AUTHOR BIOGRAPHY

R. Zamora Linmark was born in Manila, educated in Honolulu, and resides in San Francisco. His work has appeared in numerous anthologies and journals, such as The Best Gay American Fiction of 1997, Flippin': Filipinos on America, Premonitions, *and* Charlie Chan Is Dead. *His novel,* Rolling the R's, *was published in 1995.*

11

Where Are You Now?

Thomas Sze Leong Yu

Packing the last of my books into the back of the rented moving van, I run back up to my apartment for the last time to make sure I did not forget anything. I pause as I hold the cool bronze doorknob, seeing my distorted reflection on its scratched yellow surface. Slowly, I twist the knob open. Familiar smells of oil, from countless nights of cooking in the wok, rush around the door into my nose. I walk with heavy steps into the apartment and through the halls, inspecting the empty rooms, the naked white walls stripped of posters and calendars of Hong Kong actresses. All over the walls there are still little messages that my little brother, Ricky, and I wrote to each other a long time ago. They read:

> To that retard Ricky,
> Go eat shit.
> Your Master Thomas Yu
> 3/23/87

On the same message the word *retard* is crossed out. So is *Master*, which is then replaced by the word *Slave* in crude blue ink. The reply, slanting upward from mine:

> I found your note.
> Fuck you.
> Your Eternal Emperor Ricky Yu
> 3/31/87

I find myself smiling as I read all the messages on the walls. Near the light switch in our room, I discover my brother's last message.

To this Shithole of a Room,
Goodbye, and sorry about the walls.
Ricky Yu— 12/11/95

I take out a pencil from my pocket and add my name below his.

The date, 12/12/95.

Even after ten years of living here, the place still looks pretty much the same as the time my family first moved in. I search every corner, and seeing nothing left behind I lock the door and leave. Instead of taking the elevator I walk down the dark stairs, stinking of pot, spilled beer, and old urine. These are the smells of young men breaking up with their girlfriends, the tears that fell on this floor. These are the smells of fathers getting assaulted coming home late from night shifts, the blood dripping on the tiles. And these are the smells of the many times I walked into homeless people making love on the steps, panting with sour breaths, or of the addicts shooting up on the roof. These stairs were theaters of the things strange, passionate, and violent of my childhood. Walking down, I notice something on the far wall, a word in faded black marker. CRAZE: The image slowly came back to me, of when that word was scrawled on the wall. That was Carlos's tag. Damn, Carlos, I knew you so long ago. Where are you now?

The first time I saw Carlos I was watching him from my second-story window facing the empty gray yard. I first learned Carlos's name when the other kids would shout for him from the other side of the yard, crooning the last syllable as wolves would howl at the pale moon. But even before I knew his name I had distinguished him from the other kids by his peculiar hair. Back then, my brother, Ricky, and I never knew that such a hairstyle existed. We just assumed that Carlos thought it was funny to wear a dark mop on his head, like the old used ones Mom kept in a blue bucket by the toilet. I sat by the window watching his ropey head, waiting to see if the mop would fly off in the sudden gusts of summer winds. Instead, the black octopus gripped his head as if his head was a sinking ship, the dark arms clinging on as he swung like a human pendulum near the neglected metal slide.

That day by the window a year had already passed since all of the tenants settled into this new Loisaida project in the Lower East Side. Ricky and I used to go down to the new yard early in the morning to avoid the crowds in the spring of that year. But by summer all of the swings were broken. The only thing left was the sticky metal slide that was more fun to stomp on than to actually *slide* through. Carlos had nothing to do by himself down at the broken yard; he was just a lonely urban Tarzan swinging on chain vines that were once real swings.

Johnny, Kris, Julia, and the usual pack of kids that played downstairs after the morning cartoons did not come out. Too shy to go down and play with them, I usually just sat by the windowsill watching them run around in the yard. I didn't know how well Chinese boys like my brother and me would mix with Puerto Rican kids. That day I was thinking about how to figure out Spanish, since it sounded so goddamn different from Chinese, or how I would look with hair like that when Carlos saw me at my window and called, "HEY CHINO! Come down and play!"

Carlos said that I was the first chino he'd ever met in real life because Bruce Lee on TV didn't count. We kung fued the garbage can as if we were real renegade shaolin monks who'd had too much rice wine to drink. Tottering to the ground in painful submission, the dented garbage can fell, and the beer bottles that rolled out smashed like tinkling fireworks. The ones that didn't break we threw against the wall until the ground was covered in sparkling brown and green. Both of us sporting bastard smiles, Carlos rasped with pride to the other kids that we kicked ass good today as the others scattered the glittering glass across the whole yard. Gathering around, the other kids asked, "Hey chino, where you live, man?"

"He lives right in our building," Carlos answered for me. I pointed out my window among many others, and they did the same. Pretty soon we would be going to each others' apartments and spending more and more time playing down in the yard.

I remember some of those days and forget the others. Sometimes, we were inside the yard. Other days we were scaling the black metal spires of the yard fence and going into the streets or roaming around in other buildings' backyards and empty rubble lots. Looking back now, all of the fun days merge with the other days when we just sat around lazying in the summer heat. My mind no longer distinguishes each individual day. Now, they all seem like one big hazy memory.

I will always remember the first summer as the time when we looked for Johnny's red dodgeball as we climbed over the concrete walls to get into other yards of adjacent buildings. We lost it the day before when Carlos spun the ball around with his arm like an outta-gas helicopter and let it fly over the wall into some deserted rubble lots. We searched for it by guessing how far the ball must have bounced or by checking behind overgrown, smelly weeds that might have hidden it, only to be driven away by swarms of shiny green flies. As a replacement we played dodgeball with a softball, but it hurt too much when someone got hit by it. Carlos had to make Julia stop crying when he accidentally smacked her in the shoulder with it before she would run to her mom to tell on him. We had no choice but to stop playing dodgeball. Besides, the softball broke too many windows. For a few days we sat around catching many flying, brown beetles or knocking them out of the air with a quick slap. At noon, when we had decimated most of the beetle population in the yard, we lay on wooden benches and exchanged idle talk.

"Man, I'm thirsty," complained Carlos.

"Yeah, I know, right," replied Johnny.

"Why don't we go to the lady that sells the ice down near Avenue D?" suggested my brother.

"How much does it cost?" I asked.

"I think it's a quarter," Kris replied. "Or we could buy the bigger ices for fifty cents if you want to walk a little farther."

"Hmmm. I wonder if I have money," said Julia. She checked her shorts pockets, producing nothing. When she got up the wood of the bench she was lying on creaked as she walked toward our building side of the yard.

"MA!" Julia shouted. "MA!"

After a brief pause Julia's mom peered out of the third-story window wearing a light-blue cotton sleeping gown. Her curly brown hair was flattened on the left side of her head from just waking up.

"What?" Julia's mom shouted back.

"I need some money," answered Julia. "I wanna buy some ice."

Julia's mom disappeared into the cool recesses of the dark window. This time only her hand stuck out between the window bars, dropping a bunch of jingling coins in a white sock.

"THANK YOU!" shouted Julia, picking up the sock. "C'mon, let's go buy ice."

My brother Ricky, Johnny, and several other kids, led by Julia, climbed over the black fence and disappeared from view into the street. Meanwhile, Carlos, Kris, and I stretched our bodies across the wooden benches, too lethargic to do anything. We just lay there for a while until Kris staggered up, as if his body weighed several tons. He climbed the concrete wall opposite the black fence, and undid his zipper.

I watched a great golden arc curve over the wall and heard it splatter on the thirsty weeds growing in the other lot. The line of piss undulated as Kris danced along the top ledge. Many sparkling dots reflected back as the summer sun climbed higher and higher over the yard, too intense for me to look at for long. With my eyes closed, the sunlight shone brilliantly through the blood-red film of my eyelids. Even the heavens persuaded me to start drifting away into sleep.

But before I could, in a tiny place between consciousness and dreams, I heard Kris's whooping call from the top of the wall. "The dodgeball! The dodgeball! I found it!"

Carlos and I sprang up and climbed the wall next to where Kris stood. Peering in the direction of Kris's pointing finger, I spotted the red dodgeball in a dusty ditch, covered with broken concrete blocks and assorted plastic garbage. It laid half buried in the dry sand, gleaming with urinated moisture, like a fossil making a debut after being shadowed by eons of evolution and cataclysmic disasters. Carlos jumped down into the ditch and was already thinking of how to dig it out for a game of dodgeball when the others came back.

Sitting on that concrete wall I saw my brother Ricky, Johnny, and Julia climbing the black fence across the yard. Kris couldn't wait to tell Johnny the good news.

"You found my dodgeball?" asked Johnny.

"Yeah, it was right there in the ditch," Kris replied.

"At least you don't have to piss on it, dickhead," said Johnny.

"If I didn't piss on it, we never woulda found it. Then it would be covered in dust forever. So you should be thanking me," Kris answered.

"Okay, fucking thank you, you ass," Johnny said, laughing. He rolled the dodgeball to Carlos, who kicked it back inside the building.

"I'll be right back!" shouted Carlos.

After several minutes we heard the springy bounces of the dodgeball echoing through the buildings. Carlos came back with the red ball after washing it in his apartment. He threw it hard coming up the stairs to the yard, aiming for Johnny. Johnny ducked, and it nailed Julia right in the back of her head, popping the blue-colored ice out of her mouth onto the hot ground. Crying doubly hard, for having been hit on the head and for dropping the ice, Julia wailed to her mom at the third-floor window. Carlos ran up apologizing profusely, trying to shut her up at the same time, as things in the yard slowly flowed back to normal.

Another summer I remember Carlos and me sitting down by the yard early in the morning leafing through a bunch of old porno magazines someone had dumped out the window. It was still a time when we didn't understand why we had erections every time we looked at those pictures. As Carlos studied the pages intently, I asked him what he wanted to be when he grew up.

"I don't know," he said. "All I know is that I'll be pretty damn rich."

"That's it?" I asked.

"Yeah. But I'll also have a wife like this white girl here," he said, pointing at the picture. "Don't you think she's pretty?"

"I guess so."

"I mean, don't you wonder what it's like sleeping with one of them?"

I shrugged. "But what you gonna do with all your money?"

"I don't know. I probably give some to my mom . . ."

"Yeah . . ."

"Then I'll buy this whole building and the yard, and you could have a floor for yourself, and I'll have a floor for myself, too."

"Sounds good," I said, thinking of how nice that would be when we would each have a floor. We had such bastard smiles on our faces.

"We could play dodgeball every day, don't hafta go to school, don't hafta work. Damn . . ."

Each day ended for me when my mother called from my second-story window. Carlos tried imitating Chinese, but I told him, dammit, you'll never get it right. Chinese to him sounded like a bunch of kung fu sounds, like Bruce Lee kicking butt. Spanish to me sounded like someone speaking English really damn fast, with a lot of gargling sounds. Even with all of my exposure to Spanish, like my neighbor's constant, earth-shaking merengue music, I never really picked up the language. Maybe it was because I always waited for Carlos to translate the Spanish spoken to me, and Carlos waited for me to translate Chinese for him. Or maybe it was because Carlos and I only came together during the day to play in the yard, but at night we went back to our separate worlds. On most nights I would eat dinner by my windowsill, looking down at the yard already blue-dark, and I would hear Mrs. Rodriguez's cackling voice shouting "CAR-LOS," echoing it through the canyon of project walls. I heard Carlos shouting back "ALRIGHT, MA" and the soft thudding of the abandoned dodgeball, bouncing in the empty yard.

For the rest of the summer we played and played, thinking those days would last forever even in the autumns of our youth. We hardly thought about how the sun waned earlier at the end of each day until it became too dark to play outside. Our shorts turned into long pants, and our T-shirts became coats. School came back, and we saw less and less of each other down at the wintry yard. Carlos, though, still wanted things to be the way they were in the summer. Wearing a thin jacket, Carlos sat shivering on the wooden benches, waiting each day for us to come down into the yard to play. But by then we all went to different schools, and everyone began hanging out with different people. Sitting near the window, scrambling to finish my homework, I heard Carlos calling me, almost begging, "C'mon, chino. Come down here. Come down and play." I still feel that heavy weight down in my gut as I remember the gloom in Carlos's face when I excused myself, telling him I had too much homework. After a while, I didn't see Carlos down at the yard anymore. He gave up trying to keep us all together.

I remember Kris telling me once that Carlos was two grades behind, even though we were all the same age. Carlos didn't seem to care about school as much as the rest of us. Once, he ripped some tattered yellow pages from his outdated public school social studies textbook so we would have something to play fire with. Huddled around, we watched in primal rapture as bright orange flames ate away the pages stamped with "New York City Board of Education." We all made fun of Carlos's report cards then, always the worst of the whole gang. Little did we know we were leaving him behind, abandoning him to the streets forever, forgetting about him hanging out alone in the deserted yard of broken swings.

Riding away in the back of the moving van, I watch the dwindling mirror reflection of the brown project disappearing behind me. I think back to the last time I saw Carlos, probably last winter, I'm not really sure. Maybe it was the time the maintenance man caught him spray-painting the staircase wall.

I can still see the maintenance guy grabbing Carlos's slightly bent elbow as he put the finishing touches on the "E." But then again, I think I saw Carlos down at the street some months after that.

Looking much older, Carlos had stubbles of hair that were trying to grow into a goatee. I didn't recognize him at first among the crowd of laughing teenagers throwing dirty street snow at people walking by. He recognized me, though, and told his friends not to throw any at me. As he walked up to me, I thought he was some stranger from another building. "Hey chino," he said to me. I looked closer, and I discerned him: that smile, that face I knew under that bristly, square jaw, and that kid I had once laughed with behind this deep voice of a young man I saw. "Thanks," I said back to him, and we separated again as I went up to the building and Carlos returned to the streets. He still remembered me and those summers we played together after all this time. I am ashamed that only now am I returning the favor.

AUTHOR BIOGRAPHY

Thomas Sze Leong Yu is a native of Hong Kong who grew up on New York City's Lower East Side. His interests include Asian American political activism and New York City government. He has occasionally contributed creative works to New York Newsday *and various journals. He is a member of the undergraduate class of 2000 at Harvard University and is majoring in government and East Asian Studies.*

12

The President's Palace

Dianne Monroe and Nguyet Lam

When I drive down this street in Atlanta, East Ponce de Leon Avenue, I always remember my country and the day we went to see the President's Palace. It was the day we went to Saigon for our final interview to leave Vietnam and come to America.

See how the trees bend inward, draping the road in shade. It is the same on the street to the President's Palace in Saigon. You feel as if you can travel forever, deeper and deeper into the green. Then you feel as if you are falling into a tunnel of green. You feel as if you will fall forever, become lost in the green, and never again emerge into the blinding white of the sun.

Everywhere now in Atlanta they are building. Tearing into the earth with claw-tooth monster machines that smell of diesel oil. Buildings of steel and cement, chrome and glass stretch skyward, welcoming the world to Atlanta for the Centennial Olympics. Everywhere the city is cleaning itself and putting on new clothes, preparing to welcome its guests, as we do in our country to celebrate the New Year.

Everywhere machines are slashing the earth, the faces are brown. They are Mexican people who come as strangers to build the structures of glass and steel that touch the sky and welcome the city's guests. Now I know that in the villages of their country, as in mine, the people speak of a gold mountain. Those who are young and strong and brave will journey far in search of their mountain of gold. I learned this the night a man and his son knocked on the door with something to say, even though the man spoke only a little English and his son spoke none at all.

I have lived in this city, this country, now for seven years, and I have seen many things. Things the Olympic guests will never see. Things I never would have believed could happen in this country I now call home. You were my first American friend, and by now you are like a sister to me. So I want to tell you the thing that now chokes my heart.

Do you remember a young man, you must have seen him talking to me once or twice. He came by my nail shop often when he was lonely or sad. Sometimes he came every day. He was tall, like you, and seldom smiled. Today his mother is preparing for his funeral.

His father was from your country and came to mine to fight in the war that joined our countries together forever in shared blood. When our two countries agreed that the children of American fathers and their families could come here, this young man was so excited. But his mother did not want to come. She was content in her country, surrounded by her family, her friends, and the spirits of her ancestors.

The young man would not let his dreams rest. "Come with me, Mother," he said again and again. "America is the land of opportunity. I will work hard and become rich and take care of you always." Finally, the old woman agreed to go with her son.

But there were things they did not know. Like how your language does not sing like ours but cuts hard along the edges and is so difficult for many of us to learn. That if one does not have a good education and good English, the only jobs you can get will not pay enough to live, and your family will be very poor.

They did not know these things because when one American dollar travels to Vietnam it becomes many dollars. Vietnam is poor and the United States is rich. We do not know about international exchange rates. We only know that when a person leaves our country for yours, he soon sends money home. In Vietnam, American dollars are like magic. A few can do so many things. We do not know that in your country those same dollars will not even pay for one trip to the grocery store.

These things the young man and his mother did not understand. So they came.

They lived on a side street in a neighborhood where the tiny apartments were stacked one atop another like empty packing crates. In them lived many other people who had also traveled far in search of their gold mountain.

So many dreams and displaced ancestors bumping into each other on the narrow stairwells while children played soccer in the parking lot below. Men leaned over the open hoods of twenty-year-old cars, coaxing them in half a dozen different languages to run just until the next pay-day.

In the windowsills people planted remnants of their left-behind lands. Basil, cilantro, and mint pushed skyward from plastic pots filled with spoonfuls of borrowed soil.

The evening air was thick with the scents of Indiri, North African bread, Mexican posole, and Pho, our beloved noodle soup. The Mexicans put tape players in wide open windows and filled the night with *música ranchera*.

It was to these apartments with their narrow rooms and thin walls that the young man brought his mother, the spirits of his ancestors, and his dreams.

He worked so hard. His first job was in a poultry plant. There he cut the carcasses of dead chickens until his arms burned and his fingers curled like chicken claws when he slept. Next he got a job in the fish department of a farmers' market. There he worked all day with his hands in packed ice until the fish scales ate into his skin and the cold bent and twisted his fingers and his dreams.

Finally, he got a job chopping vegetables in the kitchen of the Chinese restaurant next to my nail salon. He was so happy to be working where his hands were warm that he got a second job washing dishes in a Thai restaurant until one or two in the morning. He hurried home for a few hours sleep before returning to his first job at seven the next day.

He was glad to be working so many hours because for the first time he was able to save a little money. Then the Chinese restaurant next to my nail salon closed. Today it is a taco stand. The young man's small savings were soon gone, and he began to fall behind. Luckily, he found another daytime restaurant job. It did not pay as much as the first, but he was happy to again have two jobs. He was certain that he would soon be able to start saving again. He was young and strong. He was determined to build his American dream.

Then his mother became ill, and he stayed home several days to nurse her. When he returned to work one of his jobs belonged to someone else. Again he began to search for a second job. Again he began to fall behind.

The young man began to feel that no matter how hard he tried, he would never succeed. He felt the walls of his tiny apartment closing in on him. He pushed hard against those walls, but his arms were too weak and he soon became tired. He saw his American dream disappearing down a long tunnel, slipping further and further away.

He became very sad. He felt as if he was carrying a great weight. His heart bent like an old man from carrying it. I think this young man was what you call depressed.

"I am not a good son," he told his mother, "because no matter how I try I cannot build a good life for you in this country."

"I know you are a good son," his mother replied. "I see how hard you are working. Everywhere you go, luck has closed doors it has opened for others. You must keep trying, because someday you will find a door that luck has forgotten to close, and you will be able to walk through."

No matter what the old woman said, she could not ease the pain that bent her son's heart. She, too, became bent by the burden of what she could not carry for her son.

One day this young man traveled beyond sadness. "Mother, forgive me for bringing you so far from our home, for not being a good son," he said. "My pain is too great, and I will do anything to release it. Forgive me, but I must kill myself."

Then he took a kitchen knife, went to the bathroom, and locked the door.

The old woman beat on the bathroom door with her fist balled tightly. She called out to her son, but he would only reply, "I'm sorry I could not be a good son, but now I must die."

The old woman was so frightened that she called the police to ask for their help. The police came. When they left her son was dead.

The cries of the old woman kneeling on the asphalt parking lot traveled up to where the crows perched on the telephone lines and the ancestors rattled about, lost, disoriented, and confused.

When the police cars came, wailing, the people came out of their apartments. They stood silent and still on their front stoops as the ambulance arrived. Only a small boy on a red tricycle rode 'round and 'round on the parking lot pavement, singing a tuneless little song whose words were understood only by him.

The police carried the body of the boy out from his apartment and laid him in the ambulance. When the ambulance driver leaned against the police car and lit a cigarette, the people understood that there was no reason to hurry. Only then did they begin to speak in hushed voices among themselves. Their many languages rose in smoke plumes, braided and twisted together, past the place where the crows sat looking down from the telephone wires, past the place where the ancestors hovered.

You did not need to understand their languages to know what they were saying. One of the policemen stepped forward, one thick hand resting on his holstered hip: "Ya'll disperse now. I said, everyone go on home." The people understood his rough-edged language even if they did not understand his words. They tucked themselves inside their apartment homes and continued their hushed and heated words behind closed doors, in dim stairwells, and on tiny patios where herb gardens grew in little plastic pots.

The ambulance took the dead boy's body away. All that was left in the parking lot was the wailing of an old woman and a little boy riding a red tricycle around and around in a small circle, singing a tuneless no-word song that everyone understood.

Later that night a neighbor called me. "Vinh, can you come? You were her son's best friend."

I came and held the old woman's hand, thin and dry as fine rice paper, all through that first night. She cried and asked me over and over, "Vinh, please tell me, what is an easy way for me to die?"

And I, who speak so well in both my language and yours, had no words to give her.

They came the next day—not the ones who carried away the lifeless body of her son, not the ones who spoke in angry, rough-edged words. The police who now knocked at the old woman's door wore suits of dark blue and gray. Their words slid softly from their mouths and turned to smoke in the cool night air.

Such a tragedy, they said. The boy was so young. The police officers who answered the call had done everything they could. They had acted strictly in accordance with department policy. The police department had even asked one of its doctors to examine the body. The doctor had discovered that there was something wrong with the boy's heart, a thing that made the boy suddenly quit breathing. The police had done everything they could to help her son, to save him. They were so very sorry they were unable to do more. Such a tragedy, they said again. Then they left.

Between her sobs the old woman asked me how this could be. She and her son had been examined by many doctors before they were allowed to leave Vietnam and come to America. How could all those doctors have missed something so important?

Again, I had no words to give this woman who had traveled so far and lost everything she had. What could I do but hold her hand while she cried and asked me over and over again, "Vinh, please tell me, what is the best way for me to die?"

The man and his son knocked a few days later. I opened the door and smiled a welcome. They were brown-skinned like the people you see everywhere the city is rebuilding itself for its Olympic guests. The man's face was wide and open. The boy's face was not yet formed.

"Miguel," said the man, pointing to his chest with a broad, work-gnarled hand. "Miguelito, my son," he said, pointing to the boy.

"Vinh," I said, extending my hand to him.

"I have few words in English," he said, "and my son has none. But maybe, if we try, we can understand each other."

"Please come in," I motioned toward the living room.

They sat carefully. The man spread his hands on his knees in a gesture of openness. The boy's legs jiggled beneath his chair while his father searched for the words to share what he wanted to say.

We spoke, not only with words but with our hands and our hearts. In the end I understood.

They came to this place because there was work in construction. It was hard work, but the dollars they earned here multiplied as they traveled to his village in Mexico. There, the dollars did many things for the family Miguel had left behind.

In Mexico, Miguel explained, the land and the people were warm and open, but work and dollars were scarce. An uncle in Chicago had paid a man a considerable amount to guide Miguel and his son across the border, to take them a way the border police would not see.

"*Somos indocumentados.* We have no papers to be here," the man explained. Then I understood that something as fragile as a piece of paper can determine whether or not a child thousands of miles away has food to eat.

Here, they feared to walk freely in the street because if any policeman asked to see their I.D. they might be returned to their warm and open land, where there would still be no work and their family would still be hungry. So they left their apartment only to go to work, to buy groceries, and to wire money home.

Miguelito was still young, but his father believed the boy would be a great help in this country. His son was agile and quick to learn. In Mexico there was nothing the boy could not climb, from a stone wall to a steep mountainside. Miguelito had learned to see things that others could not, to search for the tiny chinks in brick and cement, rock and stone that were perfect for finger and toe-holds, to find the pathways up and over the things that others said were impassable.

Like many boys his age, Miguelito was boastful. "I can climb up that wall," he liked to tell other boys. When the other boys said, "No, you can't. It's impossible," he would show them that he could.

So it happened that on a certain Saturday Miguelito was among a group of boys lounging on the small strip of grass in back of their apartment complex, looking for a way to fill the long afternoon. Miguelito studied the building's back wall. His eyes moved from downstairs stoops and back bedroom windows to second-floor bathrooms and balcony railings.

"I can climb up the side of this wall," he said.

"No, you can't," a chorus of boys answered.

"Yes, I can."

And so, as the police were climbing the stairs to the old woman's front door, Miguelito was stretching his legs past the apartment's back balcony railing. As the police broke down the bathroom door, Miguelito's fingertips were pulling him up to the bathroom window.

That evening Miguelito told his father what he had seen. At first Miguel told his son to tell no one because they were strangers here. Because they did not have papers to be here. And because nothing would change the fact that the boy was dead.

"Who can we tell?" Miguel asked his son, "We go to any officials and tell them what you have seen, they will ask for our I.D. When they see that we have none, they will send us straight back to Mexico."

But whenever Miguel looked at his son he remembered that the old woman was also a stranger here and also had a son. He thought, if one day my precious Miguelito is dead, and someone has seen how he died, then I would want to know.

This is what Miguelito saw through the bathroom window.

After breaking down the bathroom door the big policeman put one burly arm around the boy's neck, lifting him off the ground. The boy kicked and waved his arms about, still clutching the kitchen knife in his hand. The big policeman squeezed his arm more tightly around the boy's neck. Little by little, the boy's feet stopped kicking. Finally, the knife clattered to the bathroom floor. The big policeman released the boy's neck. He slid to the bathroom floor like a broken doll.

The smaller policeman shouted at the big one, and the big one shouted back. Then the smaller policeman knelt beside the boy's crooked body and beat on his chest. He bent low over the boy's face, placed his mouth over the boy's mouth, and breathed hard, again and again, so that his cheeks bellowed out from his face. After a long time the smaller policeman lifted his mouth from the boy's and again yelled at the big one. The big one again yelled back. Finally, the smaller policeman picked up the boy and carried him out of the bathroom.

"I don't know what we can do," Miguel said. "We are strangers here. We come with no papers, and so we cannot go to any officials. But I do know that I have a son and that this woman is also a stranger here and also had a son. If something ever happened to my son, I would want to know."

I thanked Miguel and his son for their words. After they left I fixed noodles with basil and ginger. I carried a bowl to the old woman. She lay in her bed, eyes fixed on the place where the police had beaten down the bathroom door. She had not eaten more than a few bites since her son died.

"Please, won't you try just a little," I said, placing the bowl on the small table beside her bed.

She took one small bite. "Such good noodles," she said.

But I knew she tasted nothing. She said this only to please me. I touched her hand lightly.

"I must go now," I told her. "I will come again tomorrow." Then I went home.

In my small house I feel comfortable. There I can close the door against the things that make my heart jump in my chest like I swallowed a turtle. But today that turtle feels as if it is clawing its way up my throat, gasping for clean air.

I turn on my TV to relax. I like to watch the news, to improve my English and learn more about your country. My TV is old, and the picture is always a little blurry. But that does not prevent me from seeing clearly. There's a construction site, steel girders stretching skyward from half-finished, exposed walls. To one side a large tree has been upended. Its roots reach up and out like a baby's hands.

There's the sound of sirens coming closer. Into the construction site mud drive three police cars and two white immigration vans. Even before they stop, brown-skinned men dash from the shadows of the unfinished building. White cement dust and sweat streak their faces.

Three of the men from the white van catch a wiry, brown-skinned man and push-pull-drag him toward a police car. A pair of handcuffs sparkles like jewelry as a bulky policeman wrestles them onto the wrists of the brown-skinned man. He stumbles and almost falls in construction site mud.

Then the brown-skinned man stops struggling and becomes very calm. He stares straight into the TV camera and speaks to everyone who will be watching his image that evening, gathered with their families around dinner tables or in comfortable living rooms.

"United States no good," he says. Few words, heavily accented but perfectly clear.

The turtle in my chest claws at my throat, fighting for air. For now I will say nothing. I am not yet ready to speak all that is in my heart. But the words are growing inside me. Someday, when they are ready, I will let them out.

In my country people think that if you can come here you are very lucky. They think this country is something like heaven. But now I know that for some people this country is something like hell.

You were my first American friend, and by now you are like a sister to me. So I feel this is something I can ask you—about this boy whose father was American like you, and his mother, an old woman now left alone in a land that is not her own.

I want to ask you, because you are American and we still do not know the rules of your country, although we are learning more every day. What I want to ask you is this—is there anything we can do?

AUTHOR BIOGRAPHIES

Dianne Monroe is a writer and arts educator, a former journalist, and the author of plays, fiction, and literary nonfiction. She is coauthor (with Nguyet Lam) of Scattered Children, *a collection of stories retracing the journeys of Amer-Asian and Vietnamese refugees now living in Atlanta, Georgia. As an artist-in-residence in Atlanta's public schools, she has used creative writing to enable immigrant and refugee youth to improve their English while sharing their stories with others. A long-time resident of Atlanta, she is currently working with Jump-Start Performance Company. in San Antonio, Texas.*

Nguyet Lam was born in Can Tho, Vietnam, the daughter of a Vietnamese mother and an African American father. She defied the discrimination faced by children of American fathers and traditional views of a "woman's place" to obtain an education and become a teacher. She was chosen Teacher of the Year in 1986 for her outstanding work in a rural elementary school in Huyen Zi Thanh county. In 1990 Nguyet immigrated to the United States. Today, she manages a Refugee Resource Center in Chamblee, Georgia, on the outskirts of Atlanta. She is coauthor (with Dianne Monroe) of Scattered Children, *a collection of stories retracing the journeys of Amer-Asian and Vietnamese refugees now living in Atlanta, Georgia.*

13

Dreaming All the Way Home

Leny Mendoza Strobel

> *When you wake up and find yourself living someplace where there is nobody you love and trust, no community, it is time to leave town—to pack up and go. And where you need to go is any place where there are arms that can hold you, that will not let you go.*
>
> —bell hooks, sisters of the yam

And if you have to stay in a place where you have no community, you are blessed if your dreams give you the gift of encounters with people and places that provide shelter and refuge in a world as real as the one you wake up in. My dream world has been a sheltering sky for the internal hemorrhaging of my spirit, a repair kit to the psyche invaded daily by the dominating culture that may often show signs of wanting to, but doesn't know how to make space for my kind.

The first American Methodist missionary in the Philippines converted my grandfather at the turn of the twentieth century. Never mind that the Spanish came there first and that my grandfather's first choice was to become a Catholic priest. But the white man who stood on his soapbox at the town square charmed my grandfather and seduced him into becoming one of the first Filipino Methodist pastors in the region. How different this theology of a new life of faith rather than works must have sounded to his Catholic ears. He wouldn't have to buy penance anymore or confess his sins to another person. How methodical he became, and how fanatic he was about the Protestant work ethic of pulling yourself up by your bootstraps. This often resulted in his family's alienation from the large extended family and the community, but his reference point—the U.S.—became the unconscious site where whiteness would wield its power.

Not surprisingly, one of his sons—my father—became a Methodist pastor, too. As a Methodist, my father's reference point was also Protestant America.

It is no further surprise that my older sisters taught at the U.S. military dependents' school at Clark Air Base and eventually married white men from Boston and Chicago; and that I, the third daughter, married an earth scientist from Montana.

I now teach at a university, although I did not set out to do so. What I really wanted to accomplish in my graduate work was a more personal goal: to learn how to divorce the overwhelming symbolic power of whiteness in my personal life. I wanted the recurring dreams of divorce and abandonment to stop. In time, my recurring dreams about divorce became less and less frightening. The dreams reassured me that I would make it in the world after the "white man" leaves me. This is when I started to have women dreams.

My grandmother, Apu Sinang, started to visit me in my dreams in the white man's house. She came to me and told me to plant a honeysuckle outside my bedroom window. She told me to remember the days when she and I strung *sampaguita* flowers in the late afternoon, the days when I helped assemble her betel nut chew, the nights when she put me to bed as I listened to her stories of Lola Basyang. She wanted me to remember the Old World before the white men came. She wanted me to find her again. This was the clue from my memory bank that led me in my academic pursuit.

My inner landscape is in search of the place where history, memory, language, and remembering must do their reconstructive work so I can tell my Filipina story. I need to plant the story in this space, deepen its roots until they stretch to the farthest corner of the earth and imagination, connecting all of us in the diaspora.

Over the years and through synchronicity, I believe that understanding dream images led to a harvest of relationships with four mentors whose ethnic and cultural backgrounds resonated closely with mine. The crossing of our paths forever changed the landscape of my present whereabouts, leaving clues and signposts to the next bend in the road.

*   *   *

One of the bends in the road was the decision to return to the university for graduate work where I was nurtured and supported by mentor-professors—a Mexican American, a Chinese American, an African Japanese American, and a South Asian American. They would point the road ahead.

The Chinese American professor is an interculturalist; Angie introduced me to the field of intercultural communication. This is very useful information to begin with, these intercultural competence skills required of immigrants and foreigners to function well within the dominant mainstream's ideology and values. How to understand your own cultural assumptions; how to understand the cultural expectations of others; what to do or not to do when interacting with a Japanese, an Arab, a Nigerian, a Navajo—it's all contained in those four-page brochures called *Culturegrams*, which read like tips for tourists. How should foreigners behave in the host country? How close could you stand next to an American without invading his or her space? What sort of question is taboo? Why is punctuality important? I tucked away a long list of dos and don'ts borrowed from Edward T. Hall, the guru of interculturalists.

In contrast, as a second-generation Chinese American, Angie feels quite at home as a Californian. It was difficult for me to explain to her the gnawing I felt inside in spite of the cross-cultural competence I was building. Unable to articulate these feelings to Angie in a meaningful way, I sought her mentorship thinking and hoping that her calm self-assurance and skillful negotiation of cultural borders would perhaps rub off on me. Angie took me under her wings as a reentry graduate student and taught me the ropes of career building.

We experimented doing intercultural workshops together. But I was too naive and too eager to prove myself to mainly white audiences that I did all the wrong things and left Angie to clean up the mess I had created. In one cross-cultural workshop for nonprofit managers, I came prepared with my cross-cultural communication theories on three-by-five cards. I proceeded to lecture to the white faces that stared at me in confusion but that suddenly came alive when Angie used metaphors and personal stories to talk about the pitfalls of cross-cultural miscommunication. In one illustration she drew two jack-o'-lanterns on the board—one at eye level and another from a bird's-eye view. This is the difference in the way we see the world sometimes, she said to the audience. People like me may see the pumpkin from a different perspective; how, then, shall we communicate about what we see? Simple, yet succinct. Needless to say, our collaborative facilitation didn't last long. I think I embarrassed her. I wish she had given me constructive feedback, but she only said, "You're too theoretical."

All the while I was acquiring and practicing my intercultural competence skills and functioning adequately in the white world, deep feelings of alienation and insecurity began to bubble to the surface. The Western discourse I was learning was making me miserable. In the deepest parts of myself was pain that wouldn't go away. And because I didn't have the language, I didn't know how to tell Angie what I was going through. I needed to look for answers elsewhere.

This led me to ethnic studies where I learned about Filipino American history, the master narratives of colonialism and imperialism, and the psychology of colonialism. The earlier absence of both a language and this critical discourse with which to express my feelings came from this kind of trauma. According to the poet Carolyn Forche, language fragments at the time of trauma, and the narrative won't flow again until the story is reconstituted. Inevitable in this reconstitution was a process of becoming aware of the politics of power.

As I took this turn in the road, Angie and I had less and less to talk about.

I still see her on campus. Our nods and quick hello-goodbyes are a sobering reminder of paths that cross and then part again.

*   *   *

While I was working on my master's degree, counseling at the university was free, and I used up all of my allowed sessions each semester for about three years. Francisco, my counselor, specialized in short-term therapy and conflict resolution. Francisco is Mexican American, and his manner of "detached attachment," which therapists are trained in, suited him well. Francisco is truly a compassionate, warm, genuinely interested and interesting human being. He often said he was learning much from my telling him of my Filipino American experiences. And I said I was truly benefiting from his effective short-term conflict resolution techniques. As his client I did not feel like an objectified subject of analysis. But I wonder if it wasn't the underlying, deep history we share as descendants of indigenous peoples colonized by Spain—his in Mexico and mine in the Philippines—that connected us. Even as a third-generation Mexican American, he could talk with me about the Spanish colonization of Mexico and I could talk about the Spanish colonization of the Philippines as if these colonizations had happened yesterday. Even though he used the language of psychotherapy and we seldom intentionally talked about our colonial and postcolonial histories, he seemed more at ease talking about *curanderismo*, Carlos Castaneda, and speaking of his biracial children and his wife.

"There is no right and wrong, only choices that we make for which we take absolute, impeccable responsibility!" was his favorite Castaneda line. This often came up when I talked about the difficulty of reconciling my need to be in control with the need to let things be when it came to raising my teenagers, pursuing higher education, holding down a part-time job, and remaining the dutiful wife—all at once. Add to this burden, the internalized guilt and shame carried over from my colonial past about not being as good as the people who have dominated us in the past. I think there were times when he wished he could perform a *curandero* ritual to cleanse my troubled spirit, but I sensed that would have been considered "unconventional" within the context of the university's recognized therapeutic practices. Instead, he gave me a copy of a journal article he had written on *curanderismo*.

When I told him I was worried that my son's artistic temperament and ethnicity might not serve him well in the racially biased, market-driven, materialistic world, he reminded me: "Your son has a valuable gift to share with the world. He is also Filipino, and from what I know of his mother's Filipina heart, I am sure he will do well. Do not be misled by false images. Honor your child's talent. Take care of the artist." Francisco was always more at ease speaking of the power of gentleness and generosity even though we were part of a community in which political savvy, combative assertiveness, and self-serving interests come first. Once he asked, "Have you ever given someone you love a gift so lavish, generous, unexpected, and for no reason at all?" Embarrassed, I said no. In this world, he said, everything is given to us as a gift. Your ancestors and mine understood that we don't own anything. We moderns only think we do.

Francisco helped me through a period of decolonization by truly honoring my memory and my stories, recognizing them as part of our shared history, and encouraging me to hold on to what my heart knows. Do not be deceived by images and false representations and notions of who and what has power, he often said.

*   *   *

When I completed my master's degree, I continued doctoral work at another university where I met my other mentors. One of them, an African Japanese American professor, is a philosopher trained at Oxford, a Jesuit-Buddhist, and a young tenure-track professor feeling his way around the maze of tenure requirements. John's heart is in the right place; he chose to come to a small state university to serve the Asian American and Pacific Islander students and community in northern California. He could have taught at one of the largest research universities, but he said he wanted to maintain his ties to the Asian community; to him that was more important than the promise of peer recognition and public acclaim in the ivory tower. He is also married to a Vietnamese woman and there is a large Southeast Asian community in the Napa County.

John would open many doors for me, beginning with the opportunity to become his teaching assistant and then his associate. He gave me much insight into the academic game, its politics, and its heartaches—always with the tone of someone whose heart and soul is torn between the desire to do good with the least expectation of return on one's investments and the practical material demands of raising children.

John is big on empowering students of color. He wants students to dream big, and he expects students to follow through on those dreams—all the way to law school or a master's degree or medical school. After I finished my doctorate he took me to lunch and then very subtly implied that with my doctorate in education finished I must make further inroads into an academic career by getting a "real Ph.D.," preferably at a more prestigious university, like Stanford perhaps. I think he meant this in the best possible way and he had assumed I might want to position myself as competitively as possible given the politics of academe. I couldn't make him understand the instinctual resistance I felt toward the same system that had educated me. I felt like postcolonial critic Gayatri Spivak, who wrote that just because the system enables the postcolonial critic doesn't mean the system can't be questioned. How can I position myself given the contradictions in which I find myself? John's advice makes sense. But the message from my dreams raises question as to whether I, the "wrong" woman, am willing to find the off-beaten path.

I was troubled. I had just spent six years of my life working toward a terminal degree, only to be told that I needed to keep going. Not good enough. This led to a mild depression that even my dreams couldn't pry me from. During this period in my dreams I am always wearing the wrong costume, the wrong shoes. I am always going against the direction that everyone else was going. I had dreams of reading for a part in a drama production, and I forget my lines or I fall off the stage or the words won't come out of my mouth. In another dream the pregnant Asian woman professor gives her lecture behind a podium in order to hide her pregnancy because she is afraid that her academic peers will equate her big belly with lack of credibility. Waking up I asked myself if this was my internalized colonial master who says the native will never be simply good enough. Am I, Filipino American, not as good as the "real model minority," the Oxford-educated African Japanese American scholar? Even here, in alluding to myself as different from the common perceptions about what makes a "model minority," I have already sabotaged myself.

Why, if we seek to subvert the institutions that marginalize the experiences and knowledge of people of color, do we keep playing by their rules? I realize this is the complicity that implicates good people like John. Perhaps that was his own way of saying, if we are going to be labeled the model minority, we might as well live up to it and exceed their expectations! Such predicaments always provoke me to search for a metaphor or a simple story to reconcile the conflict.

A Joseph Campbell vignette comes to my rescue. In one of his anecdotes Cambell tells of an international conference of theologians. At the end of three days the leading Western theologians tell the Japanese Zen monks, "We've been here for three days now and we still haven't figured out your theology." The Zen monks answer, "We don't have theology, we dance!" My boisterous laughter when I heard this anecdote probably reveals a truth about me as a Filipino as well. If we were asked the same question, we would probably say, "We don't have theology, we sing!" I do not need a "real" Ph.D. to sing!

The last time I saw John was before he took another job out of state. Burned by the politics of race and power, he said he would find a way to go to Japan and become a monk for a few years.

My grandmother led me to another wild woman—Roxanne, a South Asian American professor of humanities who would have the greatest impact on my life and my work. She was a Zoroastrian, she said. When I met her at the beginning of my graduate work, I was an evangelical Christian. I had just started to question the Christianity of my childhood. I had confessed to Roxanne that my white Christian friends were afraid of my plans to go back to school, to a liberal university at that. Oh no, you might become a liberal, they exclaimed. Roxanne listened without judgment, and I kept wondering why she didn't judge me, why she never said anything about my religion. She never even questioned it the way I secretly questioned hers because my evangelical faith had trained me to evaluate all faiths outside of mine as in peril of damnation. I wanted to save her. But her acceptance baffled me. What kind of faith is this that is big enough to embrace difference and not make it an issue in our friendship? What kind of faith can love unconditionally better than I, a Christian, can?

Later, when I told her that I had left my evangelical church, she merely smiled as if she knew it was bound to happen, and she reassured me that it was allright and that I would be safe. There is no fire and hell outside of these boundaries, I would soon find out.

Roxanne bought me Inanna's book, the Sumerian goddess of heaven and earth who descended into hell—killed by her dark sister—and rose again to take her place in the world above. Do biblical themes of death and resurrection belong to Christianity alone, or do they belong to all faiths and reside in our collective unconscious?

She never tells me what to do or believe, even when I wish she would. In our friendship she is like the gardener of cattleya orchids, patiently waiting through the long incubation of the next pair of purple velvet blooms. Roxanne would probably blush and *hush* me for saying so. But I know she would want me to go to a dream analyst, she herself having spent much time with her favorite Jungian analyst. The combination of Jungian analysis and her expertise in both Sanskrit literature and classic Western literature makes her one of my favorite authors and storytellers. I know she wants me to go into dream analysis so my dream life can feed the hungry child of my soul and imagination. She wants me to remember and know myself as a Filipina woman—not as a postcolonial, not as a diasporic woman, not as an exile, not as the other half of an interracial couple, not as professor. Although I am all of these she wants me to be a free woman, unencumbered by labels and categories and intellectual pretense—to be free the way my grandmother was free, the way I am meant to be, perhaps always have been and will be again.

We are all ethnic, she says. Even Shakespeare, Homer, and Dante were ethnic writers. Why, then, must we justify ourselves and seek canonization from the "center"? Why must we think of our literature and our histories as located in the "margins"? We're only in the margins if our point of reference is outside ourselves, she says. Of course, she is right. Where does she get this sense of herself, I ask myself.

I am reminded that encounters happen across different kinds of borders. And I am becoming more and more aware that my encounters with others are simultaneously encounters with the parts of myself, including the encounters with my own shadow-beast, as Gloria Anzaldua calls it. It is along the same line that I think of my sojourn in the academic world, dominated by a colonizing paradigm that wants to devour those who weren't meant to belong in its hallowed hallways. But nevertheless, in the little opening into which I have been allowed to place one foot, I leave footprints marking my presence and leaving signs along the way signifying that I have come, am here.

In a dream a Filipina angel dressed in native *sinamay* and *jusi* cloth sewn together with gold thread appears at my side and takes me onto her wings. We fly high above the desert for a long while until we come to the edge of the desert and the green stretch of land and the village and its people welcome us home.

Angie, Francisco, John, and Roxanne—each of them passed on the gifts that were given to him or her. Each of them gave me the tools, the stories, the push, the kick, the time, the energy I needed for that part of my journey. Each of them understands that we always stand on the path paved for us by others. And sometimes we have to pave our own paths and create more forks in the road for others in the future. And sometimes we have to dream our way into the future, and there meet all of the people we are yet to meet in the waking world.

AUTHOR BIOGRAPHY

Leny Mendoza Strobel grew up in the Philippines and now lives in California. She teaches at the Hutchins School of Liberal Studies and in the American Multicultural Studies Department at Sonoma State University.

Part II

The Politics of Cool—Locating a Community

14

Race Construction and Race Relations: Chinese and Blacks in Nineteenth-Century Cuba

Evelyn Hu-DeHart

"LA TRATA AMARILLA"

By the middle of the nineteenth century, Cuba had become the world's leading sugar producer. Although significantly mechanized, sugar was still produced on the traditional New World plantation model using slave labor. The planter class—epitomized by men such as Julián de Zulueta and Miguel de Aldama, who were often *hacendado*, *esclavista* (proslavery), and *negrero* (slave owner) all in one—reigned supreme. Planters' interests drove most policy-making; their authority, particularly on their estates, was largely unquestioned.

By the mid-1840s, however, due to the British embargo on the slave trade and the rapid abolition of slavery all across the Americas, Cuban planters experienced a critical shortage of labor whereas the demand for sugar continued to rise. Planter interest was represented by the powerful Real Junta de Fomento y de Colonización (Royal Office for Development and Colonization), whose agency, the Comisión de Población Blanca (Commission of White Settlement), was specifically charged with promoting the immigration of free European workers to Cuba.

But free men and women in Europe were not attracted to a plantation society with a vast slave population. In desperation, the Comisión followed the British example and turned to China for contract labor, commonly known as coolie labor. An agreement was sealed in 1846 between Zulueta and Company in London and the British in Amoy, a Chinese treaty port in Fukien province, South China. On June 3, 1847, the Spanish ship *Oquendo* docked in

Havana with 206 Chinese onboard; nine days later another British ship, the *Duke of Argyle*, arrived with 365 coolies onboard. Both human cargoes were consigned to the Junta de Fomento, which proceeded to distribute the coolies in lots of ten to a group that included the island's most prominent planters and one railroad company. Thus was initiated *la trata amarilla* (the yellow trade).

When the trade ended twenty-seven years later, 124,813 Chinese coolies—almost all male—were imported into Cuba, more than 80 percent destined for the plantations. (Many more Chinese were actually taken from China and placed on the coolie ships for the long and arduous voyage which lasted a hundred days or more; mortality was extremely high, an estimated 20 percent. A slightly smaller number of Chinese were shipped to Peru. After 1853 the Portuguese in Macao took over the shipping of coolies from the British, who quit the venture because of a tremendous international outcry over its inhumanity, although the British continued to ship large numbers of coolies from India to the West Indies colonies.)

As the African slave trade wound down, ending with the last shipments of just 145 and 1,443 slaves respectively, in 1865 and 1866, the size of the coolie imports rose correspondingly, reaching the as high as 12,391 and 14,263 in 1866 and 1867, respectively. From 1865 to the end of the coolie trade in 1874, 64,500 coolies—or over 50 percent of the total number—entered Cuba.

During this period sugar production climbed steadily, reaching a high of 768,672 metric tons in 1874. Clearly, then, coolies constituted the source of labor replenishment, delaying the crisis that would have set in with the end of the slave trade and allowing the plantation economy to continue to prosper. It is also noteworthy that after 1875, when both the slave and coolie trades had ended, sugar production displayed a pattern of general decline, a crisis brought on certainly in large part by the shortage of labor.

When the Junta de Fomento turned in desperation to Chinese coolies to meet the planters' enormous demand for labor, it is not clear that they seriously considered the social consequences of introducing a third racial element and a new labor system to Cuba's plantation society. During the subsequent decades, therefore, both formally and in informal daily interactions, Cuban society had to learn to deal with this new racial and labor element that had been thrown rapidly and rather haphazardly into what had become a rigidly constructed social system divided into slave and free, with its corresponding and reinforcing racialist ideology of black and white. In other words, what were the Chinese coolies, who were neither black nor white, neither slave nor free?

This essay seeks to explore how Cuban society dealt with this dilemma, by examining these questions: What kind of legal status was defined for the coolies, what kind of racial identity was constructed for the Chinese, and finally, how did the coolies' racial identity and legal status affect race relations in

Cuban society—with blacks and with whites—and particularly on the plantations where coolies and slaves were concentrated?

THE COOLIES' LEGAL STATUS

From the beginning, the Junta de Fomento (later changed to Comisión de Colonización presided over by the eminent planter Julian de Zulueta) supervised the importation of coolies. Its agency, which had the explicit title of Comisión de Población Blanca, did not even change its name to more accurately reflect the race of the people it was importing.

To further uphold the illusion that this was an immigration project, the Chinese coolies were almost always referred to euphemistically as *colonos asiáticos* (Asian colonists), occasionally as immigrants, rarely as workers, and never as coolies. The coolie contract, accordingly, was entitled "Libre emigración para la isla de Cuba" (Free immigration to the island of Cuba). The Chinese version was more accurately entitled "Voluntary Labor Contract."

The contract stipulated a service term of eight years, with weekly wages of one peso plus food, clothing, housing, medical attention, and holidays and Sundays off. In addition, it included the provision that upon completion of the eight-year term the coolie would be "free to work as I wish without being forced to extend this contract, not even under the pretext of debt, obligations or promises that I might have made." Regulations issued in 1854 specifically prohibited the use of corporal punishment on coolies—that is, the use of shackles, floggings, stocks commonly meted out to slaves. These regulations also included provisions for *coartation* by a fair indemnification to the master. They attributed a legal personality to the coolie, who as a free man could contract marriage, control his reproduction and assume parental authority over his offspring, and preserve his marital relationship and familial obligations (married colonos with children could not be forcibly separated); he could also acquire and dispose of private property, bring charges against his master in due course, and be given recourse to the colonial authorities in the event of abuse—which, when severe enough, could result in the recision of his contract.

If the terminology, the contract, and the series of regulations issued by the colonial government in Cuba were meant to create the impression that the coolies were free men and immigrants, the practice was a different matter. It was quite clear from the beginning that the planters found it only natural to model the coolie trade after the familiar slave trade and to ease the coolies into the existing slave regime of the plantation. Coolie traders were known as *negreros*, or slave traders. Those who bought coolie contracts were known as *patronos*, or masters. In China poor young men were rounded up by force or deception by *corredores* (Chinese agents) and sent to barracoons to await embarkation and packing on coolie ships that had recently served as slave ships. Upon arrival in Havana, they were sent to the *depósitos* (holding cells) located in the central slave market, where they were auctioned off in lots of ten. Although technically their contracts and not their persons were sold, in fact, ads in newspapers spoke directly of "venta de chinos" (Chinamen for sale). Coolies who ran away were simply tagged *chino cimarrón*, or runaway.

In other words, from the moment of their recruitment in China and throughout the duration of their lives on the plantations, the coolies were regarded and treated no differently from the slaves because the *esclavista* (slaveowner) mentality on the part of *negreros*, planters, *mayordomos* (plantation manager), and the other personnel on the plantations—including the slaves themselves—was simply extended to cover the coolies as well.

Finally, the hypocrisy was exposed, and the fate of the coolies consequently sealed, when the regulations were revised once again in 1860 to require that coolies recontract indefinitely once their original eight-year term expired, or leave Cuba at their own expense. Only those whose original contracts expired before 1861 were exempted, so as years went by a few coolies did obtain residency permits and were allowed to stay in Cuba as free men; some recontracted, and most eventually opened small businesses in provincial capitals and in Havana. Recontracting was just another way to effectively keep the coolies from ever gaining their freedom and from working and living in Cuba as free men. For all practical purpose and to all appearances, Chinese coolies were slaves. This fact was not lost on the eminent Cuban historian Juan Perez de la Riva, who concluded that the coolie system was barely disguised slavery, a ploy to prolong slave labor for the plantations.

THE COOLIES' RACIAL IDENTITY

In a society that recognized only black and white, despite the close correlation of their treatment to that of slaves, Chinese coolies did not immediately assume the slaves' racial identity. Put more accurately, the racial identity constructed for and imposed on the Chinese was not automatically, necessarily, or consistently the same as that of slaves.

In other words, there was a great deal of ambivalence when it came to which racial category to fit the coolies into. To be sure, they were sometimes lumped with blacks, but on other occasions they were identified as whites. Complicating the matter was the fact that neither the contracts nor the many regulations mentioned a racial identity for coolies, although one could infer that as long as they were legally defined as free men, their immigration to Cuba as free, they could be considered white. The only way to address this issue is to examine how the Chinese were identified racially in certain social transactions in which race was important.

If we examine various censuses taken during the mid- to late nineteenth century, we typically notice the following categories—in the 1862 census *blancos* (whites), *de color libre* (free blacks), *esclavos* (slaves), *emancipados* (freed slaves), *asiáticos* (Asians or coolies). In the 1877 census (after the cessation of the coolie trade), the category *asiático* was divided into *asiático libre* (which included coolies serving recontracts) and *asiático colono* (coolies still serving the original term). In these official censuses, then, whereas free blacks were identified explicitly by race (*de color*), race was generally avoided for the Chinese.

Cuban historian Fe Iglesias, however, in several detailed studies of different kinds of censuses, did discover in some accountings that recognized not fine distinctions but rather the conventional divisions of whites and slaves that Chinese coolies were included in the count for *blancos*. Even in the official counts, free Chinese were often included as *blancos*.

Even more interesting than censuses were the baptismal and marriage records of local parishes in the plantation zones. In most cases it appeared that when coolies were baptized they were recorded in the *libro de bautismo de color* (baptismal registry for blacks).

Then there is the fascinating story of "asiático Julian Guisen," age thirty-three. (Not always, but frequently, coolies were given Christian first names, sometimes the master's surname as well, as early as onboard the coolie ships or soon after their purchase.) Guisen's contract was originally sold to a priest, Rodrigo Alonso Delgado of Bejucal, who transferred it in 1861 to Dona Cruz Crescencia Perez, who immediately married Guisen. In preparation for marriage Guisen was given religious instruction by the priest, who subsequently baptized him. His marriage to Dona Crescencia was duly registered in the *libro primero de matrimonios de blancos* (marriage registry for whites). In 1863 Dona Crescencia petitioned the authorities to release Guisen from the remainder of his contract (*recisión de la contrata*) and to grant him his naturalization papers so that he could "do the things that other free men can"[1] and not be forced to leave Cuba. Dona Crescencia was *the hija legítima* (legal offspring) of Don Jose y Dona Concepcion Hernandez of Bejucal, both of whom agreed to the marriage. In several documents on this interesting case, no direct reference is made to what could have motivated a white woman to marry a Chinese coolie, unless it had something to do with the 306 pesos that Guisen had somehow managed to amass.

Besides priests who performed baptisms and marriages, other authorities were also called on to make judgments about the racial status of the Chinese. In 1864 an official of the Sección de Agricultura, Industria y Comercio forwarded an inquiry from the provincial government of Oriente to the judge of the Consejo de Administración on "whether or not it is permitted to transfer *asiáticos* to *personas de color*" (blacks or mixed race persons, i.e., nonwhites).

The case concerned an *asiático* named Ricardo or Pedro who was detained by local police for fighting with the *moreno* (mulatto), Sebastian Sánchez, whose wife, *la negra* Antonia María, held his contract, having bought it for 300 pesos from Don Gervasio Martínez Alarcón. The judge ruled that given the *asiático's* resistance, "because he considers himself superior by race to the black who has him," it was best to return him to his original master. He reasoned that in order to maintain social order, it was not convenient to allow colored folk *(gente de color)* to enjoy the same superiority as white masters over the *colonos asiáticos.*[2]

Race relations between slaves and coolies were complicated and interesting. Placed in a competitive situation—sometimes subjected to divide-and-conquer manipulation, and given the fact that no matter how the Chinese were treated in daily routines, slaves probably knew that the Chinese were not consistently classified as black *(de color)*, with all its attendant stigma and problems, and were not slaves—the relationships between the two races were generally strained. Even if slaves could see that the daily treatment meted out to them and to the coolies was not substantially different, they also observed the somewhat greater facility with which coolies were able to free themselves from the plantations and open small businesses nearby; it was, to be sure, a poor existence, but at least it was autonomous and independent. Esteban Montejo's memoirs, as brought to life by Miguel Barnet, contain several antipathetic remarks about the Chinese.[3] Chinese testimonies and criminal records show numerous conflicts—including assaults and murders—between Chinese and slaves on the plantations.

Certainly, the coolies never forgot the fundamental distinction between them and slaves, and whenever possible reminded everyone on the plantations that they were free men rather than chattel for life. On the other side, because they had been on the plantations longer and had a long collective experience that gave them a sense of belonging to Cuba, were far more numerous in numbers, and were more assimilated (in language, culture, and similar factors), slaves naturally felt a sense of superiority to the alien coolies. Further complicating the situation was the fact that, on some plantations at least, slave and coolie labor was not totally undifferentiated. That is, more coolies began to be moved into semiskilled work in the purging and evaporating rooms *(casa de calderas and casa de purga)*, where they worked alongside skilled and much better paid white workers. Slaves, by contrast, greatly outnumbered coolies in less skilled, less mechanized, and more manual labor such as cutting and transporting cane from the field to the mill. This situation began to set up a kind of hierarchy within the slave and semislave population that drove further wedges between the two races and at the same time enabled the Chinese to become more closely identified—and to identify themselves—with white, skilled labor.

All of this natural tension notwithstanding, it must be emphasized that at the most crucial moment of their existence, slaves and coolies—blacks and Chinese—in Cuba were able to transcend their differences, their antipathy toward each other, and all other sources of conflict to join in the struggle for Cuban independence from Spain. Both groups understood that independence would lead to their personal freedom. Coolies—called *chinos mambises* (Chinese freedom fighters)—joined with black *mambises* and white Cubans in the Ten Year War, the Guerra Chiquita, and the final war for independence under Jose Martí, Cuba's greatest national hero. They marched under Maximo Gomez, Antonio Maceo, Thomas Jordan, Henry Reeve, Carlos Roloff, and many other independence movement leaders. They provided not only rank-and-file men, but a significant number rose to positions of leadership. Some Chinese commanders, such as José Tolon, recruited and formed their own all-Chinese units, but others, such as Jose Bu and Tancredo, led mixed units. Some lived and were honored during their lives; others died as martyrs for the cause. In Cayo Hueso, there is a monument to the *chinos mambises*. After independence, Jose Bu was accorded the same right as Maximo Gomez and Carlos Roloff as "having the right to be elected president of the republic."

CONCLUSION

With the sudden and rather massive introduction of Chinese coolies into Cuban plantations during the third quarter of the nineteenth century, Cuba must have found itself much in the same situation as South Africa—that is, in an apartheid system (or what Franklin Knight terms a "caste system" for Cuba)[4] divided between black and white, slave and free and disrupted by a third racial element and a third legal status that are neither black nor white, neither slave nor free. The result is an inconsistent adjustment to the reality of this new admixture without, however, disrupting the preexisting ideological structure of race.

NOTES

1. Archivo General de la Nación—Havana. Gobierno Superior Civil 641/20.248 (1861).

2. Archivo General de la Nación—Havana. Consejo de Administración. 12 September 1864.

3. Miguel Barnet, ed. *Autobiography of a Runaway Slave: Estevan Montejo* (New York: Vintage, 1973), 94–96.

4. Franklin Knight, *Slave Society in Cuba During the Nineteenth Century* (Madison: University of Wisconsin Press, 1970).

AUTHOR BIOGRAPHY

Evelyn Hu-DeHart is professor of history and ethnic studies and chair of the Department of Ethnic Studies at the University of Colorado at Boulder. Trained in Latin American and Caribbean history, her current research and publications focus on the Asian diasporas in Latin America and the Caribbean, with particular attention on the Chinese in Mexico, Peru, and Cuba from the colonial period to the present.

15

Japanese Peruvians and Their Ethnic Encounters

Ayumi Takenaka

Since the Japanese first immigrated to Peru in 1899, they and their descendants have maintained a cohesive community with a distinct identity from others as "Japanese." Why do even later-generation Peruvians of Japanese descent maintain and try to preserve an identity distinct from other Peruvians? To examine this persistent ethnicity, I discuss Japanese Peruvians' interactions with others based on my fieldwork in Lima during 1996 and 1997.

Even though I grew up in Japan, the "Little Japan" created by 80,000 Japanese Peruvians struck me because of the number of community institutions and the insularity from the surrounding society. Throughout the 100 years of their presence in Peru, the Japanese have continued to thrive as a community without melting into the larger society. Even though the majority of Japanese Peruvians are second- and third-generation Peruvian citizens born in Peru, many marry within their own group (Morimoto 1991) and maintain an identity as "Japanese," or Nikkei (Peruvians of Japanese descent). Many young Nikkei continue to dance traditional Japanese dances and sing songs in Japanese even though they may not understand the words. I wondered what it meant for them to dance to and sing Japanese music even though they knew nothing about Japanese language, history, or geography. One community leader said, "It is important to sing in Japanese even though we don't understand what the songs are about. This is how we try to preserve a little bit of our culture and Japanese language." Why do they try to preserve the culture of their ancestors?

Ethnic encounters help to explain we can see why and how Japanese Peruvians have preserved their tight-knit community and distinct identity in the ways they have been treated by others and in their reactions to that treatment. People become aware of differences through direct interactions with others (Barth 1969) and choose to preserve, abandon, or absorb some of their old and new customs in distinction from others (Cohen 1982). Over the course of their 100-year immigration history, Japanese Peruvians have come to draw group boundaries between "us" and "them" by internalizing and institutionalizing cultural differences in response to the ways they are treated by others.

ETHNIC ENCOUNTERS: JAPANESE PERUVIANS AND THE "OTHER"

Japanese Peruvians' first cultural encounter with others occurred when they immigrated to Peru as contract laborers on sugar plantations. Japanese immigration lasted from 1899 through the first half of the twentieth century. Migration from one place to another makes cultural encounters inevitable; cultural encounters, in turn, make migrants aware of cultural differences. The hardships Japanese immigrants experienced in general, and the discriminatory practices and internments they suffered during World War II in particular, have served as important historical and symbolic landmarks of their collective memory and distinct identity even today.

Historical Legacy

The most vividly remembered historical event is the *saqueo*. In May 1940 Japanese properties were confiscated and their stores looted by a mob of street protesters. When anti-Japanese movements peaked during World War II, the Peruvian government mandated that Japanese community activities cease and that Japanese schools be closed and media shut down; further the use of the Japanese language was prohibited. Policies were enacted (in 1906, 1932, and 1936) to limit and halt the entry of Japanese immigrants, deny Japanese access to property and business ownership, and require that at least 80 percent of the employees of every business enterprise be Peruvian citizens. The deportation of 1,800 Japanese business and community leaders to U.S. detention camps, carried out in collaboration with the U.S. government, further weakened the Japanese community. Anti-Japanese sentiments increased, in part because of the relative economic success of Japanese immigrants. As the owners of small businesses the Japanese, known as *chinos de la esquina* (Chinese at the street corner), became influential; they ran over half of Lima's bakeries and three of every four small coffee, candy, and refreshment shops (Suzuki 1992).

These discriminatory practices, in particular the *saqueo*, have a lingering impact on the Japanese Peruvian community as a painful memory for those directly involved and as symbols of victimization for later-generation Japanese Peruvians. First-generation and second-generation Japanese Peruvians have passed on their wartime experiences to their children and grandchildren, and many still remember those times vividly and with a lot of emotion. A second-generation Japanese Peruvian man in his fifties asked me during an interview, "Do you think you can trust those people who once attacked us and confiscated all of our properties?" "Imagine," he continued, "we couldn't vote until the 1950s because they didn't issue us a registration card. We even had difficulty entering universities just because we were Japanese."

Even half a century later many Japanese Peruvians continue to live in fear of anti-Japanese sentiments. In the 1990 national election few Japanese Peruvians voted for Alberto Fujimori, the son of Japanese immigrants, because they feared his poor leadership could provoke a revival of such sentiments. "It's better to maintain a low profile for us Nikkei," explained a third-generation Japanese Peruvian who had not experienced the wartime discriminatory practices himself, "because whatever Fujimori does affects us. During the election campaign Peruvians called us 'Fujimori' everywhere on the streets, barred us from entering some stores, and looted Japanese businesses. We were scared that at any moment anything like *saqueo* could happen again."

Racial Differences

The way Japanese Peruvians are treated by others also stems from racial differences. Japanese Peruvians' physical appearance—particularly that of those whose parents are both Japanese—stands out in Peruvian society, where 80 percent of the population identifies as mestizos, (mixture of indigenous population and European immigrants) (Apoyo 1997). Non-Japanese Peruvians often distinguish Japanese Peruvians by calling them *ponjas* (from *Japón* meaning Japan) and more often *chinos* (Chinese) because of their phenotypical features. Many Japanese Peruvians expressed discontent with this practice, like a man I interviewed at the Japanese-Peruvian Cultural Center:

> Peruvians always yell at me *"chinito"* [Chinese] on the street. I hate it. That [is why] I come to the Japanese-Peruvian Cultural Center. I feel comfortable here because it is the only place where they don't call me *chino*. When I was at school my classmates called me *"chino, chino cochino'"* [Chinese, dirty Chinese]. I knew since I was young that I looked different from others, but I hated it when others called me that.

As a reaction to the way they are treated, many Japanese Peruvians try to distinguish themselves from the Chinese. They complain that Peruvians cannot distinguish between the two groups and understand the differences in values, cultural practices, and racial features. One third-generation Japanese Peruvian who works in his parents' business said, "The Chinese are shrewd and aggressive, especially when it comes to money. They are good at business and would do anything to make money. Nikkei are not; we are more reserved and shy and not good at dealing with money." Another said, "The Chinese look different from the Japanese. Their faces are rounder, and they smile more."

Regardless of what they are called—Chinese or ponjas—Japanese Peruvians are treated differently because of their distinguishable features and thus feel rejected by the larger Peruvian society. "We are not Peruvian," said one, "because they don't make us feel Peruvian." Another added, "In Peru we are not even Japanese. We are Chinese." In this sense the distinct ethnicity Japanese Peruvians maintain is externally imposed; it is a "self-defense," according to some informants, and a reaction to the way they are treated by others.

INTERNALIZING CULTURAL DIFFERENCES

At the same time, Japanese Peruvians have gained prestige and enjoyed positive stereotypes in Peruvian society because of their relatively high socioeconomic status. Japanese Peruvian students are present in disproportionate numbers at prestigious universities and also in the country's major political and economic institutions. Peru's "Nikkei" president has apparently raised the prestige of Japanese Peruvians, as has the status of Japan as a world economic power. Consequently, many young Japanese Peruvians told me they are no longer discriminated against. "On the contrary," a young Japanese Peruvian said, "Peruvians think we Nikkei are honest and responsible so they often prefer Nikkei as their employees, particularly as treasurers. In newspapers there are lots of ads wanting Nikkei for cashiers."

Sometimes people choose their ethnicity among possible alternatives for their own perceived benefits, as explained by one student: "The term Nikkei has positive connotations, where as the term *criollo* [referring to Peruvian] is more negative-dishonest, irresponsible, unpunctual, and egoistic. So it's sometimes better to be Nikkei than Peruvian." Japanese Peruvians' relatively high socioeconomic status as members of the middle class has also promoted the maintenance of a distinct identity as Nikkei in a country where more than half of the population lives in poverty. A former editor of a Nikkei community newspaper offered this analysis: "You can trust Nikkei more than Peruvians because you can predict what kind of family background Nikkei come from and how they would behave. They are mostly middle-class people like you and share the same values." The word "trust" was used frequently when Japanese Peruvians claimed the need to maintain their community: "Since this society is dangerous and we cannot trust anyone, even the police, we must have our own locale where we can relax and leave our belongings without worrying. That's what the Japanese Peruvian Cultural Center is all about."

INSTITUTIONALIZING CULTURAL DIFFERENCES

As a result of their belief in their distinct culture or in reaction to the way they are treated, Japanese Peruvians have established a tight-knit community in Lima. With sixty-six community institutions ranging from schools to cultural centers, the Japanese community boasts some of the finest sports clubs, theaters, and hospitals in the country. The community offers Japanese language and cultural courses and hosts a variety of activities—karaoke singing contests, Japanese folklore music and dance shows, and Japanese-style athletic meets—many of which are full of Japanese cultural symbols such as food, music, and dance. Japanese Peruvians preserve and reinforce their cultural and racial heritage mainly through these community activities.

Not all Japanese Peruvians actively participate in such activities, although an estimated two-thirds of Japanese Peruvian residents of Lima belong to at least one association and participate in some community activities. I observed that those who participated most actively were "racially pure" Japanese Peruvians (i.e., those with Japanese heritage from their parents and their grandparents). The few Japanese Peruvians I met in Lima's urban slums were racially mixed, and they perceived that they were excluded from the community because of both their racial and economic backgrounds.

As a way of distinction, Japanese Peruvians have developed labels to apply to different groups; racially "pure" Japanese Peruvians are, in their own words, *Nihonjin* (Japanese in the Japanese language) or Nikkei. Racially mixed Japanese Peruvians are usually referred to as Ainoko, Peruvians of Chinese descent as *Shinajin* (Chinese in old Japanese), and other Peruvians as *Perujin* (Peruvian), *Dojin* (barbarian in old Japanese), or sometimes *Gaijin* (foreigners). Membership in Japanese Peruvian associations is usually reserved for Nihonjin. Peruvians of non-Japanese heritage can enter Japanese schools and sport clubs as long as they are accompanied and approved by members and, in some cases, pay higher fees.

The tight-knit community has established unwritten rules and codes of behavior. For instance, Japanese Peruvians have established rotating-credit unions that have helped to raise their economic status and enhance internal solidarity. These credit unions are based primarily on mutual trust and oral consent, and each participant takes responsibility for each month's payment. If participants fail to make a payment, they are punished: They are not invited to participate again. One Japanese Peruvian who has been to Japan explained the logic: "Just as the concept of *'joshiki'* [common sense] exists in Japan, there are unwritten rules in the Nikkei community. Among Nikkei you feel pressured to behave in certain ways. Peruvians, on the other hand, don't have the concept of *joshiki*, so they act in whatever ways."

These unwritten rules help to establish solidarity and trust within a group and, at the same time, to increase distance from others. Exclusive social networks, such as the Japanese Peruvian community, serve as a mechanism for protecting the privileges of a group and simultaneously as a mechanism of social discrimination and segregation by imposing their own rights, duties, norms of conduct, and entrance requirements (Figueroa, Altamirano, and Sulmont 1996). By imposing its own code of behavior, a tight-knit community can perpetuate itself.

CONCLUSION

Japanese Peruvians have preserved their ethnic community and identity through a series of interactions with others and through a sense of being different from others. Ethnic encounters have made them aware of differences, and in the process they have defined group boundaries: "us" versus the "other." Ethnic encounters have also made them aware of alternatives.

Japanese Peruvians have preserved an ethnic identity not only because they perceive differences but because they choose among possible alternatives they discover in their ethnic encounters. As long as they perceive benefits in maintaining differences from the "other," Japanese Peruvians will probably continue to dance the traditional dances of their distant ancestors and sing songs even in a language that is foreign to them.

REFERENCES

Apoyo Opinion y Mercado S.A. *Informe de Opinion*. Lima: Apoyo, 1997.

Barth, Frederik, ed., *Ethnic Groups and Ethnic Boundaries: The Social Organization of Culture Difference*. Boston: Little, Brown, 1969.

Cohen, Anthony, ed., *Belonging: Identity and Social Organization in British Rural Cultures*. Manchester: Manchester Press, 1982.

Figueroa, Adolfo Teofilo Altamirano and Denis Sulmont. *Social Exclusion and Inequality in Peru*. Research Series 104. Geneva: International Institute for Labour Studies, 1996.

Morimoto, Amelia. *Población de Origen Japonés en el Peru: Perfil Actual*. Lima: Comisión Conmemorativa del 90 Aniversario de la Inmigración Japonesa al Peru, 1991.

Suzuki, Joji. *Nihonjin Dekasegui Imin*. Tokyo: Heibonsha, 1992.

AUTHOR BIOGRAPHY

Ayumi Takenaka is a Ph.D. candidate in sociology at Columbia University. She completed fieldwork in the Japanese Peruvian communities in Peru, Japan, and the U.S. and is writing her dissertation on the transnational migration and ethnicity of Japanese Peruvians across these three countries.

16

The Great Day for Arlen

Armando Siu Lau

When you were born, your granny Demetria told me . . .
    "Today is a great day, 16th of July, day of the Virgin of Carmen."
    I didn't understand then.
When you were growing up, you gave me happiness,
    with your sweet smile, you sang, you danced, you painted
    pretty drawings and played the guitar.
When you studied at La Escuela Normal de Señoritas,
    you wanted to be a good teacher to show the poor peasants
    who didn't know how to read.
When you at Christmastime made the piñata for the poor children
    of the La Pila Grande barrio.
When you wrote the song "María Rural" to show solidarity with the
    peasant mother on the 30th of May.
When you left for that great destiny, you left me your guitar, your
    unfinished painting, your poem of prophecy and the book
    Juan Salvador Gaviota so that I could feel your love beyond
    the heavens and earth.
. . . After nearly twenty years from the day you were born . . .
When in a summer night, I, on an airplane, crossing the sky of the North
Pole,
    heading toward the Far East . . .
    I saw you in a dream . . .
        Your body stained with blood!!!
        And your beautiful long black hair cut short!!!
        Sitting on a Lotus Flower going up to heaven,
        like the Virgin Buddha Quan Yin.
When I woke up, in the middle of the flight, over the North Pole,
    I saw outside the window a pale sun on one side of the sky.
    I looked at my watch marking 3 in the morning,
    between the 31st of July and the 1st of August.
I said: "Today will be a great day."

Nicaragua, December 1975. Translated by Jaime Cham and Lok Siu.

119

Arlen Siu Bérmudez was born and raised in Jinotepe, Nicaragua. She was already a celebrated musician, poet, and writer when she joined the FSLN (National Sandinista Liberation Front) at age 18. Her artistic works and critical essays on Marxism and feminism served as inspiration to both the Sandinista revolutionary movement and the Nicaraguan women's movement. She died in combat at age 20. As a popular leader of the National Liberation Sandinista Front (FSLN), she was martyred and became a symbol of the revolution. This poem was written by her father, Armando Siu Lau shortly after her death on July 31, 1975.

AUTHOR BIOGRAPHY

Armando Siu Lau was born in Guangdong, China and served in the Communist Revolutionary Army before he immigrated to Nicaragua in the late 1940s. He lives in Jinotepe, Nicaragua.

17

Land, Culture, and the Power of Money: Assimilation and Resistance of Okinawan Immigrants in Bolivia

Kozy K. Amemiya

A problem arose for Mr. Hiroshi Kochi, an immigrant farmer in the Department of Santa Cruz, Bolivia, one day in June 1994. A native Bolivian was claiming the land Mr. Kochi had been cultivating for almost three decades. This was not Mr. Kochi's first problem over land. Mr. Kochi was an Okinawan from Chatan Village on Japan's southernmost island of Okinawa whose family land had been taken away by the U.S. military to construct the Kadena Air Base. He had immigrated to Bolivia in 1954 as a single man with 400 other Okinawans as part of a program sponsored by the governments of the Ryukyu Islands and the United States. He and his fellow immigrants had endured many hardships, and Mr. Kochi had finally become a successful farmer. With that success came problems very different from the ones he had experienced in Okinawa. The Americans took away the land his family had cultivated for generations in Okinawa. In Bolivia a Bolivian tried to claim the land Mr. Kochi had received legally and on which he had toiled. The problem that arose in 1994 was not his first; nor was he the only one who faced such a problem. Many immigrants in Bolivia have had similar experiences.

The immigrants' lands, once part of a hostile jungle, are now a fertile ground for the creation of wealth and have often been the cause of dispute. The immigrants have experienced numerous disputes with native Bolivians over land, which commonly fall into two categories: (1) Bolivian migrants from other regions occupy the unused land, and (2) claims are made, often by powerful Bolivians, against the immigrant's land currently in use. Mr. Kochi's problem belonged to the second category. Okinawan immigrants, including Mr. Kochi, had settled previous cases with payoffs. This time, however, Mr. Kochi decided to fight back. He took his case to the Bolivian courts, involved the Japanese ambassador and the Bolivian president, and won his case.

The case of Mr. Kochi's land dispute provides a snapshot of the current relationships among the Japanese and Bolivian governments, the Japanese government and Japanese immigrants, and the Japanese immigrants and Bolivian communities.

THE FIRST JAPANESE IMMIGRANTS IN BOLIVIA

Compared with their counterparts in Peru, Brazil, and Argentina, the number of Japanese immigrants in Bolivia is small. Although nearly a quarter million Japanese (including Okinawans) immigrated to Latin America before the Pacific war began in 1941, less than 1 percent went to Bolivia.[1] This number does not include the Japanese who entered Bolivia through Peru. Ninety-one Japanese men who had originally immigrated to Peru to work in the sugar-cane fields crossed the border into Bolivia in 1899 and arrived in the Amazon region as rubber tappers.[2] They were followed by many more who also worked as rubber tappers and as carpenters, boat operators, and other skilled laborers. Some ran shops to cater to the growing population in the region stimulated by the rubber boom. Although their exact number is not clear, these immigrants left footprints in such places as Japón, Tokio, Yokohama, Mukden, and Puerto Arturo in the northernmost tropics of Pando.[3]

As the natural rubber industry in the Amazon region declined after World War I, some Japanese immigrants left the area for cities in other regions—such as La Paz, Oruro, Cochabamba, and Santa Cruz—or reimmigrated to Brazil. The majority, however, remained in the region as merchants or independent farmers and married local Bolivian women, thus blending into local communities. Isolated in the most remote region of Bolivia and with no official ties to the Japanese government or contact with the outside world, these Japanese and their descendants did not form a distinct "Japanese immigrant community." Their "Japaneseness" disappeared within one generation. Only a few traces, such as Japanese surnames, were left in the community.[4] It is estimated that in 1997 their descendants numbered about 1,000 in Cobija, the Department of Pando, and 7,000 in Riberalta, 1,300 in Trinidad, and 500 in Rurrenabaque, all in the Department of Beni. About 200 descendants remain of those who moved out of the northeastern region to Oruro and Cochabamba. The number in La Paz includes later arrivals and was 800 in early 1997.[5]

Most descendants of Japanese immigrants in Pando in the Amazon region are a quarter Japanese racially and Bolivian culturally. They have little contact with other Japanese communities in Bolivia. Likewise, they had no contact with Japan until the acute labor shortage during Japan's bubble economy in the late 1980s gave their Japanese surnames economic value by granting them special status to work in Japan. A number took advantage of this status and went to Japan to earn money.

POSTWAR IMMIGRATION TO BOLIVIA

Two Japanese immigrant communities in the Department of Santa Cruz, where Mr. Kochi lives, were established after World War II. One is Colonia Okinawa, located in the northeast of Santa Cruz, consisting of immigrants from Japan's southernmost islands of Okinawa; the other is Colonia San Juan Yapacan', located northwest of Santa Cruz, consisting of immigrants from all over Japan. The immigration to both Colonias began separately in the mid-1950s when Okinawa was still under U.S. occupation. The immigration of Okinawans was organized by the government of Ryukyu Islands (GRI) and was encouraged by the United States Civil Administration in Ryukyu Islands (USCAR) in the early 1950s. The GRI pushed the overseas emigration to alleviate population pressure, high unemployment, land shortages, and increasing social discontent. The USCAR sponsored Okinawan emigration to reduce the social tension caused by land appropriation by the U.S. military for the purpose of constructing military bases.

At the same time, the United States wanted to make Bolivia self-sufficient in terms of food supply and pressured the new Bolivian government to accept Okinawan immigrants. Financially dependent on the United States, Bolivia had no alternative but to follow the United States' intention. Thus, the thread connecting Okinawa and Bolivia was strung by the U.S. at the height of the Cold War.

The immigration program was hastily organized, and immigrants were recruited. Lured by the promise of 50 hectares of free land, about 4,000 people applied for emigration to Bolivia, out of whom 400 were selected. They arrived at the first settlement site west of Santa Cruz in 1954. Mr. Hiroshi Kochi was one of them. Almost immediately a strange illness, later called Uruma Disease, struck the settlement, affecting half of the immigrants and killing fifteen. Within a year the entire colony moved to another site, and then to another. Finally, the group settled in the current site of Colonia Okinawa in October 1956 and started over. It was only another beginning to their hardships.

Another immigration program, parallel to the Okinawa immigration, was arranged by the Japanese government a few years later. The Japanese immigration to Bolivia was first organized by an industrialist named Nishikawa who envisioned a sugarcane factory in the Santa Cruz region. He brought eighty-eight Japanese men, women, and children into San Juan Yapacan' in

July 1955, but the colonization plan soon fell apart, and the immigrants were left in the jungle. The Japanese government took over and recruited immigrants from all over Japan. In 1957 the first government-sponsored immigrant group arrived in San Juan. Although they had no major outbreaks of disease, these Japanese immigrants experienced as much hardship as the Okinawans did, with no roads, decent housing, hospitals, or schools.

A disparity in overall aid grew between Colonia Okinawa and San Juan Yapacan', which were sponsored by the different governments. Colonia Okinawa with its Okinawan immigrants initially received bulldozers and other heavy machinery from the United States, but the U.S. aid was short-lived and provided no technical assistance. San Juan with its immigrants from all over Japan, on the other hand, had no big machinery, but as Japanese government aid increased in quantity and quality conditions improved, which widened the gap between Colonia and San Juan. Okinawans appealed to the Japanese government for the same aid as that given to San Juan. As a result, Colonia Okinawa was placed under Japanese government protection in 1967, five years before the reversion of its homeland of Okinawa to Japan.

Meanwhile, both communities battled a series of disasters (crop failures, droughts, floods, and the remote locations). The majority of the immigrants left the *colonias* and moved to towns, returned to Japan, or reemigrated to other Latin American countries. As of April 1, 1997, about 770 immigrants and their offspring remained in in Colonia San Juan, and about 850 in Colonia Okinawa. About a thousand Japanese and Okinawan immigrants and their descendants live in the city of Santa Cruz and vicinity.[6]

Ironically, the exodus of immigrants out of the *colonias* helped those who remained to expand the farmland needed for mechanized farming. They grow rice, citrus, and macadamia and raise chickens for eggs in San Juan. In Colonia Okinawa, which is drier than San Juan, they grow mostly soybeans, wheat, sorghum, and sunflowers for oil and raise cattle. With the world demand for soybeans soaring, Colonia Okinawa finds itself a part of the world market. A gap no longer exists between the two communities—the Okinawans and mainland Japanese—in terms of the amount and quality of Japanese government aid. Still far from self-sufficient, the Japanese-Bolivian Association in San Juan stated in 1984 in a petition to various branches of the Japanese government that it would need financial and technical aid from Japan because under Bolivian policy it would be impossible to arrange and maintain the infrastructure and superstructure (such as roads, education, health care, social order, and economic development) needed in Bolivia with immigrants alone. This basic premise has not changed, although the degree of need may have declined in the 1990s.[7]

At the same time, the Department and the City of Santa Cruz, Bolivia, are also very dependent on Japanese aid. With their well-publicized aid, as well as the world reputation of Japanese economic power, and with their success in agriculture (albeit with Japanese government aid), the Okinawans and Japanese enjoy prestige. Both Colonias attract a flow of internal migrants, as well as the attention of schemers who wait for opportunities to snatch away the fruits of the migrants' labor. That is what happened to Mr. Hiroshi Kochi.

THE LAND DISPUTE

On June 8, 1994, Mr. Hiroshi Kochi heard from a Bolivian who owned farmland adjacent to his that a survey was going to take place on the 911 hectares of land in the middle section of Colonia Okinawa II. He was told that Mr. Walter Bruno Banegas Espinoza had purchased the land in May 1992 from Manuel Espinoza.[8] This surprised Mr. Kochi. He had never heard of either Mr. Banegas or Espinoza. The 911 hectares included the 527 hectares he had title to and had been farming since 1968.

Mr. Kochi was one of the first immigrants who arrived in Bolivia from Okinawa in August 1954. He has lived in Colonia I since it was set up in August 1956, and he purchased 100 hectares in Colonia II from fellow immigrants. Gradually, he expanded his farmland to the current 527 hectares by purchasing surrounding lots from immigrant farmers who had left the Colonia. All of this land had been granted to Colonia Okinawa II by the Bolivian government. Mr. Kochi obtained the legal right to all of the 527 hectares and acquired the certificate of ownership in September 1976 with then Bolivian President Hugo Banser Suàrez's signature. With that certificate he registered his ownership at the Property Registrar's Office (Derechos Reales) in Santa Cruz in June 1977. The notice of Mr. Walter Bruno Banegas Espinoza's land survey made Mr. Kochi realize that there was a double registration of the ownership of the land.

On the scheduled date Mr. Kochi sent his eldest son, accompanied by a policeman, to the survey site. Neither Mr. Banegas nor his representative was present. It was discovered that about a kilometer of the boundary line had been surveyed in two days. Mr. Kochi went immediately to the office of Warnes Province and reported that his land had just been invaded. Several days later the Office of Province sent officials to inspect the land, although the office took no further action. Instead, it recommended that the matter be settled between Mr. Kochi and Mr. Banegas. "I realized then," said Mr. Kochi, "that Mr. Walter Banegas had already made an arrangement with the province about this matter."

"Not again," Mr. Kochi thought. He had experienced similar land problems twice in the past and had seen other immigrants involved in similar disputes. Immigrants—Okinawan Japanese, any others—who are successful and becoming affluent have had similar problems with someone claiming their land and demanding money for "compensation." All such cases had previously been settled with payoffs, and Mr. Kochi himself had settled two previous cases with money. From those experiences he knew his opponent would demand a large sum of money, and this time he was not inclined to settle the matter with payoffs. If he paid Mr. Banegas off to settle this dispute, another claim would be made sooner or later against him or against another of his fellow immigrants. Thus the immigrants would be endlessly victimized. Mr. Kochi decided to put an end to it.

Mr. Kochi consulted the Bolivian-Japanese Association of Colonia Okinawa, and with its promise of full support and cooperation, he decided to take the case to the court. That was a bold decision. No one in the Okinawan immigrant community had ever fought a land dispute in the courts. In spite of all the legal documents and proof that Mr. Kochi had farmed the land in dispute since 1968, there was no guarantee that he would win the case. It would have been less troublesome and probably less costly to pay off Mr. Banegas, which seemed to be exactly what Mr. Banegas wanted.[9]

Still, Mr. Kochi was resolved to fight back. He might have had the typical experiences of an Okinawan immigrant in Bolivia, but he was no ordinary man. He had always had a strong sense of justice. When the first group of immigrants arrived in Bolivia and were stricken with Uruma Disease, which killed fifteen people, Mr. Kochi secretly helped a fellow immigrant who had suffered a nervous breakdown join his relatives in Brazil. He had been a leader in Colonia Okinawa and had served as president of both the Bolivian-Japanese Association and the Okinawan Association of Bolivia. His friends refer to him as "Caballero" (gentleman). Mr. Kochi wanted to fight this battle not just for himself and his family but also for his community.

Soon Mr. Kochi learned he was facing a very powerful opponent. Mr. Banegas was a judge in Santa Cruz and was so well connected politically and socially that he had influence over the governor of Santa Cruz. In addition, his sister was a member of the Lower House of the National Congress. He knew how to work the Bolivian system and had gone through all of the necessary formalities to justify his claim to the disputed land. According to Mr. Banegas's claim, Manuel Espinoza had acquired the 911 hectares in question from the central government in September 1988. He had allegedly proceeded to obtain the title, which had yet to be issued. Mr. Banegas claimed he had purchased the land from Espinoza for 5,000 bolivianos in May 1992 and had registered it as his property without a certificate of title at the Property Registrar's Office in July 1993. Espinoza reportedly died that year.

Mr. Kochi filed a complaint in the criminal justice system (Policia Tecnica Judicial) against Mr. Banegas for having violated his property rights. The trial began in July 1994 but was suspended in September 1995. Mr. Kochi also appealed to the National Agrarian Reform Arbitrator (Interventora Nacional Reforma Agraria) in November 1994 to reaffirm his legitimate right to the land in dispute, to invalidate Mr. Banegas's registration of the land, and to reject Mr. Banegas's application for a certificate of land title. In April 1995 the arbitrator handed down a judgment in Mr. Kochi's favor. Through his lawyer in May 1995 Mr. Kochi appealed to the Agrarian Judiciary (Asesor Juridico Agrario) in the presidential office in La Paz. Meanwhile, Mr. Banegas started a civil action against Mr. Kochi. The trial for that case began in August 1994, and a decision was handed down in Mr. Kochi's favor in November 1995. Mr. Banegas appealed the case to the Superior District Court in December that same year.

Both sides used every possible channel to win their case. Mr. Kochi had received some favorable rulings, but he was at a disadvantage because as an immigrant he had no ties to Bolivians in power. In other words, he lacked political clout. He had the support of the Japanese community, represented by the Bolivian-Japanese Association of Okinawa, the Okinawan Association of Bolivia, and the Bolivian-Japanese Association of San Juan Yapacan'. These groups, however, were helpless vis-à-vis the Bolivian power structure in spite of the growing importance of the Okinawan and Japanese communities in the development of Santa Cruz. Mr. Kochi and the Bolivian-Japanese Association were well aware that the trials in Bolivia were influenced by money. The associations had petitioned the Japanese Consulate in Santa Cruz to help Mr. Kochi. The Japanese consul visited the governor of Santa Cruz twice on Mr. Kochi's behalf and asked for proper treatment of his case. That was not enough, however, for Mr. Kochi to win against Mr. Banegas's network of influence.

Mr. Kochi needed something more effective and authoritative that could affect Bolivian society in general. He concluded that the best and ultimate result would be possible only with the president's signed declaration of support validating Mr. Kochi's position. He appealed to the Japanese Embassy to intervene on his behalf. Ambassador Shizuya Kato was reluctant to help and told Mr. Kochi he did not want to get involved in such a "personal matter." The ambassador's indifference to his plight caused Mr. Kochi to feel the same indignation he had felt in the 1960s when Okinawa was still under U.S. occupation. "An official of the Japanese aid agency told us Okinawan immigrants that we had no right to complain because we were not paying taxes to Japan," Mr. Kochi recalled. "I was incensed. At that time we were not even recognized as Japanese nationals. We couldn't pay Japanese taxes even if we wanted to."

On August 3, 1996, the Departmental Inspector of Agrarian Labor and Peasant Judiciary (Inspectoria Deptal. de Trabajo Agrario y Justicia Campesina) in Santa Cruz handed down a decision against Mr. Kochi. It was a terrible blow, and he decided to appeal to the ambassador who had recently replaced Ambassador Kato. The new ambassador, Michisuke Tateyama, was different from his predecessor and took an interest in Mr. Kochi's case. He summoned Mr. Kochi to La Paz in August 1996 to personally assess the case and Mr. Kochi the man. Assured of Mr. Kochi's integrity and honesty, as well as of the solid legal footing of his case, the ambassador began to play an active role in solving the problem. The Japanese Embassy had immense clout in Bolivia because of its economic and technical aid, and Ambassador Tateyama was ready to use it.

In November 1996 Bolivian President Gonzalo Sanchez de Lozada was invited to Japan by the Japanese government. Tateyama notified the Japanese government beforehand of Mr. Kochi's land problem so the Japanese government would call President Gonzalo Sanchez's attention to the issue. Japanese Minister of Foreign Affairs Ikeda did just that. In his meeting with Chancellor Antonio Aran'bar, who had accompanied Gonzalo Sanchez, Ikeda brought up the case of Mr. Kochi's land dispute as the first item of discussion. He asked Aran'bar for the Bolivian government's help solving this problem expeditiously, to which Mr. Aran'bar responded that "the problem shall be considered with transparency."[10] Ambassador Tateyama met personally with the Bolivian minister of foreign relations and the minister of the president to immediately and definitively settle this dispute.

Nonetheless, four months passed with no apparent progress toward a solution. With President Gonzalo Sanchez's term approaching an end, Ambassador Tateyama pressed for a solution to the land dispute by making the situation known to the public. The daily newspaper *El Deber* reported in March 1997 that he had said he would have to "take some action to the present Bolivian administration in a few weeks." Such action would include suspending all new Japanese government aid to Bolivia, although Tateyama promised that aid to the projects already signed would be delivered. Once Mr. Kochi's case was made public, the President's Office issued Gonzalo Sanchez's signed declaration validating Mr. Kochi's claim on March 18, 1997. Thus the land dispute between Mr. Kochi and Mr. Banegas was resolved not in the courts but through the Japanese ambassador's intervention, using Japan's economic and political power over Bolivia, particularly Santa Cruz.

CULTURAL CLASHES AND ASSIMILATION

Mr. Kochi's land dispute with the Bolivian elite shows that Okinawan and Japanese immigrants need Japanese government protection not only financially and technically but politically as well. The dispute also reinforced the negative view, widely held by first-generation immigrants in the Colonias, of the Bolivian elite and the government. These immigrants have less daily contact with Bolivians, and with a more limited range of Bolivians, than their urban counterparts in the city of Santa Cruz. Most Bolivians they associate with are the workers they employ and a few merchants they do business with. Very few in the second generation married local Bolivians. The immigrants come into indirect contact with the Bolivian elite through the government, which in their view does little for them or even for the Bolivian people. Hence, their views of Bolivians are dichotomous. They regard the Bolivian working class and peasants, whom they employ and work with, as docile (*oto-nashii*) and good-natured and Bolivian society as accommodating, whereas they tend to view the Bolivian upper classes as greedy and dishonest. Mr. Kochi's land problem with Mr. Banegas reinforced the "us-versus-them" framework through which they view land disputes between themselves and Bolivians as a clash of cultures.

Nevertheless, Okinawan and Japanese immigrants in both the rural and urban regions of Bolivia are grateful to Bolivia for having accepted them into its society and provided them with opportunities for a new life. On their return visits to, or while working in, Japan and Okinawa, these immigrants find themselves not completely comfortable in the places that were once their homes. They now consider Bolivia their home.

NOTES

This study was made possible by grants from the Japan Foundation and the Japan Policy Research Institute.

1. According to the records of the Ministry of Foreign Affairs, 244,536 Japanese immigrated to Latin America during the twenty-five years between 1916 and 1941; of these, only 202 went to Bolivia. Kunimoto Iyo, *Boribia no "Nihonjin mura"—Santa Kurusu shu San Juan ijuchi no kenkyu* (Tokyo: Chuo Daigaku Shuppankai, 1989), 57.

2. Hence Japanese immigrants in Bolivia regard 1899 as the beginning of their history and commemorate it.

3. Kunimoto, *Borinia no "Nihonjin mura*," 61–62.

4. Wakatsuki Yasuo, "Boribia no Nihonjin Ijuchi no Gaiyo," *in Boribia ni okeru Nihonjin Ijusha no Kanyo to Kenko*, Ishii Hiromasa and Tsugane Shoichiro, eds. (Tokyo: Keio Gijuku Daigaku Chiiki Kenykyu Senta, 1990), 18.

5. The pamphlet of the Federacion Nacional de Asociaciones Boliviano-Japonesas (April 1, 1997).

6. Pamphlet of the Federacion.

7. Wakatsuki, "Boribia no Nihonjin Ijuchi," 34.

8. This section was reconstructed mostly from an interview with Mr. Kochi, documents of correspondence of the Bolivian-Japanese Association of Okinawa with the Japanese Embassy in La Paz, and the legal documents related to this dispute.

9. Sure enough, Mr. Banegas offered to withdraw his claim in exchange for U.S. $150,000 as "compensation." Mr. Kochi refused. Eventually, Mr. Banegas reduced his demand to U.S. $33,000, but that did not change Mr. Kochi's mind about not settling the case with payoffs.

10. This section was reconstructed from *El Deber*, a Bolivian daily in Santa Cruz, March 18, 1997.

AUTHOR BIOGRAPHY

Kozy Amemiya is a research associate at the Japan Policy Research Institute and is studying the postwar emigration of Okinawans to Bolivia. She holds a Ph.D. in sociology from the University of California, San Diego. She is the author of "Woman's Autonomy Within the Community: The Contextual Argument of Japanese Pro-Choice Women," American Asian Review *13, 2 (Summer 1995), 97–142, and of many articles in Japanese on population control policies, women, the family, and cross-cultural issues.*

18

Spanish

Feroza Jussawalla

They always speak to me in Spanish
Until I say
"Soy de la India"
Then it's always a shock
A sense of betrayal
But I didn't ask for it
It's that dark hair
And dark eyes
The oliveness of complexion

And, in the grocery store
The indigent immigrant asks for directions—
While a student asks me on campus,
"Dondé está la Business building?"
"Ay!" I say, "It's very far!
Pero, no habla espanol."
Indignant, she says
"Oh! You can talk to me in English!"
But I didn't initiate the conversation
I think

"Que! I've never seen a young one of us Re-public-ano"
he says
in the swimming pool
"We need to put our Chicanitas ahead in the party
You need to come and see me
My father was chair of the Republican Party in Taos County
All his life
Mas of the Republicanos in Dona Ana County are gringos
Pero, where are you originally from
Hatch? You look Castillian"

131

No hablan border Spanish, verdad?
"Soy de la India."
"Mande?"
And I'm not invited anymore

The old white Democrat
whose mother was Spanish
laughs
"You need to change your name . . ."
and he laughs some more
"Rosita Balboa
Something like that . . .
Rosita is appropriate for you
Indians and Mexicans all have long, dark, wavy, hair
Yes, you could pass
for a Mexican Señorita."

Solidarnos
No solidarnos

AUTHOR BIOGRAPHY

Feroza Jussawalla is professor of English at the University of Texas El Paso. She received her Ph.D. from the University of Utah in 1983 in English and American literature. She specializes in postcolonial studies, composition, and children's literature. In 1996 Jussawalla codirected an National Endowment for the Humanities summer seminar on postcolonial literature at the School for Oriental and African Studies in London. She has published a variety of works including Conversations with V. S. Naipaul, Interviews with Writers of the Postcolonial World, The Hold Guide to Writing in the Disciplines, Excellent Teaching Essays in Honor of Kenneth Eble, *and articles in the* Massachusetts Review, Public Culture, Third Text, *and the* Journal of Indian Writing in English.

19

Chattanooga Days

Jay Chaudhuri

In 1991 I wrote my senior thesis entitled "The Political Nature and Involvement of Indians in South Africa: 1860–1985." Three years later, in summer 1994, spurred by the subject of that thesis, I helped forge an Indian-African alliance in Chattanooga, Tennessee, for an Indian American congressional candidate named Ram Uppuluri who was seeking the Democratic nomination for Tennessee's Third Congressional District. He was the only candidate of color contesting the seat. I instantly identified with him: his southern drawl, an only child, experience working in Congress, and a strong identification with both the East and the West. After I had accompanied Ram to fund-raisers in the Indian American communities of New York, New Jersey, and Connecticut (or what was jokingly dubbed the "samosa circuit" because every fund-raiser seemed to include an all-you-can-eat Indian buffet) and authored a foreign policy position paper, the campaign staff finally invited me to work for them.

From the outset Ram's campaign strategy to win the Democratic nomination required strong support in the northern part of the district (cleverly described as the RAM section, an anagram for Roanne, Anderson, and Morgan Counties). Second, we needed to split Chattanooga evenly with local contenders Whitney Durand, a Harvard-educated lawyer, and Chuck Jolly, a pharmaceutical businessman. The second objective depended on Ram receiving a large number of African American votes. If the campaign met these two goals, we would secure over 25 percent of the votes, a low percentage but sufficient to win in a crowded field of seven contenders. The campaign staff decided that Martin and I would implement the Chattanooga strategy. We had fewer than seventy days to do it.

Martin was a white, reasonably fit twenty-six year old. Before joining the campaign he had worked as a counselor to Native American children in South Dakota. Martin was race conscious, perhaps because of his relationship with the well-known Seignathaler family. John Seignathaler had been Attorney General Robert Kennedy's special assistant (and the only southerner on Kennedy's staff) during the Civil Rights movement. Martin was finishing his master's thesis at the University of North Carolina on the speeches of Martin Luther King, Jr.

*   *   *

Martin and I operated the Chattanooga campaign out of our residential house located in the city's largest African American voting precinct, Glenwood. In that neighborhood our residence was known as the Meharry House, named after the famous African American medical school in Nashville. The house also served as a metaphor for the power structure in Chattanooga. Most affluent and politically powerful whites lived on Signal and Lookout Mountains, whereas African Americans resided in the valley. The Meharry House was at the foot of Lookout Mountain.

We were essentially strangers in this clean, well-trimmed, middle-class neighborhood. We were also strangers living in one of the largest houses on the block. But our presence triggered no real disturbances because we shared the house with two medical students from Meharry Medical College. The house had always been home to transient students. Now Martin and I occupied the house as students of sorts—students of southern politics and coalition building.

We had the second floor to ourselves. We set up two telephone lines, covered the walls with maps of voting precincts, and filled our plastic shelves with placards and campaign literature. In our four-room complex we worked, ate, and slept. We would occasionally smoke cigarettes on the back porch that overlooked a big yard. A giant oak tree served as the porch's canopy and kept us cool during the hot summer nights.

*   *   *

The key political player for our campaign in the African American community was Dr. Thomas Brooks. Dr. Brooks had grown up in a Nashville housing project and had worked hard to attend medical school at Meharry. In fact, he owned the Meharry House and had named it after his alma mater. He had a long face featuring a Vandyke and wore round, dark-rimmed glasses. Part preacher and part doctor, Dr. Brooks was an outspoken, somewhat rebellious man who had battled with the city of Chattanooga over Title VI of the Civil Rights Act of 1964. Title VI required that all state agencies receiving money must develop and implement plans to ensure that no one receiving benefits under a federally funded program was discriminated against on the basis of race, color, or national origin. Dr. Brooks argued that the city was not complying with the law because minorities seldom shared in decisions about how the federal funds would be spent.

Our strategy in courting African American votes centered on issues. I felt Ram's background and experience as a minority at a minimum gave us a legitimate claim to speak about select issues. Fortunately, the twelve critical public policy issues Ram needed to address were neatly outlined by members of the Minority Economic Development Commission (MEDC), a group composed of African American leaders from across the Third Congressional District. By developing detailed responses to each issue and disseminating our positions to as many people as possible, I thought we could split the votes between our candidate and Durand and Jolly in Chattanooga.

Fresh out of graduate school, I was eager to apply my knowledge and formulate the campaign's positions by interviewing key policymakers in the African American community. Over the course of two weeks I solicited ideas and suggestions from a number of individuals active in the community which culminated in our campaign's position paper, "An Economic Development Proposal for Minorities of the Third Congressional District." The twenty-five-page proposal addressed economic development, health care, transportation, housing, education, and crime, but the foundation of the plan revolved around Title VI—the issue championed by Dr. Brooks. When I showed the finished product to Johnny Holloway, another prominent leader of the Chattanooga African American community, he responded, "This has never happened before in this town. Chattanooga has been waiting a long time for this."

The proposal appeared to be well received. In late June Ram discussed the plan on a one-hour African American radio talk show called *Let's Talk*, hosted by Ed Owens, also a preacher by profession. Ram talked about home buyback programs, cleaning up the Chattanooga Creek, welfare reform and education with the ease and love of issues I had witnessed previously in his conversations with the campaign staff.

He returned to our theme. "The top issue is Title VI. It is the overreaching issue because it says anytime you have federal money come into the community, minority groups should have meaningful participation," he said. "Housing and quality of life and education and other issues are small pieces of Title VI."

During a discussion of the need to repair and provide safe recreational centers, Darryl Clay phoned in to share his dilemma. Darryl worked and trained young kids at a local community center, but he did not have enough money to take the kids to a sports competition in Alabama. So Darryl spent money out of his own pocket. Our solution for funding recreational opportunities obviously struck a chord with Darryl.

"This is what I am talking about! This is what I am talking about! This is good in the neighborhood," Ed shouted proudly on the radio.

"Now Ram, if you keep talking like this I might elect you myself! This is a man after my own heart. And it makes you wonder where the other public officeholders are," he continued.

*   *   *

I quickly realized that in Chattanooga there was more to being a campaign worker than just meeting people during the day and writing position papers at night. You had to be a jack-of-all-trades at all hours. When Martin and I went out for drinks late at night we still campaigned, targeting twenty somethings, or what Ram called the "cool vote."

I designed and delivered invitations to our open house in the Glenwood neighborhood, only to be interrupted for an interview on behalf of Ram at the local African American radio station. Then it was back to the house where Martin and I prepared 200 pimento cheese and chicken salad sandwiches. Usually, the energy in working on a campaign is devoted to several small tasks that are not very interesting. The open house invitations and sandwiches, however, were intended for an occasion of great significance: Dr. Thomas Brooks, who had been wavering for a couple of weeks, was planning to endorse Ram.

For our open house I wore a special bowtie a friend had brought me from Kenya. It had the traditional African colors—red, yellow, and green—and I wore it with my black suit. In the early evening, just when the unbearable summer heat became bearable, our supporters started to gather. There was Reverend Fouther, a young, handsome African American minister from Chicago who had recently moved to Chattanooga and seemed to identify with our young candidate and staff. There was Trudy Hughes, whom had I called to learn about Parents Are First Teachers (PAFT), a program that emphasizes early childhood intervention. Trudy was excited about our campaign's interest in PAFT and had invited her African American baby-sitter.

Ram, his parents, and Dr. and Mrs. Caldwell (Dr. Caldwell was Ram's campaign manager) arrived after some more guests had filtered in. Then Thomas Brooks—the main attraction for the evening—arrived. He mingled with the crowd and ate some sandwiches. He praised me in front of Ram, saying, "You got a good brother working for you down here." Then Dr. Brooks spoke to the crowd. He talked about the primary, about how African Americans were being taken for granted by Democrats, and about Ram. But that was all. Nothing; no endorsement. Then he left. The rest of crowd slowly spilled out. The only thing Martin and I had were leftover sandwiches.

Although Dr. Brooks's words were positive—certainly more positive than those he had used for other candidates—they were not enough. Our campaign had a clear strategy to win the endorsement of Dr. Brooks's political group, the African-American Voters Coalition. The withholding of his endorsement became the source of intense frustration and confusion for the campaign.

Now nothing seemed to go right. In late June fund-raising began to lag.

*   *   *

Things got worse. In late June Ram did an interview on the *Smith and West* show, Chattanooga's most popular FM talk show. Parker Smith was the show's Democrat, and Kevin West was the Republican. Naturally, they argued about major policy issues and politics.

The interview started smoothly. "A lot of people have trouble pronouncing your name," Smith said. "I gotta say," he paused, "you see the name and you don't expect to see someone speak good ol' Southern like you do, Ram."

"Well, I grew up in Oak Ridge all my life," replied Ram.

Ram talked about his background, his job as a newspaper reporter, and how he ended up in politics. He discussed the role of a member of Congress and the need for reform.

The first few questions from the callers were "softballs," easy. There was one about why Democrats should represent the working middle class and one on Ram's position on education.

Then came this one: "I have a question for Mr. Uppuluri . . . actually it is a concern," said the anonymous caller in a thick southern accent. "Mr. Uppuluri was quoted in the Chattanooga paper as being against large contributions of special interest groups. But oh . . . around more than $60,000 of his campaign contributions have come from the Indian community."

He continued, "There is another fella by the name of Dhillon," referring to Neil Dhillon, the Indian American congressional candidate from Maryland, "and Mr. Uppuluri was in a meeting with him, according to the newspaper *India Abroad*. Mr. Dhillon indicated that the Indian community needed to elect Mr. Uppuluri so that federal spending for India can be increased, and there was nothing in the article that said Mr. Uppuluri countered that statement." The caller reiterated, "I am concerned about his relationship with the Indian community."

"Oh, there was something in that article," Ram replied quickly. "You should look through it . . ."

"I have the whole article here," said the caller.

"It should quote me as saying what I have said everywhere," Ram said. "That the first job of a Congressman, whether you are Indian or Chinese or African American or white or green or yellow or pink, the first job of a Congressman is to represent [his or her] constituents."

"But I think people are a little bit upset with the rumor," said Kevin West, cutting in. "We have discussed this time and time again on this show, and to be honest with you, I brought it up: It is that Indian people get 2 percent low-interest loans from the government for buying hotels. What is the deal with Indians and hotels? I thought I would ask you the question. So this is a good time to ask you."

"I don't know about 2 percent loans. I have *no* idea what you are talking about there," said Ram. "I *do* know that there are many Indian Americans who go into the hotel business. It is an interesting cultural phenomenon."

"I know that some of the callers are worried about a particular ethnic group, in this case Indians, getting low-interest loans that others can't get. Is this true?" inquired Smith. "What's happening here? It's a phenomenon that doesn't make sense to me."

"I am certain there are no federally sanctioned loans," Ram asserted. "I have no idea what that issue is about."

The show broke for a commercial. I was seething at the attack on Ram's ethnicity. I, too, had once had my loyalty and patriotism to the United States questioned by some elderly white men during a fellowship interview. No matter how refined my southern mannerisms were, the color of my skin prompted those men to ask whether I would serve in the Gulf War.

The *Smith and West* show continued. The next caller phoned in. "Ethnicity seemed to be one of the central issues in the earlier conversation," he commented. "Does Mr. Uppuluri own stock in Dunkin' Donuts?" he asked.

"No," Ram responded.

"What!" said a baffled Smith. "That went way over my head."

"Most of the Dunkin' Donuts franchises in the area seem to be owned by Indians in the area," said the caller. "All kiddin' aside, very briefly, then, Mr. Uppuluri was making a reference earlier to his admiration of John Kennedy. One of John Kennedy's problems running in the South was the pivotal state of West Virginia, and he bore the mantle of Catholicism. What is Mr. Uppuluri's religion in this fundamental Protestant congressional district?"

"I'm surprised to hear that question," Smith commented.

"I grew up, of course, in the Judeo-Christian tradition of America and have been steeped in the Judeo-Christian ethic all my life," Ram said. "As far as what it means to be American, I think it means everything you bring from your cultural heritage, as part of your family background and family values."

Ram concluded, "I think we should all be proud of our background, and I am."

In those fifteen minutes two callers blurred the line between Indian and Indian American. I paced back and forth debating whether to call the talk show. I picked up the phone and dialed the number.

"Listen, as an Indian American living here in Chattanooga," I said, keeping my identity anonymous and trying to contain my anger, "I find it offensive that ya'll harped on Ram's fund-raising in the Indian American community." I exaggerated my southern accent in hopes of portraying myself as a good ol' boy coming to Ram's defense. "You would never scrutinize an Irish American or Italian American candidate in the same manner."

"Yes we would," West responded forcefully. "But our concerns have really been raised by others, particularly the press. It is a very legitimate question."

It seemed pointless to argue. They did not understand. Yet during the attacks we endured about campaign money coming from the Indian American community, I remember one African American gentleman who stopped Ram and said, "They're trying to get you for that Indian money when you're just getting help from your brothers."

*   *   *

The press and his opponents portrayed Ram as different, almost as a for-eign candidate. This also created ripples of worry in the African American community. Just before Ram was to speak at a gathering of African American ministers, Gene McKissick, an early and rabid supporter of Ram's who was a publisher in nearby Cleveland County, shared the concerns of others in the African American community. "They don't think you can win, man," Gene told us. "They don't think you can because they are going to think you are Iraqi in the general election."

Ram paused and then responded forcefully, "Look, Gene, if they don't think I can win, then what does that say for them—that no African American can ever be elected from this district?" He continued, "When we win this primary it will be a national story because of who I am."

A number of African American ministers filled the pews of the church. Ram walked to the front of the church and stood behind the pulpit. He did not have a commanding presence, but he spoke with an eloquence that more than made up for his size. He talked about King's legacy and vision for a color-blind society and about how those principles were fundamental influ-ences both on him personally and now on his campaign. Ram spoke with pas-sion. The crowd punctuated his speech with "amens." In those few minutes Ram had seemed to address the nagging question of whether the Third Con-gressional District could elect an Indian American.

*   *   *

Political insiders and the press knew that Ram's ethnicity was a factor in his electability. So did Thomas Brooks. Chuck Jolly's ability to sink his own money into the race was enough to make anyone think twice about endorsing Ram. In Ram's hometown newspaper, *The Oak Ridger*, an article noted, "An endorsement announcement of a Third District candidate by the African American Voters' Coalition [AAVC] was canceled, and it is not clear whether Oak Ridge attorney Ram Uppuluri or former pharmaceutical company exec-utive Chuck Jolly of Chattanooga will get the nod." With our funds drying up, I had to convince Dr. Brooks and his AAVC coordinator, Linda Morris, at a scheduled meeting that we could meet the financial obligation to hire workers who would implement the plan to get voters to the polls.

In politics it is all about cutting the deal. If the AAVC endorsed Ram, I was certain he would secure the Democratic nomination. With Morris and Dr. Brooks sitting at the kitchen table in the Meharry House, I outlined our bud-get for getting out the African American vote. Dr. Brooks, with support from Linda, was satisfied, although he demanded a few minor changes. But we had cut the deal. We now needed only to make it official.

For this endorsement, there were no pimento cheese sandwiches. Instead, we lined up chairs in the downstairs living area and printed nearly to a hun-dred copies of the economic development plan. Before the press arrived,

Linda summoned our new workers. They were all African American, pre-dominantly female, and mostly from nearby housing projects. Linda's rela-tionship with them was almost motherly. Two years earlier AAVC volunteers had done remarkably well and had secured victory for the first elected African American state representative in the area. If things went well, Linda was con-fident we could send Ram to Washington.

Ram rolled in at about four o'clock. Accompanying him were Dr. Caldwell and the National Association for the Advancement of Colored People (NAACP) leader of Anderson County. Reverend Fouther and Gene McKissic arrived, and Dr. Brooks finally showed up. The NAACP head gave a fiery speech and pep talk directed to the workers. Then Thomas Brooks officially endorsed Ram. At the same time, he warned both the other candidates and the entire Democratic Party that "this is to let other candidates know that being a Democrat is not enough for African American people to vote for him or her. We want a candidate that can address our issues. We seek a candidate like Ram Uppuluri." It was official. With the many labor union endorse-ments from the north and now the AAVC endorsement in Chattanooga, Ram was the only candidate openly supported in both parts of the district.

*   *   *

In political parlance it's called GOTV, "Get Out The Vote." This literally means leafleting neighborhoods with campaign literature, phoning likely vot-ers, and making sure they show up at the polls on election day. In close races such as the one we expected, GOTV could decide the fate of the campaign.

Our task was to call almost 5,000 African American voters, but to reach that many voters in two weeks we needed volunteers, lots of volunteers. It would be impossible to achieve this goal in such a short time without the help of the Indian American community in Chattanooga. The number of paid vol-unteers from the African American community simply would not suffice.

With the help of Sheila Boyington, a politically active Indian American resident, I relied on twenty-five Indian volunteers. Sheila was like an older sister who reintroduced me to the Chattanooga Indian American community. She also convinced a large number of community members to help with Ram's campaign.

I arranged for these volunteers to make phone calls in shifts over the next two weeks. A local Indian businessman allowed the volunteers to use his four phones in the evening. I briefed each group on the status of the campaign, Ram's position on minority issues, and his AAVC endorsement. It was impor-tant for the callers to convey those points to the voters. Then I gave each volunteer a handful of cards with the phone numbers of potential African American voters.

I was usually busy making calls myself. But in the other rooms I would hear the voices of first- and second-generation Indian Americans persuading African Americans to vote for Ram Uppuluri. The cultural differences, mostly between first-generation Indian Americans and low-income African Americans, were often amusing. I remember one Indian American woman who emphasized her professional title of "Doctor" to each voter—a title that holds great prestige in the Indian community. Unfortunately, her thick Indian accent did not help communication between her and the targeted voter. First, the typical African American voter thought a doctor was calling to confirm an appointment; then he or she had trouble understanding the Indian callers' long, unpronounceable last name; finally, the voter could not comprehend the candidate's long, unpronounceable name.

In spite of those difficulties, the environment was empowering. The volunteers had passion and persuasion in their voices, and we made progress toward reaching close to 2,500 voters (AAVC workers helped reach the other 2,500). In those final weeks my senior thesis about South African blacks and Indians working together to achieve victory had come to fruition.

As the phone banks were operating, AAVC volunteers blitzed key precincts—especially housing project areas—with campaign literature. On the two Sundays before the election they littered African American church parking lots, flyers that said "VOTE FOR THE RAM. Endorsed by the African American Voters' Coalition." Under "THE RAM" was a picture of a ram's head—a clever way for voters to remember Ram's name when they went to the polls.

* * *

In the final week of the campaign I traveled to Atlanta with Ram and some campaign staffers for the final Indian American fund-raiser. Ram made his last stump speech to an Indian group. He put the primary, now less than ten days away, in perspective. "In less than two weeks," Ram said, "I will be the first of three Indian Americans running this year to face an election. I will also be the first Indian American since Dilip Saund of California to do so. We will be making history."

History arrived on August 4. While Ram visited some of the African American precincts, I attended the phone for voters requesting rides. Our system to transport voters was composed largely of first-generation Indian American volunteers who staffed two- to three-hour shifts. Because we had devoted all our resources to pamphleting precincts, our ride system was less aggressive than those of other candidates.

As the polls closed, Martin and I picked up Napoleon Rutledge—a devoted AAVC volunteer—and his girlfriend. We dropped them off at the downtown Holiday Inn, where the Chattanooga Democrats were gathering, and proceeded to the Board of Elections to monitor the voting results. As ten o'clock approached it was apparent that we were falling significantly short of our 40 to 50 percent goal in the African American community. Although Ram did well in the largest precinct where the Meharry House was located, he split the rest of the African American votes with Jolly and Durand. It would take a strong showing in Oak Ridge and the northern part of the district to achieve victory. The rest of the night did not look promising.

We walked into the Holiday Inn disappointed, knowing defeat was at hand. Napoleon and the other AAVC volunteers awaited us. They had optimism in their eyes. They believed Ram Uppuluri could pull off the win. As the news kept indicating Ram's fourth-place position, our volunteers still thought victory might come. "It ain't over yet," Napoleon told me as we left the hotel to go home. But it was.

*   *   *

Two days later, on August 6, the *Chattanooga Times* ran a column by editor Paul Neely entitled "Bitter Pills to Swallow." For "Best Losers" he wrote:

> Sen. Steve Cohen [fifth place in the Democratic gubernatorial primary] . . . and Ram Uppuluri, fourth place in the Democratic congressional primary brought intelligence, wit and candor to otherwise scripted races. Months ago, for instance, I asked Uppuluri what he thought would be the major obstacles to his winning. His answer: "How about the last name Uppuluri?" Maybe risk of a mistake makes it impossible to give spontaneous, conversational answers when you're in first and second place. But these two men give hope that there's a place for something beyond the public pabulum of campaign rhetoric.

In spite of Ram's defeat, I rejected forever the prejudices of the South, the region in which I have spent virtually all of my life. I have become a crusader of sorts. For me, the campaign became more than just electing the first Indian American in three decades; it was a movement that included the voices of the unheard. I had selected the road of brotherhood, which affirmed that between African Americans and whites there are browns. During those days in Chattanooga I believed Ram Uppuluri and I could change the world.

AUTHOR BIOGRAPHY

Jay Jyoti Chaudhuri was born in Chattanooga, Tennessee, and was raised in Fayetteville, North Carolina. He holds an undergraduate degree in South Asian Studies from Davidson College and received a master's degree in international affairs from Columbia University through a Jacob K. Javits fellowship. Active in the Democratic Party, he has served as field director for congressional candidate Ram Uppuluri, legislative aide to U.S. Senator Russell D. Feingold, and director of issues and research to U.S. Senate candidate Charles Sanders. His writings have appeared in several North Carolina newspapers and Indian American publications, including India Abroad *and* Little India. *Currently, he is a student in the North Carolina Central University School of Law.*

20

On Ice Cube's "Black Korea"

Jeff Chang

LOCATING THE SPACES OF STRUGGLE

In the anxious period between Du Soon Ja's conviction and sentencing in late 1991, Los Angeles rap artist Ice Cube issued a brutally terse judgment of his own in a song called "Black Korea." With an audio snippet from Spike Lee's *Do The Right Thing*, he placed himself as a customer in a Korean American–owned corner store trying to purchase a 40 ounce bottle of malt liquor. What should have been a simple transaction was about to become a moral lesson in interracial relations.

As the music bursts forth, the scene is set for an ugly confrontation. Ice Cube confronts two prejudiced, "Oriental, one-penny-counting" proprietors who follow him closely as he walks through their store. Their scrutiny infuriates the rapper, who turns and leers at the woman storekeeper, "Bitch, I got a job." At the song's bridge, the shop erupts into argument when his friends raise their voices in his support.

By now, the original Spike Lee scene has been fully stripped of all its irony and humor, left with only the raw racial conflict. Then the bass surges back, and the song rushes to its conclusion. First, Ice Cube issues an economic threat: "Don't follow me up and down your crazy little market, or your little chop suey ass will be the target of a nationwide boycott." In a final defiant gesture, he raises the prospect of a racially vengeful conflagration. "Pay respect to the black fist," he yells, "or we'll burn your store right down to a crisp, and then we'll see ya because you can't turn the ghetto into black Korea." The Korean store owner has the last word: "Mother fuck *you!*"

Tension between African Americans and Asian Americans is a subtext running throughout the album, *Death Certificate*, which finds Ice Cube partially repudiating his previous street gangster pose and replacing it with an emerging nationalist perspective. But his new embrace of blackness is coupled with

143

an antipathy toward Asians. In "Us" he fumes at bourgeois black "sellouts" and calls for racial solidarity when he sees "Japs grabbing every vacant lot in my 'hood to build a store and sell they goods." In "Horny Lil' Devil," a track about black male emasculation, he gets so energized from wiping out the "devils" (variously seen as white sexual harassers of black women, racists, and "fags") that he runs out to the corner store to beat up the "Jap" owner.

Ice Cube's comments on Asians were not a new development in hip hop music. Dating to the 1990 Red Apple Grocery boycott in the Flatbush section of Brooklyn, rap sometimes served as a kind of sounding board. Queen Mother Rage, a rapper affiliated with Sonny Carson's blackwatch Movement, denounced "the Orientals hungry for each piece of our prize." In a single called "To Be Real" she cautioned, "Check the incidents and the innocence. Ignorance is no defense." Special Ed's teen rewrite of a James Bond fantasy, "The Mission," found the young rapper traveling to Japan to confront a Chinese nemesis. When he discovers that his enemy not only possesses amazing "black belt karate" skills but also catches bullets in his teeth, Ed gets down and defeats his opponent "Flatbush style." (The conflation of very different Asian American stereotypes into a new myth of a threatening, as opposed to a model, minority was a recurrent theme.) And during the hot summer months, Chubb Rock led a New York concert crowd in chants of "Fuck you, egg roll."

These created musical spaces of struggle arose from real urban spaces of increasing racial strife. In south-central Los Angeles, a number of large plant closings contributed to a black male jobless rate of about 50 percent in some areas.[1] The poverty rate of Asians in Los Angeles County grew to twice that of whites, whereas the poverty rates for blacks and Latinos each swelled to more than three times that of whites.[2] At the same time, the succession of Korean immigrants into small businesses previously owned by Jewish immigrants in the south-central Los Angeles area created a new ethnic petit bourgeoisie or a "middleman minority."[3] And new conflicts between Korean Americans and African Americans were only beginning to peak at the start of the 1990s. In 1991 three firebombings of Korean American stores took place during the month of August alone. By 1992 a survey of racial attitudes in Los Angeles conducted before and just after the April uprising showed that more than 41 percent of blacks and 48 percent of Asians felt that it was difficult to get along with the other group. Blacks felt worse about Asians after the riots; Asians, too, saw blacks more negatively.[4]

Ice Cube's one-minute rap was a concise evocation of interracial conflict in an environment of deteriorating opportunities. But it was also an artifact of popular culture. *Death Certificate* was number two on the *Billboard* charts a week after it was released and went on to sell over one and a half million copies. The album's explosive content ignited a searing debate in the mass media. Feeling materially targeted, Korean American community leaders and grocers initiated economic boycotts against Ice Cube's album and the St. Ides malt liquor he endorsed. Thus a musical work was transformed into a political cause.

"Black Korea" and the chain of events it unleashed represent a moment in which issues of interracial conflict and political empowerment crystallized in a clash of what Edward Chang calls "strategies of survival" for Asian Americans and African Americans.[5] The struggle for power was waged on two fronts: on the media front for social power and on the market front for economic power. "Black Korea" left a flood of critical interpretations in its wake, but not all readings were covered equally. Whereas whites and blacks held a one-sided debate over the merits of Ice Cube's work, Korean American opinion was marginalized. At the same time, the song's lyrics created material stakes. Korean Americans saw the boycotts as a strategy for material protection and political empowerment. Yet some members of the African American community saw the final success of the boycotts as proof of African Americans' economic disempowerment. And neither African nor Asian American tactics and strategies yielded substantial gains to their respective groups.

I am writing about this set of events because I think they reveal much about the future. As urban and, indeed, rural spaces diversify, power will be increasingly contested along racial lines. When such contests are between communities of color, they are inevitably represented as anomalous to a civil society or as an object lesson to the more stigmatized ethnic group. But structures of white privilege still define the limits communities of color resist and set the terrain on which they clash.

In spaces of struggle such as south-central Los Angeles, political organizing to expand minority access and power has become increasingly complex. Organizations working to empower communities of color have drawn on two coexisting and sometimes compatible but basically divergent approaches to organizing. The anticolonial approach has sought unity of racially colonized peoples against a white ruling class. The nationalist approach has sought racial solidarity for collective group advancement. I suggest utilizing a recognition of "differential disempowerment" as a way to reducing opposition between disempowered racial groups and creating new space for those groups to move towards full access and participation.

BUT YOU DON'T HEAR ME, THOUGH: RACIAL POWER IN CRITICAL INTERPRETATION

Theodor Adorno once called popular music "a social cement" that strips listeners of their individuality and binds them by their psychological needs. Mass audiences for popular culture, in Adorno's estimation, were an ignorant horde sharing a low tolerance for style, subtlety, and significance; a need for instant gratification; a blind submission to commodification; and a passive acceptance of demagoguery masquerading as culture. Youth are particularly prone to becoming "slaves to the rhythm."[6]

Yet this analysis is inadequate to understand the impact "Black Korea" has had on well over one and a half million listeners. Some scholars see audiences not as passive subjects but as creators of their own political meanings.[7] Dick Hebdige, for example, explains punk music and style as a calculated subcultural act of "noise," which he defines as "interference in the orderly sequence which leads from real events and phenomena to their representation in the media."[8] Rather than support authoritarian power, he concludes, punks use their subculture to actively resist it. By exploring punk music from its audience's perspective, Hebdige dissects power and ideology. Such an approach highlights who shapes discourse about popular culture, how that discourse is shaped, and what that discourse says.

I find Hebdige's approach much more useful than Adorno's for examining power in multiracial Los Angeles. Separating audience reactions to "Black Korea" along racial lines can, in fact, reveal the multiple ways in which social power is wielded, contested, and negotiated. In examining what I term *social power*, I look at three distinct, if not completely homogeneous, audiences: the black rap music audience, the mainstream white media, and the Asian American audience.

White male writers defined the mainstream debate: Should "Black Korea" be censored?[9] *Los Angeles Times* rock critic Robert Hilburn set the stage in *Death Certificate*'s first review, stating, "Ice Cube . . . continues to make albums that spark debates over just how far pop music should go in chronicling frustration and rage."[10] The debate intensified greatly three weeks later in a precedent-setting *Billboard Magazine* editorial. Editor Timothy White called for record store chains to boycott the record, writing, "[Ice Cube's] unabashed espousal of violence against Koreans, Jews, and other whites crosses the line that divides art from the advocacy of crime."[11] In a trade magazine that normally avoids controversies over artistic merit or lyrical content, the editorial was extraordinary. *Death Certificate* remains the only album in *Billboard* history singled out for condemnation.

"Black Korea" even inspired political magazines not usually known for comment on "low" popular culture to address the apparent threat of rap music to society. An article in *The Economist* recalled Adorno's criticism of popular music, evoking "rhythmically obedient" but uncritical fans. "In rap as in rock, rebellion sells," the editorial read. "Sadly, too few fans distinguish between the rebellious and the reactionary."[12]

David Samuels, writing in *The New Republic*, also depicted rap fans as passive, mindless consumers: "This kind of consumption—of racist stereotypes, of brutality toward women, or even of uplifting tributes to Dr. Martin Luther King—is of a particularly corrupting kind. The values it instills find their ultimate expression in the ease in which we watch young black men killing each other: in movies, on records, and on streets of cities and towns across the country."[13] Thus the other defining perspective of "Black Korea" commentary was whether being a rap fan constituted socially acceptable behavior.

It was a line familiar to the young African American audiences for rap music who played the central role in the legitimization of Ice Cube from his early days as a "gangsta" hero to his rise to a kind of modern-day griot status. They formed his core audience when he was rhyming "To a kid looking up to me, life ain't nothing but bitches and money."[14] Later in his career, after two platinum albums and success among white crossover audiences, they stood by him strongly during the controversy over *Death Certificate*. Many fended off criticism of his work by claiming it was as representative of their own experiences and by suggesting his detractors were motivated by racism.

Angela Griffin wrote in the *Los Angeles Sentinel*, "Since Cube is trying to kick it on the positive side, trying to wake us up to the conspiracy against blacks, and how the White man is both brainwashing and using us so we can ruin each other, someone wants to cause an uproar. Why? Because they're getting scared. They don't want us to realize what they're trying to do— capture us in a mental slavery."[15]

James Bernard, senior editor of hip hop magazine *The Source*, defended Ice Cube against calls for boycotts: "Yes, Ice Cube is very angry, and he expresses that anger in harsh, blunt, and unmistakable terms. But the source of his rage is very real. Many in the black community, particularly Los Angeles, Cube's home, feel as if it's open season on blacks with the Rodney King assault and the recent murder of a young black girl by a Korean merchant."[16]

Hip hop is an American subculture developed by marginalized African American and Puerto Rican youth in New York ghettoes during the 1970s, including turntablism (or DJing), spray can art, break dancing (or b-boying), and rapping. As David Toop has demonstrated, rapping fits into a cultural line that can be traced back through the African American historical experience to the preslavery West African oral tradition.[17] One of rap music's many functions is to continue the long, rich line of African American social commentary and protest. The modern popularization and commodification of African American music have greatly transformed but not erased this basic cultural function.

But for many disenfranchised youth of all colors, hip hop is simply a stylistic revolt against limited opportunity and racism. In this sense, social commentary can often look like a reckless, even fatalistic indulgence to those nonconversant with rap's language. For instance, rhymers often convert peer group competition into violent metaphor. Real or invented enemies are routinely and mercilessly slaughtered in the record grooves. "Gangsta" rap can thus be compared to action-adventure movies, of which Gina Marchetti writes:

Particular genres tend to be popular at certain points in time because they somehow embody and work through those social contradictions the culture needs to come to grips with and may not be able to deal with except in the realm of fantasy. As such, popular genres often function the way myth functions—to work through social contradictions in the form of a narrative so that very real problems can be transposed to the realm of fantasy and apparently solved there.[18]

"Gangsta" rappers argue that their poetry mirrors their reality. But these raps are more than mirrors, they represent a process of self—myth making in a context of personal, historical, and psychological decimation. In this sense, the popularity of gangsta rap and the iconization of gangsta rappers make sense, even if one thinks musical "gangsta"-ism is insensible.

On *Death Certificate* Ice Cube attempted to move from 'hood hero to "race man" by moving the "us-them" dialectic into the realm of interracial relations. " 'Black Korea,' " he said, "holds the tone of the neighborhood and the feelings of the people."[19] He also remarked:

It's inspired by everyday life in the black community with the Koreans. Blacks don't like them and it's vice versa. The Koreans have a lot of businesses in the black community. The [Harlins] shooting is just proof of the problem, just another example of their disrespect for black people. You go in their stores and they think you're going to steal something. They follow you around the store like you're a criminal. They say, "Buy something or get out." If it hasn't happened to you, you can't know how bad it feels for somebody to make you feel like a criminal when you're in their store and you haven't done anything.[20]

Many of Cube's African American fans understand the fiery conclusion of "Black Korea" as a mythical, metaphorical resolution of the very real social problems of economic disenfranchisement and Korean American prejudice. Although rappers often claim their rhymes are a form of poetic journalism, that is beside the point. The music's liberation comes in its transposing real-life problems into terms that can be controlled. So when the debate over the merits of Ice Cube's record erupted, it was not surprising that African American music critics quickly rose to his defense in black newspapers and the vast network of hip hop zines. Chuck D of the rap group Public Enemy and Bernard was even given prominent space in *Billboard Magazine* where he challenged anti-black media bias.[21]

Hip hop music itself functions as representation—what Hebdige calls "noise."[22] Ice Cube devoted the lead cut of his next album, *The Predator*, to answering *Billboard*'s negative editorializing.[23] Yet whites still shaped the parameters within which African Americans could respond. As Coco Fusco has cautioned, one cannot "confuse the appearance of access created by the commodification of ethnicity . . . with the decentralization of wealth and democratization of political power that have yet to take place in this country."[24]

On the other hand, Asian Americans were largely muted in the debate. Korean Americans were not quoted in any mainstream news coverage until after the grocers' boycott had concluded. Most coverage appeared in the ethnic press, especially the *Korea Times* (of Los Angeles), *Asian Week*, and the alternative music press.

There, young Koreans expressed strong and contradictory emotions. Michael Park, a rapper with the group Seoul Brothers and a community activist in Seattle, was a good example. He had been a victim, along with his brother and two black friends, in a controversial incident of police brutality on the University of Washington campus.[25] A devotee of Ice Cube, he nonetheless reacted strongly to "Black Korea." "Not only is Cube offensive to Koreans and Korean Americans," Park wrote in the *Korea Times* of Los Angeles, "he has attacked Asian people as a whole."[26] Park asked the Korean community to use the incident to reflect on its own prejudices toward African Americans, but he expressed support for the boycotts.

High school student Henry Yun argued, however, that "Black Korea" was "a death threat to all Korean American merchants in this country," but he also reported that most of his friends felt Ice Cube should not be banned.[27] Dong Suh, the son of a grocer, attempted to "move away from the issue of censorship and the stereotyping of rap as violent and move toward addressing the core problem." He contributed an emotional and articulate analysis of the tensions between Korean and African Americans.[28] Suh stated,

> Several years ago, a prominent radio personality in Philadelphia, where my family operates a small corner store in a predominantly African American neighborhod, expressed a similar sentiment. I clearly remember his warning that if Koreans did not respect blacks, firebombings were likely. Although it's hard not to react personally to such statements, the problem lies neither with that radio personality nor with Ice Cube. His statement is merely a symptom of a more systematic problem that goes beyond the tension between African and Korean Americans. [29]

Suh also discussed the realities of social power in the 'hood: "When compared to Korean Americans, African Americans are a numerical and political majority. [Ice Cube] does not realize that as a member of the majority, he wields real power against Koreans."[30]

Korean American community leaders also struggled with this quandary. Jerry Yu, executive director of the Korean American Coalition (KAC), stated, "Ice Cube kept saying that this is social commentary. And I think it's true, he's expressing a certain sentiment that's out there. But not everybody might understand; some people might take it that he's encouraging or advocating violence against Korean store owners."[31]

Community leaders also recognized that tensions were increasing in October and November 1991. As they waited for the Du sentencing, they were locked in difficult negotiations with African American activists who were boycotting another liquor store in which an African American had been shot by a store owner. But they decided Ice Cube's free speech rights were irrelevant. Ice Cube, Yu said, was obliged to take a moral position: "When there's people in a position to affect a nationwide audience, they have a higher standard of responsibility to be fair, not to be discriminatory, or racist, or inflammatory, or to incite riots."[32] Yumi Jhang-Park, then executive director of the Korean American Grocers' Association (KAGRO), put it more bluntly: "This is a life-and-death situation. What if someone listened to the song and set fire to a store?"[33]

But Korean American activists were unable to reach the mainstream press with their message. When *Entertainment Tonight* interviewed Yu regarding the boycott, he was videotaped for over thirty minutes, yet the subsequent airing featured him only briefly, reading lyric excerpts from "Black Korea." Rabbi Abraham Cooper of the Los Angeles based Jewish human rights group the Simon Wiesenthal Center was shown explaining the boycott for most of the segment.[34]

The hierarchy of social power placed whites on top, African Americans far below, and Asian Americans even further below. Mainstream media focused coverage and commentary on "Black Korea" around themes of censorship and rebellion. Yet those themes were phrased in terms of a white-black racial axis; Koreans were useful to the discussion only insofar as they represented non-black targets of black rage. Few bothered to ask how Korean Americans might feel about the record, and even fewer gave them voice. Whereas Jewish boycott leaders were widely quoted, only two journalists felt obliged to quote a Korean American, and they did so only after the grocers' boycott had ended.[35] Some liberal music critics felt they had to qualify their criticism of the record to African Americans by addressing their status position as white males, but they nonetheless monopolized discussions.[36] They marginalized African American views by allowing only response rather than representation. They marginalized Asian American views by largely denying representation.

PAYING RESPECT TO THE BLACK FIST?

The "Black Korea" Boycotts as a Strategy for Empowerment

Upon its release on October 31, 1991, *Death Certificate* had advance orders of over a million copies, making it an instant hit. Yet the controversy around the album's content transformed the musical piece into a political issue. The rap that had threatened "Don't follow me up and down your crazy little market or your lil' chop suey ass will be a target" became a catalyst for organizing.

On November 1 the Simon Wiesenthal Center called on four major retail record chains to boycott the album, calling it "a cultural Molotov cocktail" and "a real threat."[37] Guardian Angels began to picket record stores carrying the album in New York and Los Angeles. Two days later, KAC held its own press conference, issuing a joint statement signed by the Japanese American Citizens League, the Los Angeles Urban League, the NAACP, the Mexican American Legal Defense and Educational Fund, and the Southern Christian Leadership Conference. Korean swap meet vendors and the Camelot Music chain also joined the boycott.[38]

The goal of the KAC boycott was to challenge representational problems. Yu said, "In the minds of Korean Americans, this is all part of the oppression or unfairness we face. We're constantly trampled on, nobody listens to us, we're constantly seen through distorted images in the media . . . We're not really battling against Ice Cube; all we're trying to do is get him to understand our concerns, get him to respond to our issues."[39] The boycott was in line with KAC's ongoing campaign against media stereotyping, which had included a boycott of the motion picture *The Year of the Dragon* and protests over racist coverage in *Time*, the *Los Angeles Times*, and *Rolling Stone*. But although the KAC boycott unleashed a flood of mail at Priority Records offices, Ice Cube's label, the record still sold well over a million and a half copies as mentioned previously. Perhaps, as Ice Cube had bragged on the album, he was the "wrong nigga to fuck with."

Actions were also moving on a very different front, however. On November 7 KAGRO reached an impasse in negotiations with the McKenzie River Corporation in San Francisco, the maker of the St. Ides Premium Malt Liquor for which Ice Cube was a prominent endorser. In a malt liquor equivalent of the fight between Coca Cola and Pepsi, McKenzie River's newer St. Ides brand had been competing with Pabst Brewing Company's Olde English 800 brand in a pitched battle for market share. The urban black communities of Los Angeles represented the key battleground. Beginning in 1988 McKenzie River had recruited underground West Coast rappers to record 60-second music commercials to air on the influential all-rap station KDAY.[40] When excited listeners began to request the spots more than they did some of the songs on KDAY's regular playlist, McKenzie River knew it had a winning business plan. By 1991, in no small part as a result of Ice Cube's spots, St. Ides had become the malt liquor of choice in Los Angeles 'hoods.

But now KAGRO was asking McKenzie River to withdraw all promotional materials and commercials featuring Ice Cube and to sever its relationship with him. Faced with a daunting choice, McKenzie River responded that meeting these demands would financially damage the small company and declined to do so. KAGRO had its stores return deliveries and stop ordering St. Ides. Yang Il Kim, the national president of KAGRO, expressed sympathy in the *Korea Times* for McKenzie River's business worries but remained resolute on the boycott, pointedly mentioning that the company had selected the wrong rapper to endorse its beer.[41]

At its peak, between 5,000 and 6,000 stores in Los Angeles, San Francisco, Oakland, San Jose, Seattle, Tacoma, Portland, Philadelphia, Baltimore, Richmond, and Washington, D.C., honored the boycott.[42] On November 16 McKenzie River broke down and conceded to KAGRO's demands, ending the use of all ads that featured Ice Cube and claiming it would not use him in new promotions. The company also agreed to create a scholarship fund and a jobs program for blacks from sales of St. Ides. KAGRO officially ended its boycott on November 20, only three weeks after the release of *Death Certificate*.[43]

Conciliation took place three months later. In early February 1992, McKenzie River organized a joint meeting between Ice Cube and the KAGRO leadership. Ice Cube apologized to the merchants and pledged to discourage violence against store owners and to continue "working to bring our communities closer together." He wrote to Kim, of the meeting:

> I explained some of the feelings and attitudes of black people today, and the problems and frustrations that we confront. And I clarified the intent of my album *Death Certificate*. It was not intended to offend anyone or to incite violence of any kind. It was not directed at all Korean Americans or at all Korean American store owners. I respect Korean Americans. It was directed at a few stores where my friends and I have had actual problems. Working together we can help solve these problems and build a bridge between our communities.[44]

KAGRO leaders expressed pleasure over the meeting, conceding that Ice Cube had made some legitimate complaints and expressing hope that blacks and Koreans would "help each other and learn to understand each other's cultures."[45]

Why was one economic boycott a failure and the other so successful? In the KAC boycott Korean Americans lacked the social power to sustain a lasting effect. When asked whether it might have been possible to mount the kind of protest the police associations had mounted against rapper Ice-T's song "Cop Killer," Yu argued, "There was no way we could organize that kind of impact."[46] He pointed out that the community's small size, the large number of recent immigrants, the lack of voting strength, and economic self-interest prevented KAC from forming a strong united front on this issue. KAC sought to gain legitimacy by working in concert with other civil rights organizations, incorporating the NAACP, the Mexican American Legal Defense and Education Fund, and the Simon Wiesenthal Center into the boycott. Still, as Ice Cube's publicist, Lillian Matulic, noted, "We received a lot of form letters. But in my opinion, the boycott would only affect the people who wouldn't listen to Ice Cube anyway."[47] The *Entertainment Tonight* fiasco was both ironic and symbolic; KAC's boycott against media stereotypes failed because of a lack of media coverage.

KAGRO's use of market clout in its boycott of St. Ides, however, was stunningly successful. Here the hierarchy of power changed, reversing the positions of African Americans and Asian Americans. According to Executive Director Ryan Song, KAGRO represented over 3,500 stores in southern California alone, had over 20,000 members who generated $2 billion in annual sales, and controlled roughly 7 percent of the national market.[48] African American activists noted that McKenzie River Corporation was targeting a young, urban African American male audience by using rappers such as Ice Cube to sell its malt liquor.[49] The prospect of thousands of Korean grocers in its target areas returning their orders was clearly too much for McKenzie River to bear. Yu argues that this shows that race had little to do with the boycott: "It's not that the Korean American merchants are so much more powerful. St. Ides did not respond because they were Korean Americans, but because of the economic threat."[50] Yet through the KAGRO boycott, Korean Americans were able to translate their status as small store owners into ethnic economic empowerment.

Although the controversy over the song had ended, what Dong Suh called the core issues that had created it had not gone away. Looking back a year later, Ice Cube told an interviewer:

> I live in the black community so I wanted to let the Korean community know the tension that we feel. You're in our neighborhoods, which is perfectly fine with me. I have no problem with that. But when we come into your store, you have to treat us with respect because we are putting your kids through college, we are putting food on your table and we deserve the same kind of respect [as] anybody that's going to the store. A lot of black people didn't feel that respect had been given or when the riots jumped off, Korean shops wouldn't have been a target.[51]

Many African Americans were outraged at the 1991 resolution of KAGRO's St. Ides boycott, tying it to the light sentencing for Soon Ja Du in the murder of Latasha Harlins, which had taken place only five days before. Sonny Carson, the leader of the New York-based blackwatch Movement and an organizer of previous boycotts against Korean stores, called for a one-day moratorium on the purchase of Korean-sold goods and services on Martin Luther King, Jr. Day, telling the *New York Amsterdam News*: "We buy fruits, leather, jewelry, they sell us vegetables, repair our shoes, dry clean our clothes, but they have no respect for us. We should spend money with people who respect us, not those who shoot us down . . . we will not tolerate their endorsement of murder in L.A. or anyplace else because that is what their boycott infers."[52] Although some thought that this was an extreme position from an opportunistic activist, other progressive African Americans shared the same opinion. Sheena Lester of the *Los Angeles Sentinel* wrote an editorial angrily excoriating McKenzie River Corporation and KAGRO:

> Mind you, this is the same beer company . . . who shrugged off black folks' com-plaints about those offensive St. Ides radio ads. . . . These are the same weasels who now are bowing to the demands of insensitive, poison-pushing merchants, who are apparently more outraged about being called names than they are about a dead black child. . . . As for KAGRO, I s'pose it's business as usual for them, too—back to following us "county recips"[53] around their respective stores, awaiting the opportunity to catch us being the untamed, non-civilized mongrels we are, right?[54]

Lester brought together the Du sentencing, the issue of alcoholism in the African American community, and the lack of black-owned stores in a dia-tribe against Korean American prejudice and relative economic empower-ment. For her, the resolution of the boycott was yet another example of Afri-can Americans being stepped on by everyone.[55]

Even noted Berkeley professor and writer Julianne Malveaux had told a conference of black scholars in December 1991:

> [Ice Cube] is saying what we all feel. Where is there space for us in this econ-omy? Where is there space for us in this society? Can you value my life? A Ko-rean woman—and this is not race-bashing—got off with five-hundred hours of community service for killing a fifteen-year-old black girl. Community service! Give me a break. And Los Angeles is about to pop right now.[56]

Los Angeles finally "popped" on April 29, 1992, leaving the charred shells of Korean liquor stores as proof of the currency of her sentiments.

Its leaders felt that the Ice Cube boycotts might empower the Korean American community. Yu had stated, "By expressing how we feel, we are making constant progress towards being equals in this society."[57] These goals, however, were problematized by the role that class played in Korean American ethnic interests. KAGRO national president Kim recognized such problems when he told the *Korea Times* during the boycott, "We're trying to negotiate, not to expand tensions."[58] Even after the boycott was over the *Washington Post* portrayed Kim as hoping to avoid further conflict. He was quoted as conceding that the rapper was not condemning the entire Korean American community but only a few merchants, and was shown pleading with the writer, "I personally ask you to make a good article, a good comment between the communities."[59]

Where do inner-city Korean American grocers fit in a class framework? The prevalent view has been that they are a "middleman minority"—a small, distinct cultural group located between wealthy elites and the subordinate majority. As providers of goods and services, Korean Americans constitute a petit bourgeoisie. As recent immigrants they inevitably come to feel their marginal social status when the poor majority targets them through political discourse and hostile incidents.[60]

Edna Bonacich argues that immigrant and ethnic entrepreneurs are actually "cheap labor," exploited by capitalists just as other workers are.[61] Most Korean small business owners do not make large profits, and they face a grueling host of difficulties, not the least of which is the constant threat of violent crime. Yet Bonacich and Light find that as a petit bourgeoisie, Korean Americans are likely to act like "quintessential capitalists with respect to their clients" who will "provide whatever service or commodity will sell" and who take little interest in the "impact of their businesses on that community."[62] These authors find that the nature of Korean American exploitation is much different from the exploitation of "local workers and the local poor."[63]

Asian Americans in this position maintain ethnic and class solidarities that are difficult to separate.[64] Although they organize around representational issues, organizers may not have taken into account the important class issues. KAC saw "Black Korea" as part of a line of racist, stereotypical portrayals of Korean Americans. Yu stated:

> What I'm trying to say is that what's right is right and what's wrong is wrong. So if someone is spouting hate and violence or something, and I'm not saying that Ice Cube necessarily did that, but if someone is calling for violence against a certain group, then it's wrong. No matter who that person is, whether that person is black, white, Asian, Korean, whoever, it's wrong.[65]

Korean American attorney T. S. Chung was quoted in the *Korea Times* as saying that *Death Certificate* "reflects an attitude urging blacks to take the law into their own hands by burning down stores if they don't like the store owners. I don't think that is the kind of society we want to have."[66] Unfortunately, these arguments could be read as suggesting that "Black Korea" represented the threat of racial conflict and not of class conflict—a "spin" on black-Korean tensions commonly used by the white mainstream media. Such an argument was a dead-end, a reduction of complex circumstances into a reversal of the old black-white paradigm. As conservatives had done with affirmative action and welfare, Korean Americans, as "honorary whites," could be cast as racial victims; African Americans could be cast as racial aggressors. By flattening the complexities of the situation, real economic issues were covered over with inflammatory racial overtones. All that was left was April's downward spiral into violence.

In the same press conference Chung had said that although there was "some justifiable anger . . . Koreans didn't have anything to do with the creation of that situation."[67] Undeniably, in the zero-sum game of racial struggle

in the ghetto, neither Korean Americans nor African Americans were successful in empowering themselves. They found themselves in an isolated
space, thrown into battle, fighting for no real prize. Yu sadly characterized
the boycotts' end: "No way do I see it as a victory. If there was a victory it
would have been that [Ice Cube] wouldn't have released the album in the first
place."[68]

ENVISIONING COMMON GROUND

Professor Manning Marable, writing for the *Korea Times of New York*, called
for African American self-criticism in regard to Ice Cube and the boycotts of
Korean stores. In doing so, he also eloquently summed up the difficulty of
finding common ground amid shrinking resources. He stated:

> Certainly, Ice Cube reflects much of the righteous anger and hostility of our
> people . . . But to target our anger against Asian Americans does not, in the long
> run, resolve the crisis of poverty, economic oppression, and a lack of black own-
> ership, which is the consequence of a racist, corporate system. Attacking petty
> entrepreneurs who are also people of color only permits those who directly ben-
> efit from the oppression of both groups to get away unscathed. The second
> problem presented by Ice Cube's lyrics involves the promise of a truly progres-
> sive Rainbow Coalition. People of color must transcend the terrible tendency to
> blame each other, to emphasize their differences, to trash one another.[69]

How are we to transcend? We may need first to revisit our primary assumptions on political organizing.

An anticolonial approach has guided progressive people of color in organizing for empowerment. This approach is rooted in the idea that racial minorities in the United States are, and have historically been, colonized peoples who share a similar situation of oppression and thus have a common
natural unity against the white colonizers.[70] Yet this approach has been made
problematic by immigration policy and demographic shifts. Within Asian
American communities, class stratification and ethnic difference have increased since the 1965 Immigration Act. In inner-city spaces like south-central Los Angeles, race and class intertwine to create tension and unrest between Asian Americans and African Americans.[71]

Korean Americans and other Asian Americans form a petit bourgeoisie
able to exploit an African American and Latino poor. In Donald Noel's conception, this situation meets two of the three criteria needed to establish ethnic stratification: ethnocentrism and competition over scarce resources. The
third criterion is the establishment of power by one group over another.
Until this occurs, Noel argues, there will be a destabilizing conflict.[72] Edward
Chang argues similarly: "In the Korean-black relationship, the dominant-

subordinate position has not been established between the two groups. When the perceived or real power of [the] two groups is equal, or if each group believes that it is superior over the other group, there is a high probability for violent and direct confrontation."[73]

Strategies for political empowerment must therefore be examined closely. If Asian Americans extend their economic power to include social power over African Americans, the situation in south-central Los Angeles may stabilize at the cost of ethnic stratification. At the same time, continued Asian American social marginality demonstrates that the costs of disempowerment are far too serious.[74]

But if the white-nonwhite axis of the anticolonial approach is increasingly difficult to apply in the emerging multiraciality, a purely nationalist approach, centering an ethnic-nonethnic opposition, is also problematic. The blackwatch Movement's one-day moratorium on Korean goods hoped to demonstrate symbolically to African Americans that their interests can be served only by their own. But such tactics beg the questions of whether resources might be better spent in starting black-owned businesses and from where the capital to start such businesses would come.

KAGRO's nationalism provided a different set of problems. Yang Il Kim's dilemma was how to prevent a possible backlash from African Americans, so he downplayed the resolution of the boycott. The meeting with Ice Cube was not reported by *The Korea Times* for three months and then only as a balance to the traumatic April riot headline "Cry Koreatown." Kim was forced to snatch defeat from the jaws of a pyrrhic victory.

Especially in spaces abandoned by whites and left to communities of color, it is unrealistic to hope to promote the interests of one group without the other. Outdated binary oppositions of white-nonwhite or ethnic-nonethnic must be discarded in favor of more complex approaches to understanding power. Michael Omi argues for an understanding of "differential racialization" to help explain how class affects a diverse Asian American experience.[75] Similarly, a notion of "differential forms of disempowerment" among communities of color might help organizers and public policy analysts grapple with complex interracial conflicts. Growing multiplicities of race and culture, further complicated by class, argue for a focus on where and for whom power lies and on where and for whom it does not. This analysis must also be situational; it would be an obvious mistake to assume the hierarchies found in south-central Los Angeles apply everywhere. History, space, and context shape power relations and attempts to redistribute power.

For Asian Americans it is no longer (if it ever was) enough to claim similarity and solidarity with African Americans; difference and divergence must be acknowledged. In discussing alternative jurisprudential methods, Mari Matsuda argues: "Our various experiences are not co-extensive. I cannot pretend that I, as a Japanese American, truly know the pain of, say, my Native American sister. But I can pledge to educate myself so that I do not receive her pain in ignorance."[76] Matsuda warns Asian Americans against allowing themselves to "be used" by whites against other groups of color.[77] Asian Americans must work with other communities to mitigate points of difference and minimize points of tension.

Calls for multiracial unity and cross-cultural understanding without an understanding of the specific ways in which relative power is manifested and used can become pointless exercises. Claims to empowerment can become tools to maintain historical forms of subordination. We cannot move forward until we are more aware in our movements of the different paths that have brought each of us to this common space. Only then can we take the necessary steps to shape and share our spaces in common.

NOTES

My deepest appreciation to Kyeyoung Park, Russell Leong, Edward Chang, the UCLA Asian American Studies and Afro-American Studies reading rooms, Bill Adler, Marcy Morgan, Michael Park, Adisa Banjoko, Sheena Lester, Jerry Yu, Lillian Matulic, Nate Santa Maria, Joseph Ahn, and the URB massive. This chapter first appeared in *Amerasia Journal* 19:2 (1993): 87–107. It has been revised slightly for inclusion in this book. Reprinted by permission.

1. James Johnson, Cloyzelle K. Jones, Walter Farrell, and Melvin Oliver, "The Los Angeles Rebellion, 1992: A Preliminary Assessment from Ground Zero," UCLA Center for the Study of Urban Poverty, Occasional Working Paper Series 2, 7 (Los Angeles: UCLA Center for the Study of Urban Poverty, May 1992), 6.

2. Research Group on the Los Angeles Economy, *The Widening Divide: Income Inequality and Poverty in Los Angeles*. (Summary of Findings) (Los Angeles: UCLA Graduate School of Architecture and Urban Planning:1990), 8.

3. On Korean Americans, see Ivan Light and Edna Bonacich, *Immigrant Entrepreneurs: Koreans in Los Angeles, 1965–1982* (Berkeley: University of California Press, 1988); Kyeyoung Park, "Placing the Korean Petit Bourgeoisie in the Los Angeles Crisis: The Interpenetration of Race and Class," unpublished paper, Los Angeles. 1993. For recent work on the middleman minority theory applicable to Asian Americans, see: Jonathan H. Turner and Edna Bonacich, "Toward a Composite Theory of Middleman Minorities." *Ethnicity* 7(1980), 144–158; Edna Bonacich and John Modell, *The Economic Basis of Ethnic Solidarity: Small Business in the Japanese American Community* (Berkeley: University of California Press, 1980).

4. Lawrence Bobo, James Johnson, Melvin Oliver, James Sidanius, and Camille Zubrinsky, "Public Opinion Before and After a Spring of Discontent," UCLA Center for the Study of Urban Poverty, Occasional Working Paper Series, 3 (Los Angeles: UCLA Center for the Study of Urban Poverty, September 1992), tables C27 and C28.

5. Edward Tea Chang, "New Urban Crisis: Korean-black Conflicts in Los

Angeles." Ph.D. dissertation, Ethnic Studies, (University of California at Berkeley, 1990), 23.

6. Theodor Adorno, "On Popular Music," in *On Record: Rock, Pop and the Written Word*, Simon Frith and Andrew Goodwin, eds. (New York: Pantheon, 1990), 311–312. See also Herbert Gans, "Popular Culture in America: Social Problem in a Mass Society or Social Asset in a Pluralist Society?" in *Social Problems: A Modern Approach*, Howard S. Becker, ed. (New York: John Wiley and Sons, 1966), 549–620.

7. Simon Frith, "Music for Pleasure," *Screen Education* 34 (Spring 1980), 53.

8. Dick Hebdige, *Subculture: The Meaning of Style* (London: Methuen, 1979), 90.

9. See also Robert Christgau, "Me and the Devil Blues," *Village Voice* (December 17, 1991); Dave Marsh, "Record Review of 'Death Certificate'," *Playboy* 39 (March 1992), 3; R. J. Smith, "The Racist You Love to Hate," *Los Angeles Weekly* (November 15–21, 1992); Jon Pareles, "Tales from the Dark Side, Spun by a Reluctant Outlaw," *New York Times* (November 11, 1992); Jon Pareles, "Should Ice Cube's Voice Be Chilled?" *New York Times* (December 8, 1991); Joe Queenan, "Hate on Ice: Taking the Rap on Racism," *Washington Post* (December 29, 1991).

10. Robert Hilburn, "A Crucial Message, a Crude Delivery From Ice Cube," *Los Angeles Times* (November 3, 1991).

11. "Editorial," *Billboard* (November 23, 1991).

12. "Cracked Ice," *The Economist* 321, 7735 (November 30, 1991).

13. David Samuels, "The Rap on Rap," *New Republic* (November 11, 1991), 29.

14. N.W.A., "Gangsta, Gangsta," on *Straight Outta Compton* (Ruthless Records Recording, Compton, 1988).

15. Angela Griffin, "The Iceman Cometh, and So Does the Controversy," *Los Angeles Sentinel* (December 5, 1991).

16. James Bernard, "'Death Certificate' Gives Birth to Debate," *Billboard* (December 7, 1991).

17. David Toop, *The Rap Attack 2: African Rap to Global Hip Hop* (London: Serpent's Tail, 1991), 19.

18. Gina Marchetti, "Action Adventure as Ideology," in *Cultural Politics In Contemporary America*, Ian Angus and Sut Jhally, eds. (New York: Routledge, 1989), 187.

19. Ice Cube interview tape (Priority Records, Los Angeles, 1992).

20. Quoted in Dennis Hunt, "Outrageous as He Wants to Be," *Los Angeles Times* (November 3, 1991).

21. *Billboard* (December 7, 1991).

22. Hebdige, *Subculture*, 90.

23. The chorus of "The Predator" is a characteristically blunt "Fuck Billboard and the editor. I am the Predator." Ice Cube, *The Predator* (Priority Records Recording, Los Angeles, 1992).

24. Coco Fusco, "Pan-American Postnationalism," in *Black Popular Culture*, Gina Dent, ed. (Seattle: Bay Press, 1992), 281.

25. Michael Park, "A Night of Terror," *Korea Times* (Los Angeles) (April 24, 1991).

26. Michael Park, "Ice Cube Stereotypes All Asians, Not Just Koreans," *Korea Times* (Los Angeles) (January 20, 1992).

27. Henry Yun, " 'Black Korea' " Is a Death Threat," *Korea Times* (Los Angeles) (November 11, 1991).

28. Dong Suh, "The Source of Korean and African American Tensions," *Asian Week* (February 21, 1992).

29. Ibid.

30. Ibid.

31. Author interview with Jerry Yu of the Korean American Coalition, March 1993.

32. Ibid.

33. Quoted in John Leland, "Cube on Thin Ice," *Newsweek* 118 (December 2, 1991), 69.

34. Yu interview.

35. Lynne Duke, "Rapper's Number Chills Black-Korean Relations," *Washington Post* (December 1, 1991); Leland, "Cube on Thin Ice," 69.

36. In particular, see Christgau, "Me and the Devil Blues."

37. Chuck Philips, "Wiesenthal Center Denounces Ice Cube's Album," *Los Angeles Times*, (November 2, 1991).

38. Sophia Kyung Kim, "Chilling Fields: Ice Cube Rap," *Korea Times* (Los Angeles) (November 11, 1991).

39. Yu interview.

40. Author interview with King Tee, May 5, 1998. King Tee was the first Los Angeles rapper to do a St. Ides commercial, with his partner and future *Death Certificate* producer DJ Pooh. He told me, "We do a commercial anytime we want, and they're paying top dollar. They got a lot of respect for me. And St. Ides take care of a nigga, 'specially when they broke. They put like 50 [grand] in a nigga's pocket."

41. Quoted in Richard Reyes Fruto, "KAGRO Puts Freeze on Ice Cube," *Korea Times* (Los Angeles) (November 18, 1991).

42. Duke, "Rapper's Number," A9.

43. Richard Reyes Fruto, "St. Ide's Cans Ice Cube," *Korea Times* (Los Angeles) (November 25, 1991).

44. Quoted in Sophia Kyung Kim, "Ice Cube the Peacemaker," *Korea Times* (Los Angeles) (May 4, 1992).

45. Ibid.

46. Yu interview.

47. Author interview with Lillian Matulic, publicist for Priority Records, March 1993.

48. Speech by Ryan Song at "Conference on New Directions for the Korean-American Community," University of Southern California, Los Angeles. March 1993.

49. Carla Marinucci, "Malt Liquor's Rapper Ads Changing Tone," *San Francisco Examiner* (December 15, 1991).

50. Yu interview.

51. Ice Cube interview by Ruben Martinez, *Life and Times* TV show, originally aired on KCET Los Angeles, January 20, 1993.

52. Quoted in Vinette K. Pryce, "Carson and 'Blackwatch' to Boycott Koreans on MLK Day," *New York Amsterdam News* 82, 52 (December 28, 1991).

53. A reference to welfare recipients in Ice Cube's "Us" on *Death Certificate*: "Too much backstabbing/ While I look out the window and see all the Japs grabbin'/ Every

vacant lot in my 'hood/ Build a store and sell they goods/ To the county recips/ You know us poor niggas/ Nappy hair and big lips/ Four, five kids on ya crotch and you expect Uncle Sam to help us out?"

54. Sheena Lester, "Youth Ideas Section: From the Editor," *Los Angeles Sentinel* (December 12, 1991).

55. Author interview with Sheena Lester, former Youth Ideas editor of the *Los Angeles Sentinel*, February 1993.

56. Julianne Malveaux, "Popular Culture and the Economics of Alienation," in *Black Popular Culture*, Gina Dent, ed. (Seattle: Bay Press, 1992), 207.

57. Yu interview.

58. Quoted in Fruto, "KAGRO."

59. Duke, "Rapper's Number," A9.

60. See Bonacich and Modell, *Economic Basis of Ethnic Solidarity*, Turner and Bonacich, *Toward a Composite Theory*.

61. Edna Bonacich, "The Social Costs of Immigrant Entrepreneurship," *Amerasia Journal* 14, 1 (1988): 120. See also, Pyong Gap Min, "The Social Costs of Immigrant Entrepreneurship: A Response to Edna Bonacich," *Amerasia Journal* 15:2 (1989): 187–194. Edna Bonacich, "The Role of the Petite Bourgeoisie Within Capitalism: A Response to Pyong Gap Min," *Amerasia Journal* 15, 2 (1989): 195–203.

62. Light and Bonacich, *Immigrant Entrepreneurs*, 433–4.

63. Ibid, 366–370.

64. See Park, "Korean Petit Bourgeoisie"; Bonacich and Modell, *Economic Basis of Ethnic Solidarity*; and Bonacich, "Social Costs."

65. Yu interview.

66. Kim, "Chilling Fields."

67. Ibid.

68. Yu interview.

69. Manning Marable, "Black Prof Sees America Belonging to People of Color, Criticizes Ice Cube," republished in *Korea Times* (Los Angeles) (February 18, 1992).

70. Robert Blauner, *Racial Oppresion in America* (New York: Harper and Row, 1972), 52. See also: Albert Memmi, *The Colonizer and the Colonized* (Boston: Beacon Press, 1965); Stokely Carmichael and Charles Hamilton, *Black Power: The Politics of Liberation in America* (New York: Vintage, 1967).

71. Park, "Korean Petit Bourgeoisie," 5–7.

72. Donald Noel, "A Theory of the Origins of Ethnic Stratification," *Social Problems* 16, 2 (Fall 1968): 157–172.

73. Chang, "New Urban Crisis," 28.

74. A 1993 study by the Korean American Inter-Agency Council showed that only 28 percent of the stores that were burned down were being rebuilt.

75. Michael Omi, "Out of the Melting Pot and into the Fire: Race Relations Policy," in *The State of Asian Pacific America*, J. D. Hokoyama and Don Nakanishi, eds. (Los Angeles: LEAP Asian Pacific American Public Policy Institute and UCLA Asian American Studies Center, 1993), 207.

76. Mari Matsuda, "When the First Quail Calls: Multiple Consciousness as Jurisprudential Method," *Women's Rights Law Reporte* 11, 1 (Spring 1989), 10.

77. Mari Matsuda, "We Will Not Be Used," from a speech April 1990, at the Asian

Law Caucus, reprinted in *Asian American Pacific Islands Law Journal* 1, 1 (February 1993), 79–84.

AUTHOR BIOGRAPHY

Jeff Chang has written extensively on race relations and music. He is assistant editor of ColorLines Magazine, *a national periodical exploring race, culture and community organizing. He writes a popular music column for the* San Francisco Bay Guardian, *and has written for* XXL, Vibe, Rap Pages, Warp, Urb, *and the* San Jose Metro. *He has produced over a dozen records, and he ran the influential hip hop indie label SoleSides. Born of Chinese and Native Hawaiian ancestry and raised in Hawaii, he currently lives and writes in the San Francisco Bay Area. His "Local Knowledge(s): Notes on Race Relations, Panethnicity, and History in Hawaii" appeared in* Amerasia Journal 22, 2 (1996). *He is currently working on a book on Ice Cube's* Death Certificate *album.*

21

Trial and Error: Representations of a Recent Past

Laura Hall

DARK DAYS

Here we are in the Guyana National Archives, a mother and daughter combing through documents, correspondence, and newspapers for anything pertaining to the lives of the Chinese in Guyana. These textual insinuations in the archives, libraries, and churches are the traces of something like a history. My mother is looking for her ancestors; I am trying to add their voices to the postcolonial narrative of the nation.

The published record on the Chinese is silent after the well-documented indenture period in the second half of the nineteenth century. There are occasional references to certain wealthy merchants, but on the whole the literature of the social sciences and history relegates the Chinese to a footnote or a few paragraphs at best. Leo Despres describes them as "the least identifiable of Guyana's six ethnic groups." Brackette Williams suggests that they could be considered model Guyanese in being "fundamentally 'English' and superficially ethnic." Most writers base their statements on a study undertaken in 1954 by Morton Fried. Noting an absence of Chinese cultural practices and observing that they lived "essentially as Guianese" Fried concluded that "these people are scarcely Chinese."[1]

There is some truth in all these statements. The Chinese immigrants readily took to Creole culture—converting to Christianity, supporting freemasonry, learning to play cricket, and intermarrying with other Guyanese. They became unidentifiable and thus uninteresting to anthropologists. Now those families are scattered around the world, part of the growing Caribbean Diaspora. Between the boat from China in the 1860s and the planes to Lon-

163

don, Toronto, or Miami over a century later, many stories great and small are waiting to be told.

Lights dim, the fan slows to a halt, and the indifferent clerk announces a blackout from her table by the door but makes no move to eject us, power cuts being part of the daily routine. Natural light and fresh air regularly flow unimpeded into this archive, so the blackout does not have too much effect on our work except that the unreliable photocopier will now certainly cease to function at all. We sweat with the exertion of copying by hand. We have returned unopened many of the leather-bound volumes. Their crumbling pages are not only the frail repository of the nation's history but have also nurtured generations of tropical insects.

The pages of the 1866 issues of the *Colonist* newspaper are a litany of criminal activity. My mother diligently copies all of the items mentioning the Chinese, exhorting me all the while not to say in my "book" that our ancestors were all criminals. I assure her that my "book," as she likes to call my dissertation, will put the information in a proper context.[2]

> January 29th. Wong a Yeune and Kong a See . . . indicted for the murder of La-A-Isung . . .
> May 5th. A Chinese woman named Wong-A-She murdered by a Chinaman named Kong-A-Cheo at Plantation Blankenburg . . .
> June 12th. A Negro named Damon Lewis of Phoenix Village, Leguan, was found murdered near his house of stab wounds. A Chinese man Chong-A-Hong was arrested on suspicion of murder.[3]

The editorial pages fulminate over the hardened criminal nature of the Chinese.

> June 28th. Ordinary prison life seems to be nothing very unpleasant to the Chinaman. Accustomed to be ruled with the rod of iron in his native country, he thinks lightly of confinement so long as it is accompanied by tolerably good fare and not a little repose from labour.
> September 12th. Yk-A-Kow, Chin-A-Ping and Tan-A-Hok were flogged yesterday . . . for plantain stealing. We understand that Hamlet, the executioner . . . urged that it was only proper that . . . when any remunerative business of a respectable and pleasant kind, bearing upon criminal reform, was to be done, it should also fall to his lot. Amongst the latter class of job was ranked naturally enough by Mr. Hamlet, the flogging of a few celestials for plantain stealing.[4]

Happily for my transcriber, Chinese names disappear from the crime columns by the early twentieth century. Now they can be found among the lists of qualified voters and jurors, buyers and sellers of properties, holders of mining claims and timber grants, and advertisers of businesses.

Phyllis Hall, née Lee, is my mother and the great-granddaughter of Chinese indentured laborers who arrived in the 1860s. The children of that first generation of immigrants met with varying degrees of success in their attempts to escape the economic confinement of the sugar estates. My mother's paternal grandfather, Thomas Lee A Pen, a man of very modest means, is remembered mostly for his excellent roast pork and harmonium playing in church. Isaac Fung Teen Yong, her mother's father, was a successful businessman. Isaac's grandchildren reminisce about his cocoa and rubber plantations, his mining enterprises, and his many properties in town, but without documentation their existence is merely conjecture; for little remains of his fortune. How the son of indentured laborers acquired so much property is a mystery; details of Isaac's early life have disappeared.

My second cousin Andy Lee has compiled an extensive genealogy of the descendants of Isaac and his seven brothers and sisters, a family that has branches throughout Guyanese society and whose members are now scattered around the globe. Next to Isaac's name is that of his wife, Mary, about whom less is known. Mary's name has no branches. No parents, brothers, or sisters appear by her name on the family charts. No one is even certain of her family name. Like most women of her generation her activities are not commemorated in public documents; only anecdotes remain.

Once long ago, when the family lived in the country near Suddie on the other side of the Essequibo River, Mary took ill. When word reached Isaac who was in Georgetown attending to business, he lost no time in commandeering one of the ferries that plied the Essequibo between Parika and Suddie to bring Mary to the hospital in Georgetown. The story was told to my mother by her mother, Dora, the fourth daughter of Isaac and Mary. I like to think of Isaac's gesture as a measure of the affection that he had for his wife, but my grandmother's point in telling the story was to substantiate the family's former wealth.

Phyllis's diligence finally pays off when she finds a transaction of one of her grandfathers in the *Official Gazette*. An estate owned by Quintin Hogg, a partner in one of the large sugar firms was being subdivided and sold. The buyer of one lot was the impecunious Thomas Lee-A-Pen. She takes down the details of the transport for "the East half of lot No. 96, part of that Plantation La Penitence, situate on the East Bank of the River Demerary, in the colony of British Guiana, called Albuoy's Town . . . 9th day of October, 1889, to and in favour of Thomas Lee Appen."[5]

My mother is disappointed that our delving into the archives casts little light on Isaac's business activities, but she dutifully notes the constant activities of other eminent Chinese families whose names do appear in the records: "Evan Wong, Evan Wong, that's all I'm seeing. I don't see any mention of my grandpa here, and he was rich, too, you know." The two families were once close, sharing residences in town and going on picnics up the Demerara River. My grandmother Dora and Evan Wong's daughter Flo were "grow-

Isaac Fung Teen Yong, Georgetown, Guyana. Date unknown. Reprinted courtesy of Laura Hall.

match," as they say in Guyana, close friends who were born on the same day and grew up together. Isaac may have been rich, but his friend Evan Wong was considered one of the wealthiest men in the colony; thus his name was featured prominently in the reports of business activities of the day. Whereas Isaac's fortune disappeared with the next generation, the Evan Wong family fortunes were maintained by the activities of his children—particularly the eldest, Robert Victor.

A NOTABLE FAMILY

In his account of the Chinese in British Guiana, Cecil Clementi devoted several pages to the story of Evan Wong, describing him as the "most noteworthy" of all the notable Chinese immigrants—those who had made good in the colony.[6] Yan Sau Wong was ten years old when his parents emigrated to British Guiana from Hong Kong onboard the *Dartmouth* in 1879. They were part of a group of Hakka Christians who came to labor on the sugar plantations. At some point he took the name Evan, a name that remains in the family to this day. Like many other Chinese immigrants, his first venture away from the plantation was shopkeeping, and from there he went on to acquire other shops and businesses around the country and in Georgetown. He invested in rubber, cocoa, coffee, and coconut estates and in the profitable balata, timber, and mining industries. In his leisure time he indulged in breeding and racing horses, the favorite pastime of gentlemen of means in the colony. When a fire struck the Chinese commercial district of Georgetown a few days before Christmas 1913, Evan Wong's enterprises suffered $40,000 in damages, a huge sum at the time; the losses, however, were deemed insignificant to the overall Evan Wong enterprises, which by then were very diversified.

In his private life, Evan Wong and his wife Sarah Leung, a Creole-born Chinese woman, raised ten children—five girls and five boys. The eldest, Robert Victor, attended Bristol University in England, where he read civil engineering. On his return he married Cheu-leen Ho-A-Sho, the daughter of another "notable" Chinese patriarch, John Ho-A-Sho. When Evan and Sarah died suddenly within days of each other in 1924, Robert was left to care for his young siblings and his father's extensive business interests. But Robert was more than a businessman; he was imbued with a sense of the possibilities of the land of his birth and was active in the social and civic life of the colony. He ventured into politics and succeeded in being elected to the Legislature in 1926, making him possibly the first person of Chinese descent to become an elected representative in the Americas. In 1928 he was appointed to the Executive Council. He lost his seat in the 1931 election but decided to run in a by-election in 1934. Playing on the initials of his name, his slogan, "Right

The Evan Wong Family, Guyana. Circa 1919. Robert Victor Evan Wong stands in the back at the far left next to his wife Cheu-leen. Courtesy of the Evan Wong family.

Vanquishes Every Wrong," was an optimistic assertion that was not borne out by his experiences in that election and its aftermath.

ELECTION PETITION

The sudden death of the Honorable E. F. Fredericks, representative for the Essequibo River District, precipitated the by-election on May 28, 1934. The Essequibo River constituency was composed of the islands of Leguan and Wakenaam at the mouth of the river and Bartica, a town at the confluence of the Mazaruni, Cuyuni, and Essequibo Rivers. Alfred Railton Crum Ewing, a descendant of Scottish planters, was R. V. Evan Wong's only challenger for the seat. On May 29, Frederick Low, the returning officer for the district, announced the results of the previous day's poll. Of 677 registered voters, 443 had cast their vote; 236 had voted for Robert Victor Evan Wong and 199 had voted for his opponent, Alfred Railton Crum Ewing, eight ballots were spoiled.[7] Wong had defeated Ewing at four of the five polling stations.

A few weeks later, on June 18, Ewing filed a petition to have the election declared void, alleging corrupt practices by Wong's agents and canvassers: Walter Chee-A-Tow, Frederick Sue-A-Quan, Abdool Majeed Khan, Simon

Yhap, Robert Rose Chung, Eric Leung Walker, Issri Persaud, Lilliah, Ellen Whyte, and Kassim Kamal.[8] The election petition was heard in the Supreme Court of British Guiana by Chief Justice Crean. Four months and sixty-three witnesses later, he rendered his verdict: Crean concurred with Ewing that Evan Wong's agents had engaged in "treating, undue influence, bribery, and personation."[9] The judge praised Ewing's witnesses as "creditable," whereas those testifying for Evan Wong were characterized as "unreliable" and untruthful. He allowed that R. V. Evan Wong himself had not authorized or consented to the offenses, "yet, he is responsible for them as if they were his own acts . . . and on account of these acts this election must be declared void."[10] The election was held again on December 10 with the same two men contesting the seat, and once again R. V. Evan Wong was the victor—this time by a slim majority of one vote. Wong served out the term in the Legislature but never ventured into politics again. Though the election of R. V. Evan Wong was clouded by the petition, the fact remains that a Chinese candidate was elected in a district where the Chinese population formed less than 1 percent of the total population.

Guyana's common division between Africans and Indians was not the fault line in this case.[11] Each candidate drew support from both communities. On the stand witnesses seemed motivated less by ties of ethnicity or by loyalty to either candidate and more by the distinctions of religion and class within their respective communities, as well as by long-standing friendships and rivalries. In the public forum of Justice Crean's courtroom, the islanders' envies and admiration cast a shadow over "the truth." The consequences, after all, would be borne by either Ewing or Evan Wong—both "big men" in the colony but both outsiders on the islands.

POLITICS OF DRINKING

Walter Chee-A-Tow and Frederick Sue-A-Quan were charged with supplying free drinks at two locations in order to influence voters. According to the Honorable R. E. Brassington, a longtime member of the Executive and Legislative Councils and Wong's last witness, elections in the country's districts had always had a festive aspect. In the old days there had been a lot of drinking, and it was a habit that would die hard. This had held true on the election day in question. African and Indian men had gathered at different provision and rum shops—run mostly by Chinese families—to have a few celebratory drinks and wait for rides to the polling stations. Walter Chee-A-Tow, a shop owner, was ferrying voters to the polls at Enterprise and Richmond Hill. Since the advent of the motor car, voters expected candidates to provide transportation whether they lived five miles or fifty yards from the polling station.

At Louisiana Village on Leguan a group of men, mostly Africans, gathered at the local shop managed by Frederick Sue-A-Quan. The men were rice planters, public works contractors, and the laborers who worked for them. Voters and nonvoters alike were drinking and gossiping. Sue-A-Quan knew most of the crowd well; some bought drinks there often, and others had accounts in the shop, which they charged and paid off at the end of the month or when their padi crop was harvested. A few had bad credit, but in the morning's goodwill they managed to obtain a drink or two by hanging around with their friends. When called to the witness stand, their memories were influenced not only by the alcohol they had consumed but by their relationships to one another and to the owners of the shops they were drinking in.

John Archer, a laborer, and Joseph Stanton, a rice planter, were summoned to testify for Ewing. Both said that they each had ordered about five bottles of beer and wine, which they had mixed together and shared with others. The most critical part of their testimony was their claim that they had not been charged for their drinks. Another Ewing witness, Benjamin Nurse, the sexton of the church at Enterprise, had stated earlier to Ewing's agent that he, Stanton, and Archer had received free drinks. On the stand he changed his story, saying that Sue-A-Quan had refused to serve him any drinks because he was in debt to the shop and he was no longer sure whether the others had paid for their drinks. When Ewing's lawyer pointed out the discrepancy between his account on the stand and the original statement he had signed, Nurse pleaded that he could not read or write too well; after all, he reasoned, he was only a sexton in the church, not a *reader*. Ewing's frustrated lawyer had Nurse declared a hostile witness.

Josiah King, a woodcutter and rice planter with outstanding debts, also testified for Ewing. King no longer bought goods at Chee-A-Tow's shop because he owed too much money, but he had stopped by on election day and alleged that he drank without paying. King then rode in Chee-A-Tow's car to Enterprise polling station where he voted for Ewing. He insisted "it was a custom" to take drinks from a candidate even if one did not vote for him, although he would have preferred money.

Frederick Sue-A-Quan, the shop manager, was not a voter, but he and his family had known R. V. Evan Wong for many years and supported his campaign. His older brother, William Sue-A-Quan, was Evan Wong's polling agent at the Richmond Hill station on election day. Frederick admitted that he had encouraged people he knew to vote for Evan Wong but he asserted that he never gave free drinks to voters and produced account books to show that the drinks had been paid for. Some of the drinkers remembered being at the shop at around midday or later, however, Sue-A-Quan stated emphatically that he had closed the shop at eleven A.M. in order to go to Enterprise to help in his brother's shop.

A few miles away at Enterprise, a group of Indian men gathered near William Sue-A-Quan's shop. A woman named Rasulan and her son Abdool Samad testified that they had seen Balgobin, Hogg, Kaow, and Sookdeo drinking half a bottle of rum provided by Chee-A-Tow, but none of those men was called to verify her statement. Rasulan's neighbor, Ousman, said that a wedding had taken place the day before the election. Afterward, as was the custom, he and the other men—including Abdool Samad—went to the bride's house, and Rasulan went with the women to the bridegroom's house. At the time the next day that the mother and son claimed they saw the men drinking, Ousman said they were still at the wedding celebrations. Nevertheless, Justice Crean found "no reason for disbelieving the woman Rasulan and her son."

Wong's case was not helped by the testimony of his supporter Walter Chee-A-Tow whose elusive replies and contradictions irritated the judge. Chee-A-Tow said he had known Wong since he was a boy, and when Wong's candidacy was announced he deemed it a matter of "national feelings and friendship to help Mr. Wong in every way possible during the election."[12] But he also claimed, perhaps out of a desire to protect Wong, that he had never spoken to Wong directly about the election either before or afterwards—a claim that even Wong refuted. Although Wong said he had not appointed any election agents, Crean considered both Chee-A-Tow and Sue-A-Quan to be his agents in practice; thus through them Wong was guilty of treating voters to drinks.

Crean's view of Chee-A-Tow as untrustworthy was reinforced by the latter's inability to describe clearly his business relationships with either his father-in-law, William Sue-A-Quan, or his shop manager, Frederick Sue-A-Quan. What Crean was unable to grasp and none of the shopkeepers was able to convey to the judge was the very fluid and informal way that many Chinese families handled their business affairs. Whereas one relationship might exist legally and on paper, the understanding of the relationship by those involved might be very different; this discrepancy was viewed by the judge as an attempt at obfuscation.

The shop in Louisiana represented both the vagaries of the shopkeeping business as well as the closeness of the Chinese community. Walter Chee-A-Tow was married to William Sue-A-Quan's daughter Dorothy. William had owned shops in Louisiana, Enterprise, and elsewhere on Leguan for many years. William's younger brother Frederick had managed the Enterprise shop for a few years, and Chee-A-Tow had officially managed the shop in Louisiana and lived above it with his family. He left the running of the shop to others, as his main interest was his rice mill. By 1934 William Sue-A-Quan's finances were in trouble, and his creditors were pressing him. At that time he transferred the license for the Louisiana shop to Chee-A-Tow. Although the license was now in Chee-A-Tow's name, William Sue-A-Quan retained ownership of the land and the shop building, which explains Chee-A-Tow's denial in court that he owned the business. Chee-A-Tow hired the younger Sue-A-Quan, Frederick, to manage the shop for him in return for free board and lodging and half of the profits, so Frederick considered himself a partner. Chee-A-Tow also denied that this was the case pointing out that Frederick had not supplied any of the capital.

Cane Cutters to Shopkeepers

The Sue-A-Quans, like R. V. Evan Wong and Walter Chee-A-Tow, were the grandsons of indentured immigrants. The Sue-A-Quan family arrived with the *Corona* in 1874. The arrival of this group of immigrants caused much comment in Georgetown. Unlike other raw recruits for the plantations, these immigrants did not appear to be awed in the least by their new surroundings. The *Royal Gazette* exclaimed that the immigrants had been

> Promenading the city with all the airs and eagerness of a body of Cooke's tourists visiting some celebrated continental city for the first time. . . They have pried into the stores, the churches, the Public Buildings; they have patronized the cabs to a liberal extent, as many as 10 of them airing themselves in one vehicle at the same time . . . Amongst the lot there is scarcely a man who has the appearance—not of being an agricultural labourer but of being a likely person to be converted into one.[13]

A laborer named Soo A Cheong, his wife, Yau She, and their nine-year-old son, Soo Sam Kuan, were among the *Corona* passengers. According to their contract of indenture, they were assigned to Plantation La Grange on the west bank of the Demerara after they landed where they served out the terms of their indenture. The boy Soo Sam Kuan became known as Henry Sue-A-Quan. He married Mary Hoee (originally Ho Yee), and they had five sons and two daughters. "Not much is known of his life except that he later operated a small store serving labourers on the plantation selling staples. . . . It is said that his wife Mary would call him 'Hakka' in a derogatory tone whenever there was a difference of opinion between them."[14] William, born in 1888, was the eldest of their seven children and Frederick, born in 1908, was the youngest.

William Sue-A-Quan moved to Enterprise, Leguan, and by 1913 had become a local merchant and proprietor.[15] Over the years he acquired several shops and a number of properties on the island, including several lots that were part of former plantations. Among them were several lots at Anna Maria which he probably bought from Evan Wong, the father of R. V. Evan Wong. Wong had reclaimed buildings, land, a rice factory, and a provision shop at Anna Maria from a man named Chung Le Pow when the latter defaulted on his mortgage in 1913. In June 1934, just before the election petition hearings were to begin, the misfortunes of trade came full circle. William Sue-A-Quan, pressed by his creditors, the Honorable Francis Dias and G. R. Reid, put some of his properties up for auction. Most of his land and property on Leguan, along with the "buildings and erections" except for "one trash building thereon owned by Sunny Forthy,"[16] were placed on the auctioneer's block.

The Skulking Absence

Although Alfred Railton Crum Ewing appears to have left few traces other than the lengthy election petition, the Crum Ewing name had a long association with the colony of British Guiana. The Glasgow company of H. E. Crum Ewing and Alexander Crum Ewing was one of the seven largest concerns dominating the sugar industry during the indenture period. The Crum Ewings took an active interest not only in the technological improvement of their properties but also in the moral improvement of their workers. As Scottish Presbyterians, they actively supported missionary endeavors and contributed to the maintenance of a Canadian Presbyterian missionary on their estates from the early 1860s onward.[17]

The Canadian missionaries concentrated their efforts on the Indian population, providing schools and schoolteachers for Indian children on the Crum Ewing estates and elsewhere in the colony. One such school was the Canadian Mission School at Ridge on Wakenaam, where Goolab Abraham Jowahir was the head teacher. Jowahir was Ewing's most convincing witness. He testified that the week before the election the tailor Lilliah had approached him and asked him to vote for Wong, adding that Wong had promised to give a dinner for his supporters thirty days after the election. Another Ewing supporter, Buddha, said Lilliah had also asked him to vote for Wong and told him there would be a free dinner afterward.

Lilliah's testimony was quite different. He agreed that he had seen Jowahir and Buddha at a wedding in Ridge, but he added that he had not spoken to either of them in over a year, much less spoken to them of free dinners. The rift was precipitated by a debate over an inflammatory pamphlet about Hindus written by an Indian Christian convert named Harripaul. Lilliah had led the Hindu side of the debate, which had ended in a fracas with police called in to restore order. Since then, Jowahir, Buddha, Harripaul, and other Christian Indians had not spoken to him. Lilliah suggested that Jowahir and Buddha had lied about him simply because he was a Hindu. Justice Crean was clearly more impressed by Jowahir than by Lilliah. Because Jowahir was "a school teacher and a leading man in his district,"[18] Crean saw no reason to disbelieve him. He concluded that Lilliah and others had indeed attempted to bribe voters with the promise of dinners.

In summing up his client's case, the Honorable E. G. Woolford, counsel for R. V. Evan Wong, addressed the multitude of allegations against his client. Finally, he turned to the character of the petitioner: "I ask your Honour to note his skulking absence from the witness box."[19] Ewing's absence leaves him a shadowy character in the courtroom drama, represented only in the testimony of his enemy, R. V. Evan Wong. On the stand Wong recounted with some bitterness that the two men had not been great friends before the case—he had regarded Ewing as an employee of his father's estate. They had been enemies ever since Ewing had brought a case against the estate of Evan Wong. When Ewing won he continued to taunt Wong by carrying the judgment around with him.

REMAKING THE NATION

My mother and I search for her mother's shop at Diamond each time we pass the spot on the road along the east bank of the Demerara. We know the approach well by now, having traversed the road a couple of times. When the odor of rotten eggs assaults our nostrils, we know we are almost there. The smell permeates the air around the sugar refinery where the cane is processed into the famous Demerara sugar and its by-products, molasses and rum. Nearer the factory the canals turn viscous and black from industrial waste. A little further along, Phyllis identifies the mosque and movie theater which she is convinced were on either side of Grandma's shop. Something about them is different now, and no building resembling the shop is anywhere in sight.

Her mother, Dora, daughter of the merchant Isaac Fung Teen Yong and his wife, Mary, married Alexander Lee in February 1918. Alex was a shop clerk and a son of the not very well-to-do Thomas Lee-A-Pen and Elizabeth Leow. Isaac endowed the newlyweds with a car and several shops. A combination of bad luck, poor business sense, and a love of gambling whittled away the inheritance until only the shop in Diamond remained. There were several other Chinese shops in Diamond when Phyllis was growing up. Dora's sister Jane owned one close by, and some people named Wong had another shop on the estate. A third sister, Eva, had a shop up the road in Grove Village. The shop buildings in Diamond, like everything else, were owned by the estate and leased to the owners.

One day passing through Diamond we stop the car. Although it is a weekday it is a Muslim holiday, and many of people are promenading along the main road. Phyllis now deduces that the mosque is "in the wrong place" but says the cinema looks about the same. Outside a restaurant near the cinema, a group of young men sit on rickety bleachers sharing drinks and passing time. They are not very responsive to inquiries about a Chinese shop that was somewhere nearby sometime before most of them were born. Almost forty years have passed since Phyllis was last here. Eventually, they send her to an older Indian woman at the next house who remembers Mr. and Mrs. Lee's shop. She tells Mr. Lee's daughter that the mosque is a new one built on the same spot as the previous one but that the cinema has been moved. The Lee's old shop was torn down a long time ago, and the entire main road had been rerouted to straighten some of the bends; as a result, almost nothing on the estate is now in the same place in relation to other landmarks.

Leaving Diamond, Phyllis recollects that her father, Alexander Lee, once ran for a seat in the Legislature—a fact no one in the family had mentioned before. This little bit of family lore had disappeared, not out of a desire to repress it but because it was not considered a particularly remarkable activity for a man who always approached new hobbies with a thoroughness that he had never applied to shopkeeping. When he raised chickens, they had to be prize chickens. When his fancy turned to gardening, he imported seeds from England and grew the biggest and best flowers on the estate. His butterfly and stamp collections were a constant source of pride. He was a sociable man and loved to talk about his latest pursuits or about politics. The family regarded his decision to run as a candidate for the East Bank Demerara constituency in the 1953 as merely his latest venture.

This was the first election held under a new constitution intended to put the colony of British Guiana on the path to self-government. Universal suffrage was finally granted, and candidates no longer had to satisfy income and property qualifications.

Alexander ran as an Independent candidate and initially had the support of the managers of the Diamond Estate. When they shifted their support to another Independent candidate he continued to campaign, but he must have known that with or without the estate's support he stood little chance of winning. He garnered less than 4 percent of the vote, coming in a distant third in a field of five candidates. Alexander was not alone in his desire to be part of the process of forging the new nation; 236 candidates put their names forward for the twenty-four seats in the new House of Assembly. Among them were nine men of Chinese descent, three of whom were eventually elected—including Theophilus Lee who won the Essequibo Island constituency where R. V. Evan Wong had made his last stand in politics.

NOTES

1. Leo Despres, *Cultural Pluralism and Nationalist Politics in British Guiana* (Chicago: Rand McNally, 1967), 65; Brackette Williams, *Stains on My Name, War in My Veins: Guyana and the Politics of Cultural Struggle* (Durham, N.C.: Duke University Press, 1991), 161; Morton Fried, "Some Observations on the Chinese in British Guiana," *Social and Economic Studies* 5, 1 (March 1956): 59.

2. Laura Hall, "The Chinese in Guyana: The Making of a Creole Community." Ph.D. dissertation, University of California, Berkeley, 1995.

3. *Colonist* (Georgetown, British Guiana), January 29, May 5, June 12, 1866.

4. *Colonist*, June 28, 1866.

5. Official Gazette (Georgetown, Guyana), Vol. 18, August 31. 227.

6. Cecil Clementi, *The Chinese in British Guiana* (Georgetown, Demara: Argosy Co. 1915).

7. The franchise was limited by property qualifications that included ownership or tenancy of at least 6 acres of land or of a house or land valued at no less than $350 or annual income or salary of not less than $300. *Blue Book of British Guiana* (1936), Georgetown, The Argosy Company.

8. Details of the case of A. R. Crum Ewing versus R. V. Evan Wong are taken from the *Daily Argosy* (newspaper) and *Reports of Decisions in the Supreme Court of British Guiana in the West Indian Court of Appeal and in the Judicial Committee of the Privy Council on Appeal There from 1931-1937.* E. Mortimer Duke, ed. (Georgetown, Demerara: Argosy, 1940), 221-223, 241-252.

9. *Reports of Decisions in the Supreme Court of British Guiana in the West Indian Court of Appeal and in the Judicial Committee of the Privy Council on Appeal There from 1931-1937.* E. Mortimer Duke, ed. (Georgetown, Demerara: Argosy, 1940),241.

10. Ibid., 250

11. I have used the terms *Chinese, Indian,* and *African* to refer to Guyanese descendants of immigrants from China, India, and Africa or of slaves brought from Africa.

12. *Daily Argosy*, September 21, 1934.

13. *Royal Gazette*, March 5, 1874.

14. Trevor Sue-A-Quan, *The SAQ Tale: The Origin of the Surname Sue-A-Quan and Related Stories* (Unpublished manuscript, 1992), 105.

15. *Official Gazette*, January 25 and September 13, 1913. W. Sue-A-Quan is listed as eligible both to serve in the British Guiana Militia and to vote. Franchise qualifications in 1913 required the ownership of a certain amount of land or property or an annual income of at least 62 pounds 10 shillings.

16. *Daily Argosy*, June 19, 1934.

17. See *East Indians in the Caribbean: Colonialism and the Struggle for Identity*. Bridget Brereton and R. Dookaran, eds. (New York: Kraus International, 1982) and Peter Ruhoman, *A Centenary History of the East Indians in British Guiana, 1838–1938* (Georgetown, Demerara: East Indians 150th Anniversary Committee, 1988).

18. *Reports of Decisions in the Supreme Court of British Guiana in the West Indian Court of Appeal and in the Judicial Committee of the Privy Council on Appeal There from 1931–1937.* E. Mortimer Duke, ed. (Georgetown, Demerara: Argosy, 1940), 248.

19. *Daily Argosy*, October 17, 1934.

AUTHOR BIOGRAPHY

Laura Hall is a lecturer in American Studies at the University of California, Berkeley. She wrote her dissertation on the Chinese community in Guyana in the Ethnic Studies Department at Berkeley and has published an article on the works of Timothy Mo and Kazuo Ishiguro.

22

The Politics of "Cool": Indian American Youth Culture in New York City

Sunaina Maira

> Why Black is in style. This L.A. River is mine, I wrote
> my name on it in colors. Concrete embankments
> channel desert storms to wash teenage boys (fools)
> away. Kids never recognize limits, borders, bullshit;
>
> From a street corner, all the Chinese signs in Alhambra
> declare her love. Korean signs of Koreatown are just
> another word for feelings. Beautiful hair of Vietnamese
> noodles. Wonderful smile of oranges sold at East L.A.
> on-ramps. Big bottles of pigs' feet & giant kosher dills
> on the counter at every corner store. Every Monday morning,
> newspapers announce dozens who gave up
> loving this overpass world drenched in cooking oil.
> —Seshu Foster, from *City Terrace Field Manual* (1996)

The question that jump-starts Seshu Foster's trenchant prose-poem—"Why Black is in style"—is also the springboard from which I launch into a discussion of second-generation Indian Americans and "remix" popular culture. It is a question that is turned around in my essay, wondering not *why* black is in style, but rather, what it means for Indian American youth to emulate "black style" in music and fashion. What is the nature of the identification they are expressing with African American youth, if any? What does this imply for their own sense of racial identification, and what are some of the ways in which it is intertwined with class or gender politics? Foster's urban ode is a perfect prelude to this discussion, for he moves quickly from questioning black style to a flash of images and observations, noting the boundary crossings that underlie the appropriation of black popular culture. In dwelling on images of immigrant stores in Los Angeles—the site of the riots that drew public attention to the specter of tensions between Asian immigrants and African American residents—Foster seems to show how behind questions of style are daily realities and stories of trying to make it or just staying alive, in Asian American barrios.

Foster's lines are also a reminder that issues of style and appropriation can be superficial if not embedded in understandings of local contexts and complex class and racial politics. The second-generation Indian Americans I have interviewed and talked to in New York City have had particular encounters with African American youth depending on where they grew up, who their friends are, and a host of other factors. But even more important for this essay, their relationship with urban African American youth culture has a symbolic dimension, making it important to note the connections and contradictions in racialized images of being young and "cool" in New York. My purposes here are to explore, if only partially, the links between youth style and racial identification in the context of a particular second-generation group; to raise some key questions that emerge from these preliminary reflections; and to provoke a discussion of issues I hope will be extended and deepened in future work.

YOUTH SUBCULTURES: REMIX AND RESISTANCE

New York City is home to an increasingly visible Indian American youth subculture based in parties that resound to the beat of Indian remixes—Hindi film soundtracks or bhangra (a North Indian folk music and dance) mixed with techno, rap, reggae, and dance music by Indian American deejays. This subculture also involves constructing a culturally hybrid style—for example, wearing Indian-style nose rings and bindis with urban wear and showing ethnic identity through dance, such as borrowing folk dance gestures from bhangra while gyrating to club remixes. Moreover, bhangra remixes constitute a transnational popular culture in the Indian and South Asian diaspora that emerged among British-born South Asian youth in the mid-1980s and has subsequently flowed among local communities in New York, Delhi, Bombay, Toronto, and Port-of-Spain (Gopinath 1995a).

When I launched into my research on second-generation Indian Americans in New York City, based on interviews with college students studying in Manhattan, I realized that Indian parties were an important context in which these youth were creating and contesting a second-generation identity. I began talking to these students, some of whom are also party promoters or deejays, about the significance of this youth culture in their lives; this essay draws on those conversations and observations at clubs and parties in Manhattan.

This popular culture is significant because it provides a public space in which second-generation Indian Americans can socialize with one another, a space not created by their parents or by community institutions but by the youth themselves—with a little help from popular culture entrepreneurs (Sengupta 1996). Every weekend, there are several parties on college campuses and, more often, at clubs or restaurants rented by Indian party promoters and filled with droves of young South Asians. They move to the beat of the latest remix spun by an Indian American deejay and gather in cliques and couples, the women attired in slinky club wear—tight-fitting shirts and hip-hugger pants or miniskirts—and the men in hip hop-inspired urban street fashion—the signature Tommy Hilfiger shirts and baggy pants—or the requisite jackets and slacks. Many in the crowd are regulars on the party circuit, whereas others make occasional appearances.

Although this essay focuses on the expression of ethnic and racial identifications in relation to Indian American youth popular culture, this arena is but one of many settings in which identities are displayed; youth also move among the worlds of college, work, family, and other social events. It is illuminating, however, to consider issues of ethnic and racial identity in the context of a subculture that is shared by Indian American youth and that brings the paradoxes of identity into sharp relief.

These social events are attended almost exclusively by Indian and South Asian American youth; Somini Sengupta (1996: 1) notes that often "the only Black people are the security guards." This ethnically exclusive space reflects the nature of the social networks and college cliques among youth who participate in this "scene"; many said they came from campuses where those who are considered more "authentically" Indian or South Asian are those who fraternize only with other South Asians or only Indians. Yet as bhangra remix music gradually becomes more visible in the mainstream, the faces of those who attend such parties will possibly become more diverse. At one of the first "Bhangra Basement" nights at a world music club, now a regular event in Manhattan, a few white Americans and African Americans were getting down on the dance floor amid the sea of "desis" flailing their arms enthusiastically in bhangra or "filmi" style. This multiethnic setting, however, is probably one of the few such "desi parties" at which an African American man could sit on the corner of the stage and jam on his saxophone, adding yet another remixed layer to the already hybrid beat.[1]

The context of bhangra-remix youth culture in New York, or more generally in the United States, stands in contrast to that in Britain, where in the late 1970s and early 1980s a "new symbolic unity primarily between African-Caribbean and Asian people [referring to British South Asians]" occurred through identification with the category "black" (Sharma 1996: 39). This identification, Sanjay Sharma notes, was a political project involving "autonomous, anti-racist community struggles in Britain."(39) Hall also points out, however, that the coalitional label black, "had a certain way of silencing the very specific experiences of Asian people" (Hall 1991, cited in Sharma, 39). Bhangra remix emerged as a "new Asian dance music" that offered an Asian identity as a possible racial location but one that, in Sharma's view, "continues to be intimately tied to rethinking the possibilities of the Black anti-racist project" (34). Keeping this contrast in mind is instructive because it is a reminder that South Asian popular culture in the diaspora is not inherently allied with a particular political project but is differentially politicized depending on the historical, economic, and national contexts of particular immigrant communities.[2]

Before we explore the possible implications of this subculture for the relationship between Indian American youth and African Americans, it is important first to look at a reading of hip hop's many meanings. Tricia Rose (1994a, 1994b) suggests that hip hop, which encompasses graffiti, breakdancing, and rap music—is a youth subculture that attempts to address the specific structural conditions and life chances facing urban African American and Latino youth. She views the language, style, and attitude of hip hop as a popular critique of the condition of urban youth who face unemployment, racism, and marginalization in a postindustrial economy such as that of New York. "Hip hop," Rose writes, "emerged as a source for youth of alternative identity formation" (1994b: 34) and as a way to (re)claim their local, urban environment, fulfilling an important need in communities that have been devastated by the relocation of resources and depicted as icons of ruin (1994a: 77).

Hip hop offers an alternative means of attaining social status for youth who understand that they have limited opportunities for social mobility through traditional avenues. Rose suggests that the rituals of clothing and the creation of a distinctive hip hop style show an "explicit focus on consumption [that] plays on class distinctions and hierarchies by using commodities to claim the cultural terrain" (1994b: 36). She views hip hop as a hybrid cultural form that relies on Afro-Caribbean and African American musical, oral, visual, and dance practices. According to Rose, hip hop weaves a commentary on existing circumstances with references to ancestral cultures from the Afro-Caribbean diaspora, creating a presumably "counterdominant narrative" (1994a: 85).

Hip hop culture is now marketed as mass-produced objects by the music and fashion industries and has been adopted by youth, including young Indian Americans, with different ethnic and class backgrounds from those of its original creators. Yet the case of Indian Americans is interesting because certain themes from hip hop—such as the negotiation of contemporary and ancestral cultures—also resonate with these second-generation youth, but in a different way.

By sampling Indian music, second-generation youth draw on the sounds from Hindi movies and Indian music their parents introduced to them as children and that echo the country left behind by the immigrant generation. By remixing this music with rap and reggae and donning hip hop gear or brand-name clothes, Indian Americans display the markers of ethnicity and material status used in a multiethnic, capitalistic society. The ways in which ethnic or class identities are signaled, however, depend on the specific local community and its racial and class composition. Two Indian American women who had grown up in Florida remarked to me that the adoption of the hip hop style in New York was new to them, coming from areas where African Americans were less visible and debates over racial discrimination focused more on Cuban and Haitian populations. In contrast, youth who grew up in New York, New Jersey, and Connecticut and who had access to an Indian American social circle often said they began going to "Indian parties" while in high school. Yet within the tristate area, too, racial and class diversity varies greatly depending on the community and the family's economic resources and social networks.

The adoption of hip hop style and the construction of ethnic and racial identifications thus have varying meanings for Indian American college students. Moreover, Mary Waters (1994) argues that identifying for many second-generation youth with African American subcultures is associated with an "oppositional" stance toward mainstream white America. Does this gesture of defiance figure in young Indian Americans' identification with the hip hop subculture in New York?

WHAT SHADE IS BROWN [AND "COOL"]?

Dorinne Kondo, commenting on urban Asian Americans who identify with African Americans and borrow their dialect, observes that their appropriation of racialized style reflects "the persistence of the black-white binary in the dominant imagery and the in-the-middle position of Asian Americans and Latinos on that unidimensional hierarchy. If you are Asian American or Latino, especially on the East Coast, white and black are the poles, and if you don't identify with one, you identify with the other" (1995: 53). Gary Okihiro (1994) takes the positioning of Asian Americans within this racial binary one step further by addressing the political implications of the question "Is yellow black or white?" In the case of second-generation Indian Americans one can substitute "brown" for "yellow" or simply note that South Asians are variously classified on the basis of phenotypic features and that this question applies to all who do not fit into black or white slots. Okihiro (1994: 34) notes that Asian Americans are classified either as "near whites" when associated with model minority myths or as "just like blacks" when sharing a subordinate position to the "master class" with other nonwhite minorities.

This racial binary exerts a pull on some second-generation Indian Americans who feel they straddle the monochromatic racial boundaries of the United States. Many do not find resonant articulations of Indian American-ness until they arrive at college and find a sizable ethnic community and a specifically Indian American youth culture. Chandrika, a young Indian American woman, commented, "No matter what it is, if you haven't been accepted you're not going to be black, like all your friends, or white, like all your friends, it's not going to happen. You seek refuge." Second-generation Indian Americans who search for a category of belonging often find it provided by ethnicity, in part because of the context provided by the ethnic organizations and identity politics prevalent on U.S. college campuses. Chandrika thought this "ethnic revival" in college explained why some of her peers begin to flaunt Indian symbols of dress and jewelry and literally to perform their ethnic identity with bhangra moves on the dance floor, using these symbolical markers to assert their ethnic identity.

Some theorists who are wary of these ethnicizing moves view them as attempts by South Asians to escape racial classification in the United States by constructing, and emphasizing, an ethnic identity, particularly one that deflects identification with less privileged minority groups (George 1997; Mazumdar 1989; Visweswaran 1997). Although this may not always be an underlying motivation for second-generation Indian Americans, it is important to be mindful of the complex implications of ethnic assertions for race politics.

In the second generation, some "seek refuge" in a predominantly South Asian American community but still participate in a popular culture that draws on the music, fashion, and dialect associated with urban black and Latino youth. The question then arises: Why hip hop? It is not *just* because this is a style and expression familiar to those who grew up in racially mixed, urban areas; it is apparent that the appeal of hip hop is a more pervasive phenomenon and is a language increasingly adopted by middle-class-white-suburban youth (Giroux 1996). As Rose observes, "Black style through hip hop has contributed to the continued blackening of mainstream popular culture" (1994a: 82).

South Asian youth in the United States are influenced by hip hop style even if they do not grow up with other youth of color or in urban settings. Dharmesh, who is active in South Asian student politics on his campus, remarked that among his peers those who had grown up with blacks and Latinos, and even some who had not, often acquired "the style and the attitude and the walk" associated with those youth when they came to college. Identification with hip hop culture is also not a simple outcome of class background, as Sujata, who grew up in Connecticut, pointed out when describing Indian American "homeboys": "A lot of them are, like, total prep school, but they put on a, like, it's this preppie boy-urban look, you know, it's like Upper East Side-homeboy, you know. Huge pants and then, like, a nice button-down shirt, you know." Thus the adoption and adaptation of a style initially associated with economically marginalized youth now cross boundaries of class. Vivek, who went to a private high school in Manhattan, recalled:

> My friends were mostly, I'd say, Jewish kids and Asian kids who were into sort of like a hip hop sort of scene . . . wannabe hoods, basically, and if you want to be hoods, you know, quoting Sophocles that we'd learned in class. Which is funny because, I mean, it was mostly . . . kids from the prep schools around the area . . . and they also did the same thing.

Vivek also observed that hip hop clothing can be extremely expensive and can convey social status within this subculture; men may use name brand jackets and shoes to make others—especially women—aware of their buying power, a sign of their appeal in the dating market. This also signifies that they are "in the know," or have their finger on the pulse of current trends, and that they possess what Sarah Thornton (1997) calls "subcultural capital." Furthermore, Sheela, an Indian American woman, noted that for many second-generation men hip hop style connotes a certain image of racialized masculinity that is the ultimate definition of "cool": "South Asian guys give more respect to African Americans than to whites because they think the style is cool. The guys look up to them because it's down [fashionable]. They think, 'I'm kinda scared of them but I want to look like them because they're cool.'" Black style is thus viewed as the embodiment of a particular machismo, of the object of racialized desire, and, simultaneously, of racialized fear.

Yet in this subculture many note that a "hoody" image is not considered as appealing for women as it is for men; the image considered desirable for women at these clubs is based on a sleeker, more feminized style. This double standard does not play out only in matters of style but is embedded in deeper contradictions in the definitions of Indian American gender and sexual roles that are enacted in this space. Furthermore, these gendered and sexualized norms are contested by those who find those ideas constricting, with the most vocal critics often young women. Manisha, whose friends are mainly African American and Latino and who often dresses in hip hop gear (with a gold Om pendant around her neck) reflected, "I think the guys are intimidated by that [girls with a hip hop look]; it's taken as a sign of being closer to Latinos or blacks, of being outside of the Indian circle, as I am . . . The guys may think we're rougher or not as sweet."

This "sweet," more conventionally feminine look, with "long, straight hair," is also rife with contradictions because there is an ambivalence about the appeal of "innocent" femininity in these enactments of desire. Provocative clothing styles for women are often popular at Indian parties, yet these

The Pleasures of the Dance Floor of a Bhangra Remix Party. Photograph courtesy of Srinivas Kuruganti.

same women are considered "loose"—that is, not the type of woman an Indian American man would like to marry (see Maira forthcoming).

Furthermore, dating relationships between Indian Americans and African Americans often become the object of intense scrutiny by other Indian Americans, particularly because ethnic authenticity is embodied by the ideal of exclusively dating and eventually marrying other Indian Americans that prevails in this youth subculture and is upheld even more strongly by immigrant parents. Women repeatedly remarked to me, in almost identical words: "The worst thing that can happen to an Indian-South Asian father is for his daughter to go out with a black man." The same might be said of Indian American men who choose to date African American women; although such pairings were described as less prevalent or simply less commented on by the Indian American youth I interviewed.

It is not possible to generalize about interracial dating trends based on anecdotal reports; it is more important to note that the reason for this preoccupation with women in interracial relationships could be in part that the specter of women dating non-Indian—particularly black—men is viewed as more

Ethnic Yearnings and Other Desires. Photograph courtesy of Srinivas Kuruganti.

threatening to the "purity" of transplanted Indian culture and hence provokes greater censure. The ways in which the paradoxes of gender and sexuality disrupt a simple interpretation of subculture and style is a complex issue I cannot examine adequately here (see Maira forthcoming). It is important to note, however, that racial identification and images of gender and sexuality are always threaded through each other and wrapped in layers of dissonance that complicate understandings of this subculture.

Acknowledging these contradictions of gender and sexuality, what does it mean when Indian American men and women adapt symbols created by black youth in crafting their own popular culture? Whereas hip hop culture is now commodified and crosses class and racial boundaries, the implications of its adoption are still very much contingent on economic and political particularities, on differentials of privilege and mobility. Sunita, a second-generation woman, finds this identification through style, if unaccompanied by a shared racial or class politics, "superficial." She commented that in her view, many youth immersed in this popular culture "at the back of their minds are thinking, this is not long-term." Sunita reflected that the appropriation of what is perceived by the mainstream to be an oppositional style is mediated by the often unstated but always present location of class status. She remarked, "I know for me there's this cushion, my parents are supporting me, they're pay-

ing for my college . . . you know [the identification] is only up to a certain
point, there are big, distinct differences."

Chandrika, too, thinks that the ways in which the experiences of Indian
Americans diverge from those of African Americans and Latinos are important to note when considering the appropriation of popular culture, particularly the differences in political engagement as a result of different historical
and economic realities. Indian Americans who participate in this subculture
on her campus, she observes, do not unite with African American and Latino
students in the coalition of students of color that has been battling the university administration for adequate representation in the curriculum. In contrast, the South Asian student organization is less politicized, in her opinion,
and is more interested in organizing events largely to promote "cultural
awareness."

SURFACES OF REBELLION

Although there are contesting forces within this subculture the contradictions of mimesis and resistance clearly operate at more than one level. Indian
American youth are influenced by the rhetoric of authenticity, but in some
ways they are also engaged with the racialized identities and racism of the
immigrant generation and of U.S. society. Sunita, who has been going to "Indian parties" since she was in high school, commented that for her Indian
American peers, "identifying with hip hop is a little more rebellious" than
adopting other youth styles "because it's not the norm associated with white
culture." She pointed out that the use of style often becomes an act of defiance against parents, referring to the wave of Indian immigrants who came
to the United States in the mid-1960s and the 1970s and who were highly
educated professionals and graduate students. Sunita's comments echo the
views of researchers who argue that, for the most part, this immigrant cohort
identified with the ideology of "white middle-class America" (Helweg and
Helweg 1990; Hossain 1982). The more recent wave of South Asian immigrants that has been arriving since the 1980s, in part as a result of sponsorship
by relatives who had emigrated earlier, has generally been less economically
privileged and educationally qualified than the earlier cohort and has been
more concentrated, at least initially, in multiethnic urban neighborhoods
(Khandelwal 1995; Lessinger 1995).

Across class segments, however, identification with African Americans is
often fraught with tensions between second-generation youth and immigrant
parents. Amritjit Singh (1996: 98) is hopeful that some second-generation
South Asian Americans who turn to hip hop do so because they are resisting
the antiblack prejudices of their parents. He writes of those youth who protest the racism of the immigrant generation:

Unlike their parents, they have African American friends and have developed a better understanding of how racism and poverty operate in American society. Although their responses may not fit a sophisticated intellectual view of race and ethnicity, these young Asians appear to know at some level that the alienation they feel at work or school is experienced even more intensely by their black peers. They are also often in tune with rap and reggae; maybe the deep sense of "alienation" expressed in contemporary black music resonates with their own sense of rebellion against their parents' double standards: an insistence on seeing African Americans harshly through the prism of caste even as they cloak themselves in the highest ideals of fairness and equal opportunity. (Singh, 98)

Singh's explanation suggests a certain political and racial awareness among at least a subgroup of second-generation Indian Americans, but there is still a need to distinguish between an "alienation" felt by youth who are politically and economically disenfranchised and an alienation from parents arising out of a generational difference. Adolescent rebellion against parents and what they stand for is a common trope that has long been emphasized by coming-of-age narratives in the United States even as this has varied by gender, ethnic, and class location. It is possible, however, that for some Indian American youth there is a convergence between both kinds of responses, and a style that subverts parents' racial prejudices may *also* be an expression of their resistance to the racialized caste stratification of U.S. society. But at the level of Indian American popular culture, does identification with hip hop express a rebellion only along the surfaces of style, or is it perhaps only understood as such?

HIPSTERS AND FORGOTTEN HISTORIES

The notion of rebellion through symbols of urban black youth culture can be examined to reveal several deeper currents below its surface. One is a consideration of the ways in which this subculture is implicated in a wider discourse of what it means to be authentically South Asian by creating a space where youth can socialize and date within their ethnic group, but it also complicates this ideal by adopting an essentialized definition of what it means to be "cool" (i.e., the antithesis of unfashionable or traditional) which is linked to being black (Banerjea and Banerjea, 1996). The appropriation of black style as a guarantor of fashionability has a long tradition in white America that is critiqued by Gary Indiana:

In its most exacerbated form, this sentimental tic of the white hipster locates all "authenticity" in the black experience, against which all other experience becomes the material of grotesque irony. To be really, really cool becomes the spiritual equivalent of blackness, and even superior to it (Gary Indiana, "Racism and the Aesthetic of Hyper-Real" 1996: 81).

Rose comments that "like generations of white teenagers before them" who identified with jazz, rock 'n' roll, and R&B, "white teenage fans are listening in on black culture, fascinated by its differences, drawn in by mainstream social constructions of black culture as a forbidden narrative, a symbol of rebellion" (1994b: 5). As there has been a model of "correct white hipness" based on the "latest black style and image," a similarly constructed model of "correct brown hipness" seems to be emerging for certain second-generation Indian Americans.

At the heart of the debate over the appropriation of black popular culture is the question raised by Sengupta (1997): "Is it right or wrong for Indian Americans to consume culture in this way?" Or to push this moral dimension further, *Is* there a right or wrong in consuming "the cool"? The globalization of mass media in the era of late capitalism has resulted in the seeping of black-identified American popular culture and fashion into remote corners of the world. Indian youth living in rural areas can listen to American rap or Indian remixes from the United States as a result of media channels and family networks that span national borders. Hip hop has always been a hybrid form based on the sampling of sounds and words, and popular culture, by definition, belongs to all.

Sengupta notes, however, that an ethical dimension emerges in issues of legal property and the economics of production, where the question becomes one not of the right to listen but of the power to buy and to be compensated for creating music. She points out that many of the Indian remixes are bootleg albums that do not respect copyright laws: "The kid in the South Bronx [where hip hop was born] is not getting paid when his music is sampled by an Indian deejay. Maybe Tommy Hilfiger is benefiting [from the popularization of his fashion design]." As bhangra and Indian film remixes move into the mainstream and Indian deejays consider signing on to major record labels, as Bally Sagoo recently did, there might be greater pressure to legalize this appropriation; however, this does not necessarily translate into equitable acknowledgment or economic payback for hip hop artists, given the white-dominated ownership of the record industry (Feld 1988). The economics of appropriation are touched upon here only as the tip of a very deep iceberg, and they lead into the equally murky waters of another contextual perspective that is implicated in considering the politics of "cool."

This second layer is the grounding of particular consumptions in specific local, historical, and political particularities and in narratives that project particular genealogies of racialization. South Asian immigrants have complex and often contradictory histories of racial categorization in the United States that are often unknown to Indian American youth. I cannot explore these histories here, but it is worth remembering that the earliest Indian migrants who came to the United States in the late eighteenth century were sometimes sold as slaves and were likely to have married black women (Jensen 1988: 13). Later, Punjabi migrants in California who did not have access to Indian women married Mexicanas and Puerto Riqueñas (Leonard 1992). In Okihiro's terms, these are forgotten instances of Indian Americans who were positioned as "near-black."

At the same time, Visweswaran (1997) cautions against a romanticized reading of historical alliances between South Asian immigrants and African Americans and Latinos/Latinas, pointing out the ways in which some Indian Americans actively negotiated U.S. racial formations to improve their own situation by positioning themselves as "near-white." For example, in 1923 Bhagat Singh Thind appealed to the U.S. Supreme Court to prove that he was eligible for citizenship—which was granted only to "free white people" at the time, arguing that Indians were technically Caucasian. His plea was rejected because it was resolved that Indians were not white in the understanding of the common man.[3]

For Indian immigrants this racialized entry into the United States defined in relationship to African Americans is complicated further because according to Sucheta Mazumdar (1989: 49) the racial origin myth of the Aryan invasion of the subcontinent and the color-coded Hindu caste hierarchycontinue to influence Indian immigrants in the United States. The legacy of the racialization of Indians and Indian Americans necessarily forms the backdrop for the identification of second-generation Indian Americans with black popular culture. Those who participate in this youth culture are not unaware of the contradictions of appropriating black style.

DJ Baby Face, who has been spinning at parties and clubs for over ten years and has been a part of "the scene" since its inception, clearly articulated the paradox of racialized "cool." At an Indian party held in the cavernous tunnels of a Manhattan club, with the beat of Indian remix pounding against the walls, DJ Baby Face said, "Blacks are the scapegoat for Indians, but when it comes to fashion and style we hold them high; they have power." His succinct observation reveals the underlying politics of being "cool"—the group emulated in style is also the one on whose back immigrants tread to preserve their sense of superior status (see Morrison 1994). Among the Indian American youth I spoke with others were also critical of antiblack prejudices in various ways. The contradictions embedded in a "politics of cool" are challenged in a personal context by Indian American women who have been in relationships with African American men and who spoke of facing racist censure from their parents and the larger Indian American community.

It becomes doubly ironic to consider DJ Baby Face's observation in light of Indian American and Asian American immigrant history. Immigrants have been scapegoats for the U.S. economic woes and cultural malaise, but have they created scapegoats of their own? Remembering Sunita's remarks, if a remix culture drawing on hip hop symbolizes rebellion, does that mean that black youth culture is simply a site for fantasies of leaving a secure place, but only temporarily? Jeffrey Melnick (1996: 227) observes that the crossing of racial boundaries through music tends to wane as adolescents move into adulthood and is "temporally bounded by the fact that . . . teenagers have to grow up into a labor economy deeply invested in racial division." What will happen when Indian American youth move into the workplace and establish their own families, as is already happening across the country? What kinds of alliances will they build with other minority groups, and who will be their nemesis? This symbolic identification and appropriation by youth culture is worth noting when considering these questions, and it is also important to keep in mind the class backgrounds and educational trajectories of different segments of the second generation.

CONCLUSION

Just as one has to be critical of the implications of the appropriation of black popular culture and its impact on racial identification, one also must be mindful of the fetishization of popular cultures in academic work, especially of subcultures with hybrid appeal (Sharma, Hutnyk, and Sharma 1996). It can be argued that some cultural studies theorists have been guilty of overpoliticizing representations of youth cultures and of projecting onto them their own myths of resistance (Frith 1992). I also do not want to veer too far in the other direction, however, and underestimate the arenas in which this popular culture does have subversive potential, such as in queer South Asian subcultures where bhangra has become a signifier for the queer South Asian diaspora (Gopinath 1995b).

But it is not enough to look at style and music alone. One must look through the surfaces of rebellions for refractions of the dynamics of class mobility, racial identification, and immigration history. It is time to move toward a more complex, politically contextualized vision of these emerging subcultures. So party on, but leave the doors open.

NOTES

I would like to thank all of the students and deejays I talked to for sharing their insights and time with me and Somini Sengupta for helping me to develop some of the ideas presented here.
   1. Since I completed the research for this project, the Mutiny night hosted by DJ Siraiki, who spins innovative mixes that go beyond bhangra and Hindi film music and

draw on (South) Asian British music, has become popular among slightly older South Asian Americans and attracts a racially diverse following.

2. Although it may be obvious to many, I note the social constructedness of the racial categorizations discussed in this essay: Race represents a system of classification that is not a natural or biological given but is peculiar to specific societies and historical periods and, as this essay illustrates, is inflected by other axes of social difference such as gender, sexuality, ethnicity, and class.

3. Visweswaran (1997) also highlights that Indian-Mexican American marriages in California were born of necessity rather than choice, for antimiscegenation laws ruled against intermarriage with whites, and few Indian women were allowed to emigrate under the restrictive laws at the time. She argues that South Asian immigrant communities—or at least particular segments at particular historical moments—have long engaged in a "politics of alignment" to position themselves favorably in the U.S. ethnic and racial hierarchy and better their situation (1997: 23). At the same time, these negotiations occur in the context of long histories of racist state policies and racial violence that have targeted Indian Americans for being "nonwhite."

REFERENCES

Banerjea, Koushik, and Partha Banerjea. "Psyche and Soul: A View from the 'South.'" In *Dis-Orienting Rhythms: The Politics of the New Asian Dance Music*, ed. Sanjay Sharma, John Huntyk, and Ashwani Sharma. London: Zed, 1996, 105–124.

Feld, Steven. "Notes on World Beat." *Public Culture Bulletin* 1, 1 (Fall 1988): 31–37.

Foster, Seshu. *City Terrace Field Manual*. New York: Kaya, 1996.

Frith, Simon. "The Cultural Study of Popular Music." In *Cultural Studies*, ed. Lawrence Grossberg, Cary Nelson, and Paula Treichler. New York: Routledge, 1992, 174–196.

George, Rosemary Marangoly. "'From Expatriate Aristocrat to Immigrant Nobody': South Asian Racial Strategies in the Southern Californian Context." *Diaspora* 6, 1 (Spring 1997): 31–60.

Giroux, Henry A. "White Panic and the Racial Coding of Violence." In *Fugitive Cultures: Race, Violence, and Youth*, ed. Henry Giroux. New York: Routledge, 1996, 27–54.

Gopinath, Gayatri. "'Bombay, U.K., Yuba City': Bhangra Music and the Engendering of Diaspora." *Diaspora* 4, 3 (1995a): 303–321.

———. "Notes on a Queer South Asian Planet: Gayatri Gopinath on Queer Transnational Cultures." *Rungh: A South Asian Quarterly of Culture, Comment & Criticism* 3, 3 (1995b): 9–10.

Hall, Stuart. "Old and New Identities, Old and New Ethnicities." In *Culture, Globalization, and the World System*, ed. A. D. King. London: MacMillan, 1991.

Helweg, Arthur, and Usha Helweg. *An Immigrant Success Story: East Indians in America*. Philadelphia: University of Pennsylvania Press, 1990.

Hossain, Mokerrom. "South Asians in Southern California: A Sociological Study of Immigrants from India, Pakistan, and Bangladesh." *South Asia Bulletin* 2, 1 (1982): 74–83.

Indiana, Gary. "Racism and the Aesthetic of Hyper-Real: Pulp Fiction and Other Visual Tragedies." In *Fugitive Cultures: Race, Violence, and Youth,* ed. Henry Giroux. New York: Routledge, 1996, 55–88.

Jensen, Joan M. *Passage from India: Asian Indian Immigrants in North America.* New Haven: Yale University Press, 1988.

Khandelwal, Madhulika S. "Indian Immigrants in Queens, New York City: Patterns of Spatial Concentration and Distribution, 1965–1990." In *Nation and Migration: The Politics of Space in the South Asian Diaspora,* ed. Peter van der Veer. Philadelphia: University of Pennsylvania Press, 1995, 178–196.

Kondo, Dorinne. "Bad Girls: Theater, Women of Color, and the Politics of Representation." In *Women Writing Culture,* ed. Ruth Behar and Deborah A. Gordon. Berkeley: University of California Press, 1995, 49–64.

Leonard, Karen Isaksen. *Making Ethnic Choices: California's Punjabi Mexican Americans.* Philadelphia: Temple University Press, 1992.

Lessinger, Johanna. *From the Ganges to the Hudson: Indian Immigrants in New York City.* Boston: Allyn and Bacon, 1995.

Maira, Sunaina. "Identity Dub: The Paradoxes of an Indian American Youth Subculture (New York Mix)." *Cultural Anthropology* 14, 1 (1999): 1–32.

Mazumdar, Sucheta. "Racist Responses to Racism: The Aryan Myth and South Asians in the United States." *South Asia Bulletin,* 9, 1 (1989): 47–55.

Melnick, Jeffrey. "R'nB Skeletons in the Closet: The Men of Doo Wop." *Minnesota Review* 47 (1996): 217–229.

Morrison, Toni. "On the Backs of Blacks." In *Arguing Immigration,* ed. Nicolaus Mills. New York: Touchstone, 1994, 97–100.

Okihiro, Gary. "Is Yellow Black or White?" In *Margins and Mainstreams: Asians in American History and Culture,* ed. Gary Y. Okihiro. Seattle: University of Washington Press, 1994, 31–63.

Rose, Tricia. "A Style Nobody Can Deal With: Politics, Style and the Postindustrial City in Hip Hop." In *Microphone Fiends: Youth Music and Youth Culture,* ed. Andrew Ross and Tricia Rose. New York: Routledge, 1994a, 71–88.

———. *Black Noise: Rap Music and Black Culture in Contemporary America.* Hanover, N.H.: Wesleyan and University Press of New England, 1994b.

Sengupta, Somini. "To Be Young, Indian and Hip: Hip hop Meets Hindi Pop as a New Generation of South Asians Finds Its Own Groove." *New York Times,* The City, Section 13 (June 30, 1996): 1.

———. Personal communication, 1997.

Sharma, Sanjay. "Noisy Asians or 'Asian Noise'?" In *Dis-Orienting Rhythms: The Politics of the New Asian Dance Music,* ed. Sanjay Sharma, John Hutnyk, and Ashwani Sharma. London: Zed, 1996, 32–57.

Sharma, Sanjay, John Huntyk, and Ashwani Sharma. "Introduction." In *Dis-Orienting Rhythms: The Politics of the New Asian Dance Music,* ed. Sanjay Sharma, John Huntyk, and Ashwani Sharma. London: Zed, 1996, 1–11.

Singh, Amritjit. "African Americans and the New Immigrants." In *Between the Lines: South Asians and Postcoloniality,* ed. Deepika Bahri and Mary Vasudeva. Philadelphia: Temple University Press, 1996, 93–110.

Thornton, Sarah. "The Social Logic of Subcultural Capital." In *The Subcultures Reader,* ed. Ken Gelder and Sarah Thornton. London: Routledge, 1997, 200–209.

Visweswaran, Kamala. "Diaspora by Design: Flexible Citizenship and South Asians in U.S. Racial Formations." *Diaspora* 6, no. 1 (Spring 1997): 5–29.

Waters, M. "Ethnic and Racial Identities of Second-Generation Black Immigrants in New York City." *International Migration Review* 28(4):795–820.

AUTHOR BIOGRAPHY

Sunaina Maira did her dissertation at the Harvard Graduate School of Education on second-generation Indian Americans in New York City. She is coeditor of Contours of the Heart: South Asians Map North America *(Asian American Writers' Workshop), which received the American Book Award from the Before Columbus Foundation in 1997. Her fiction has appeared in the* Asian Pacific American Journal, Journal of Asian American Renaissance, *and* India Currents. *Sunaina is one of the organizers of Youth Solidarity Summer, a progressive summer program for South Asian youth in the United States. She fantasizes about being a deejay in her spare time.*

23

The Story of Double R

Janet Shirley

The first time I met Double R was in March 1995. A town hall meeting had been planned with Mayor Frank Jordan. The principal goal of the meeting, which had been organized by neighborhood groups, was to demand more youth services for the neighborhood. At that time 11,000 youth were living in the Excelsior District of San Francisco, and only fifty after-school recreation slots were available through the Department of Parks and Recreation.

That evening a number of youth representatives were invited to give public testimony regarding the dismal lack of resources for youth in our community. A number of these young speakers came from various youth organizations that serve the Excelsior. Among them, Double R appeared to represent United Playaz.

When I first met Double R I was immediately taken with his demeanor and bravado. Fully outfitted in gang fatigues, baggy pants, and gold chains, Double R seemed to strut up to the microphone with an unwavering air of confidence. His dark, sleek hair was neatly tucked under a blue bandanna. Double R is Filipino yet what I saw and heard that night seemed to be much more African American than Filipino. I registered confusion looking at this young man and watching his mannerisms. Two years later, when I began to interview Double R for this oral history, I discovered why.

As Double R spoke that evening, one could hear the applause and shouting from his supporters. He was obviously well loved among his fans at Balboa High School. As he spoke to the mayor there was no fear, no faltering, only pure strength. Double R's forceful manner left an impression that would remain in my memory for two years, until the next time we met.

When I began looking for a subject for a collection of oral histories, I didn't think of Double R right away. I wanted to interview an Asian gang member, but because of Double R's African American mannerisms I had forgotten that he was Asian. Through a friend, I was able to reconnect with

Photograph courtesy of United Playaz

Double R, and he agreed to share his biography with me. Fortunately, because of my previous work with youth in San Francisco and my familiarity with the staff at the Bernal Heights Neighborhood Center, I was able to establish immediate credibility with Double R. I discovered that this credibility was vital in establishing trust with my subjects. In Double R's case, it was the key for allowing me "in the door" to begin our dialogue.

*   *   *

My name is Double R. I'm an ex-gang banger, born and raised in San Francisco.

I've been in every type of lock [jail] you can think of. I've been on both sides of the gun. I took a hot one [bullet] and I've been stuck twice, all due to gang banging. I was a major drug dealer, and also I ended up becoming my best customer. This is my story.

I come from a big Filipino family with a strong foundation: my mother and father. We used to all look out for each other. My father was a sergeant in the army back then. He married my mother in the islands and brought her over here. You see, in the Philippines they think America is the land of opportunity. They believe that the streets are paved with gold and money falls from the sky. And things weren't too good there for my dad. I mean, they were poor. So my dad came over to make a better life for our family.

My father was a true soldier. He taught us kids to be soldiers: to be a man,

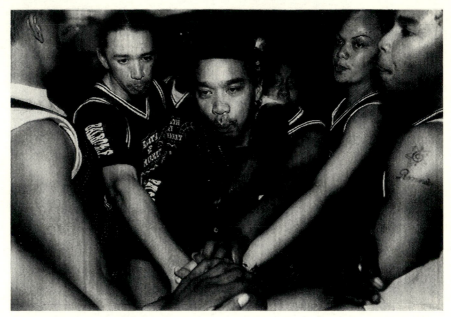

Former Gang Member, United Playaz founder, and basketball coach Double R at the heart of a game huddle. Photograph by Michael Macor. Reprinted courtesy of the San Francisco Chronicle.

to not give up, to be *down* for what you believed in. He trained us to be tough. He used to say "men don't cry, babies cry." He gave us tough love. That benefited me later when I had to be tough on the street. You need that. You need to be a soldier on the streets—that's what counts.

Anyway, my parents were very traditional, old-school Filipino. They taught me values and what was right from wrong. Every Filipino who came over to the house that was a friend of my parents I had to call "uncle" or "auntie." And there were a lot of them. I remember that when I was school age my parents tried to teach me Filipino history, but I didn't want to hear it. They would try to speak Tagalog to me, but to me it sounded weird. No one else I knew spoke it outside, so I was embarrassed. I didn't learn it and I didn't want to.

There was a curious side of me that was attracted to the outside world. I'm sure we were discriminated against back then, but I don't remember. I heard that Filipinos couldn't go to Golden Gate Park, for example. They couldn't do certain things. But my folks never talked to me about discrimination. They taught me how to believe in equal opportunity. Regardless of the skin color, it didn't matter; just be an individual.

By the time I was eight, the only time I hung with my family was when I was home. But outside of the house my brothers and I hung out with other people, our friends. There was a lot of peer pressure to be accepted. In my neighborhood, South of Market, there were a lot of blacks and there was one Latino family that I remembered. I hung out with them because they were my friends. In fact, my two best friends were black and Latino. There were Filipinos in the neighborhood, but I didn't hang with them. My older brothers, whom I respected, would hang with anybody, but they related better with blacks. I could relate better to the blacks because a lot of Filipinos spoke Tagalog or Filipino and I couldn't relate to it. I guess we were Americanized and couldn't relate. As far as ethnic groups, it didn't matter who I hung with, I didn't really trip on that.

I was very fascinated by the fast money on the streets from when I was ten years old. I was fascinated by nice cars, money, the clothes, the gold. One of my older brothers was involved with a gang at that time. I really looked up to him. He was involved in that fast life, and I liked it. He was a role model. He got so much respect. And plus, at that time there were certain movies that came out about gangs. I thought those movies were cool, so I wanted to get involved myself.

What happened is that me and a lot of guys my age in the neighborhood consolidated together to make a gang. We wanted to have power and run our territory. We wanted to be recognized and have a reputation. In fact, we'd go 'round and fight with gangs in the Mission just to get a reputation. When we first started we were just wannabees—not true *gangstas*. But later on we needed a gang to watch each other's back and to make money. That's what we wanted: to have power and make money. It's like any organized crime. You gotta have your crew: your lieutenants, your sergeants, your soldiers. You needed people to be *down* for you. So we got together and made it official. We decided then to stake out our turf.

In order to get in our gang you had to get *jumped in* or commit a felony or rob a store or do something foul. It didn't matter what color you were, what ethnic group that you came from. To join our gang you just had to be *down*. To be *down* means you have to do something that was dangerous, something you wouldn't back down on, something you'd put your life on the line for. You'd die for your gang to be *down*. To be ready to die, you gotta be *down*. To be *down* means to sacrifice, to be willing to die for your homies, for your gang and your turf. Period. In our gang there was no discrimination as long as you were willing to be *down*. I felt real close to my homies. I felt very respected around them and very powerful, very strong. The more we had in the gang, the more power we had. There were about sixty in our gang. Our turf was South of Market, but we also had guys from the Tenderloin with us.

You see, back then there were no colors. There were no Crips or Bloods—it was just people's neighborhoods. I remember one time we had a rumble in the Mission District. We went down there and there was another gang. They were all Latinos. They asked us, "Where you all from?" One thing led to another, and we ended up in a parking lot having a big rumble. There were sticks and chains and of course we were victorious because the others ended up running after we were fighting for a couple of minutes. This rumble was over turf because we were outsiders. The same thing happened with us; when anyone came through our neighborhood who we didn't recognize, who we didn't know—they'd get dealt with. It's all about having a reputation and getting respect and being feared. They need to know that nobody messes with us.

Gangs are about having the respect, about who's the baddest. When I was about seventeen or eighteen that's when crack cocaine came out. And there weren't too many opportunities out there for jobs or making money. That's when I was introduced to a big dope dealer, a *baller*, who had the nice and fancy things that I wanted. He taught me how to sell cocaine by giving me a little to take down the block to someone. I made $50 just taking it down the street. For me it was fast, efficient, and effective. So I started observing how to do it on my own.

I began to learn how to handle my own business. That's when I got with four of my main partners who would stand and sell dope on the corner—get our *grind* on. My partners were in my gang—this was still gang activity. But now it wasn't about turf—it was about making money and lots of it. Most of my partners were black, with a couple of Filipinos. I trusted them a lot. I knew they would be *down* for me. The only thing I didn't trust them with was the money because that's business. You can't mix business with friendship. I remember one time when one of my homies got shot in the process of selling dope. Revenge was on my mind. So we had to put in work—*doing dirt*, going back and settling the score. This homie was a black friend of mine, and he got shot by other blacks. But the revenge, the war was about money. Because we wanted to keep what we got.

During this time all I did was stay in my 'hood and make money. I could have traveled all over the world, but I stayed in my turf. I was addicted to the *grind*. I wasn't tripping off society, I felt I was society. I felt like I was the shit in the champagne glass. Other people weren't even in my consciousness. As far as white folk went, I really didn't care. I only ever saw white people when they came down to buy dope. I was only interested in making my money and having nice things and being down with my homies—hanging with them, partying with them, and just having fun. At the time I didn't realize I was being used. I didn't think about how the drugs got there, how the guns got there. I was just worried about making my *scratch* [money] and having more money than the next pusher. I was interested in the power. You got the money, you got the power. You got the power, you got everything.

Once we had the money, we had women and the power. People I didn't even know wanted to be my partner. We had a lot of women hanging on our drawers, even though I only had one woman. She was black and Puerto

Rican. Actually, I've never had a Filipina girlfriend. Not that I didn't try to. I did. But when I'd try to meet them it was hard 'cause I'd be talking my street talk and they'd think I was aggressive. Back then, Filipina women were quiet and submissive—that's the stereotype they had. They wouldn't hang out and party. And back in the eighties Filipinas weren't going out with blacks. And the way I talk, they just couldn't relate.

See, my background is primarily African American, even though in my life I've dated all kinds of girls: blacks, Latinas, whites. We got a lot of cross culture in our family. That's 'cause my brothers have dated a lot of black women. But I like all flavors. In some ways women is all the same—it's their backgrounds that make the difference. Most women I got together with were from the projects, from the 'hood. I relate to them best.

My girlfriend was fine—long hair, brown skin. She was everything I wanted in a woman. I loved her so much I would have fought a pack of wolves just to save her life. When we first met she was fourteen and I was sixteen. We were like each other's shadows. I got her into the drug gang. She'd do transactions for me. She'd hold my dope, my guns, and my money. We used to ride together, like Bonnie and Clyde. But she got tired of me because I kept going to jail and she couldn't hang. Looking back, I feel bad introducing her to the gang. She was a very beautiful woman inside and out.

In those times I could make $5,000 in a day or two, just over the weekend. Making that money got me the respect that I wanted. I had the power. In doing all this we had shootings, drive bys, beatings, people wouldn't pay up. But we had to handle our business. It was a serious business. By then I was eighteen, with nice cars, with *fresh-dipped gear*, with money bulging in my pockets like they had mumps in them. I wasn't only a gangster, I was a cold-stone hustler. That's until I got busted.

My father passed away in the mid-eighties—that's when I got heavy into crack cocaine. My dad was a soldier, he was a true soldier. He was a superhero to me. I kindof, like, feared my dad, 'cause he was too straight up. Me and my father never really communicated. I couldn't talk to him. We never really had a strong relationship. Like, we never told each other that we loved each other. But I knew he loved me through his actions—both him and my mom.

Anyway, when my father passed away I was so thick into the gang. And my interest in the dope gang was making cold cash, you know. By all means I did. After my father passed away, I never really talked to anybody about it. I turned to my own product. When I turned to my own product I became my best customer. So basically everything that I achieved in the gang—cars, jewelry, clothes, apartments, the fine things in life—got took because of the product. I could remember the times when people I grew up with, my best partners, I sold dope to and got them high. I didn't really care about them. I didn't even think about it. I was killing my own community, but I didn't realize it. I didn't realize how much addiction or self-destruction I was putting out until I was my own best customer.

During the times that I was involved heavily into crack, into alcohol, and marijuana I got popped for assault. I was already on probation. I was sent to North County Facility in the East Bay. While I was there I noticed the groups had their own clicks—the African Americans with African Americans, the Latinos with Latinos, the whites with the whites. There were very few Asians. If you were Asian you were up there for a serious crime because there weren't too many Asians in there for selling crack cocaine. They were usually in there for murder and strong-arm robbery. I was from San Francisco, and they locked me up in the East Bay. When you get locked up in San Bruno [jail], you usually know someone. But not here.

Anyway my bunkie was this black dude named Tom. He was from Frisco too. Me and him kicked it off real tight because we were both from Frisco. But there was animosity and player hating. Just from being from Frisco got me into fights and confrontation. But I didn't back up like no sea crab, and when I went *down* I got my respect—not from where I was from but where I was at and where I was going. Being in jail you gotta be *down* for what you believe in. You can't show no fear. You are in a eight-by-ten concrete jungle. If you showed fear you'd get beat down to the very last compound. In there people with power are the toughest group of all. The people in the institution who have the power run the place. I don't want to be explicit about this. There are inmates who would get mad if I exposed their business. The best way to handle your business is not to let people know what's happening.

I got out and went back in. The next time I went to county jail. I was familiar with a lot of my homies there. When you are in county jail you are segregated to a certain extent. There's deeper rules and consequences with the state. The difference with jail and the outside is that you can run when you are outside. In jail you can't run, you can't go home. You just go back to your ten-by-eight and marinate. Yeah, that's what happens—you marinate, like a piece of meat.

When I got out of jail I talked with this guy who had known me since childhood. His name was Dennis Ubungen. He's a Filipino who used to live in the Fillmore District and would come everyday to South of Market to work with us kids. He started telling me about school, how they can pay for your tuition. He tried to be a mentor to me. At first I didn't take him serious. I just used it as a crutch. That was in '89. I was still doing dope undercover. Crack was still calling me. I was like Dr. Jekyll and Mr. Hyde. I was Dr. Jekyll at school and Mr. Jack-Your-Ass at night, with pistols at hand. People would be at the Versatels at night, and I'd ask them to break bread, and they'd see me with my hand in my jacket. One time I did that a guy pulled a gun on me and my gun was jammed. I had to run 'cause he started firing on me. It was during that time when I really found out who my friends were. I lost self-respect. I didn't care, I was on a suicidal mission. I think it all stems back to my father's death and not talking about it, psychologically to the point of escaping reality. 'Cause communication is the key ingredient in life, as well as health awareness to stay alive. That's the major thing in life.

Around 1990 I was in a program called Horizons Unlimited, getting fresh out of jail. I was sober for quite a while in the program. 'Round this time I decided I wanted to learn more about my people because while I was in jail I began to think about my heritage. 'Cause people would ask me in jail, "Where you from?" See, I have a very ethnic look about me but I speak ebonically, real hip. Filipinos isn't identified with too much slang. People'd ask, "What are you?" And I'd say, " I'm one hundred percent Filipino with no *cut*." That's drug talk. And they'd say, "You may be brown on the outside but you black on the inside." Yeah, they'd call me an M&M—brown on the outside, black on the inside. And I noticed I got along real good with blacks. You know, the original Filipino was a Negrito—he was black. And then came the Spanish, Chinese, Japanese, American. We come in all different shapes and colors and sizes. We have a unique blend of beauty enriched in our culture.

When I started City College Dennis Ubungen was working there as a counselor. He introduced me to the EOPS—Extended Opportunity Program Services. The director of the program was Mr. Bill Chin—a Chinese guy who's probably in his late thirties. When I was introduced to him by Dennis, he told me how important education is for a person of color. You can do or be anything you want to be as long as you work hard for it. He gave me support, advice, assistance. He gave me love. He was like a father.

He was a man who believed in fairness and in helping people out. He was a great man, a superhero in my life. He spoke about how it's harder for a person of color because of the color of our skin. He'd say that education can't be taken away from you. He used to say that a person of color who has education is very important because of the way people look at you. They usually think you're ignorant or something. He used to give me a lot of talks. He seen potential in me. He would help me out even if I didn't have money for school. He'd take it out of his pocket. He'd give his right arm just to help a brother out. And he was doing this for all people of color.

During the time I knew Mr. Chin I was in and out of jail several times. I don't know what Bill thought, but he still believed in me. I'd go to jail, but Mr. Chin would be there when I got out. He got me a job. It was the support and responsibility that he gave me that made me realize what it was to make money from my own strength and sweat. I don't think I could be in the position I am now without the help of Dennis Ubungen and Mr. Bill Chin. I feel like the Lord blessed me to run into these guys.

It was during this time that I started loving to learn. That's when I began to break my code of silence to my homies, my street soldiers, about how important it is to learn and how to get the resources. I began to change when I realized what it meant to be a true gangster—that's death and destruction. I began to exercise my faith—learning about God. I started studying with Jehovah's Witnesses. That just opened so many avenues and doors to me. I got off drugs. It got me more serious about living and how precious life really is. Life is not important unless you are making an impact on other people's lives. That's a quote from Jackie Robinson.

In '94 I was still in the process of getting my A.A. from City College. I was going to school. I was involved in the truth. In that year I lost a nephew, seven years younger than me. He died of muscular dystrophy. He was twenty years old. That had a big impact on me. It made me want to try harder. It made me realize how precious life is. To me he was a hero. He was in a wheel-chair. He was on the honor roll at school. He never complained. He was a superhero to me. Dammit, I know he was suffering, but he never complained.

I began learning about the Philippines when I was still at City College. That's when I began to feel more confident, more proud of being a Filipino. I could talk about it instead of just saying I'm Filipino. I learned that we were oppressed for hundreds of years and denied our freedom. I took a course in Tagalog. It was hard for me to relate because of my slang, my language. Even some white guys were learning how to speak faster than me. That's when my Filipino teacher said I got a lot of slang in me. I got a lot of street in me. But he told me not to lose it, just study harder. That's why a lot of Filipinos I talk to now in the schools can't relate. They hear my language and they can't relate.

That same year I got a job at Bernal Heights Community Center. They were looking for a Filipino, and it fitted. Part of my job was to work with Filipino youth at Balboa High. That's when trouble broke out. I remember it was around Thanksgiving or some holiday when there was this dance in the cafeteria there. It happened that someone took the shoe off some black dude and was passing it around. So this black dude and another black started beefing over the shoes. They took the fight outside, and all their friends came around. These guys were from two separate turfs—Lakeside and Sunnydale, I believe. As they were fighting, one of their friends was standing on a car to see the action. It so happened that the car belonged to a Filipino dude who was at the party. He came out and told the guy to get off his car. And this guy, who was black, told the Filipino "fuck you" and socked him one. So then more Filipinos started coming from down the street. And the blacks who were originally fighting each other stopped and started fighting the Filipinos. There ended up being thirty to thirty-five people fighting. Someone called the police. Then the news media came and blew it up out of proportion and called it a race riot. Later the news started reporting that there were over a hundred people in the streets. It was all exaggerated.

A few days later when school began again, people started getting beat up for no reason. Everyone was jumping each other at school. And a lot of inno-cent people were getting hurt—just 'cause they were black or Filipino. It was getting out of control. So I got together with a guy, André, who was well-known with the African American kids at Balboa. We got the youth together—especially the ones who'd been fighting—and we sat around the table trying to find solutions. What we did is we sat at the table with the police present, the principal, myself, André, and at least thirty kids—black and Filipino. And we broke bread at the table and found out what really happened. We found out what transpired by communicating, although it took us at least a couple of hours to resolve the problem, which we did. We found out that the whole fight was actually started by someone who didn't even go to the school. Once people found out the whole thing was started over something really petty, they began to come up with solutions on how they could consolidate as one.

After this happened the kids came together, and it was cool. We thought about having athletic tournaments. About a month later the Latinos and Samoans got together and fought against the blacks. So what happened, although it was bad, was it brought blacks, Samoans, Latinos, and Filipinos to the roundtable. And a lot of other resources got involved—other groups, the mayor, the YMCA, Bernal Heights Community Center—and this is where the concept came up of *United Playaz*. We were thinking about how to stop the violence. We came up with the name *United Playaz* for our club.

So when *United Playaz* first got started our number-one goal was to prevent violence and promote education: to save lives, not take them. Another goal was to educate youth about different ethnic groups 'cause of all the interracial violence going on. We wanted to get kids to recognize other cultures and have respect for them. So we began forming teams for sports. What we did was combine different teams with mixed nationalities. We'd put different gang bangers on the same team. We'd hook up blacks, Filipinos, Latinos—all the kids that were at war with each other over *squat* [territory] so they got to know each other.

Like I said, we had a lot of resources, organizations, to help us out. They provided funding to our group and gave us a room at school. With *United Playaz* we started using all of our components: counseling, gang prevention, sex education, substance abuse [prevention], anger management. We had job and college information. I began to get involved with it five days a week. *United Playaz* also came up with officers, set agendas, and [had] a democratic vote. We got more organized and structured. More than half the school started to participate in our club—that includes faculty and students. That's about one thousand people a year and from all different ethnic groups. In fact, we got so many activities going on that other schools want to have a program like ours. But right now we can only do so much.

Since *United Playaz* began, I've been trying to set an example to the kids. Thinking back, I couldn't really have done what I've done without the help of other people. I had a lot of people supporting me, encouraging me,—family members and mentors—even homies, O.G.s [old gangsters] that I knew from jail. I'm talking about lifers—guys doing twenty-five to life. There was a lot of people from the South of Market that helped me—a lot of Filipinos that supported me.

You see, I believe that society is set up for people of color to fail. Like three strikes and you're out. You got programs that don't invest in the schools. There's no money in libraries, but at the same time they're flooding our communities with guns, drugs, and alcohol. They're building more jailhouses, more institutions of correction and not education. It's hard growing up, especially in the ghettos because you have very little access. It's hard getting jobs without a degree. Even just to get a street-sweeping job you need a diploma now. Society is set that way for people of color to be put down. It's set up by the white people in charge. And the way they write the laws down, like Proposition 187, it's very confusing and complicated. They twist things around to keep people of color down. As long as you have the white folks controlling things, they got the money, they got the power. They can dictate the way things will be.

If people of color stuck together they could change things, but it doesn't happen that way. For people of color in our communities you find that gangs and drugs are embedded in the ghettos. You can get drugs and guns everywhere. The cold part is that people of color are killing each other. You can't blame it on the white man. But I think that we are doing the white man's job—we're keeping our own people down. Minority means "less than," but I don't feel like I'm less than anybody.

How do I see the future for youth? The future for kids I would say is a self-destructive path 'cause there's so many programs and schools that are not being supported in the right way, and there's so many jail-houses in California. It's going to be really tough for kids in the future. Peer pressure is hard, and there's no opportunities for them. With me working with the kids, I wish I could work with every kid on this planet. But I'm only one man, and I can only help those who want to help themselves.

As for my future, I see myself in the future running my own non-profit organization. I hope I can save every kid in my community so that this becomes a domino effect. And I'm also a new father now. I know my son will make me appreciate life more and be more humble and understanding. I want my son to be happy. That's what I want for him: to live a long life and be happy and to know God and the truth. You know, just know the truth.

AUTHOR BIOGRAPHY

Janet Shirley is a youth advocate and community liaison representative for the Humanist Community Center in the Excelsior District of San Francisco. She is a member of the Mayor's Neighborhood Advisory Board and has played an active role in local city politics. Janet Shirley has traveled and lived extensively in Asia and Latin America and her major interest is in cross-cultural studies.

24

Luis Nishizawa: Portrait of a *Nisei* Artist

Ofelia Murrieta

When the first ambassador from Japan, Rocuyemon Fakicura, accompanied by Friar Luis de Sotelo, two other monks, and a retinue of 150 Japanese, arrived in New Spain (Mexico) on January 25, 1614, the canons at the fort in the port of Acapulco were fired in their honor. This date also marked the establishment of the relationship between New Spain and Asia through the voyages of the *China Ship*, the *Manila Galleon*, the *Ship of Friars*, and the *Silk Ship*—ships named for the cargo of humans and materials they carried and the ocean routes they followed. The people and materials they brought from Asia have influenced and enriched Mexican culture through the centuries.

Three hundred years later, at the end of the nineteenth century, a second wave of Japanese immigrants arrived in Mexico in search of new opportunities. Kenji Nishizawa was one of those immigrants. He married María de Jesús Flores, and their son, Luis Nishizawa, was born on February 2, 1918, in the hacienda of San Mateo in the municipality of Cuahutitlan.

At the threshold of Luis Nishizawa's house, visitors are welcomed by a picture that represents the wisdom of sparrows, which construct their nests within the security of bamboo plants. But Nishizawa doesn't paint sparrows; he paints hummingbirds because for him they represent the spirit of Mexico and of rebirth and freedom. This freedom of spirit is reflected in Nishizawa's works. He does not limit himself to one technique, expression, form, content, material, or school. His first individual exhibition was held in 1951 in the Salón de la Plástica Mexicana, and his works have been exhibited in England, Belgium, Canada, France, the United States, and Japan. He has received numerous honors including being named Maestro Emérito and Doctor Honoris Causa of the Universidad Nacional Autónoma de México and being given the Japanese government's Sacred Treasure of the Dragon award.

Nishizawa has identified strongly with the people of the pueblos and the indigenous people of Mexico. It was during the first period of his work, when he was considered a member of the nationalistic Mexican School of Painting, that he painted "La niña del rebozo" (1949), "Niña desgrandando maíz" (1950), and a series of paintings representing the annual presentation of the Passion of Jesus in the towns of Iztapalapa and Taxco (1949 and 1956). His painting of the vendors of the Effigy of Judas is from the same period. These effigies are sculptures of various sizes constructed of twigs, reeds, and paper. They are painted with bright colors and are burned during the celebrations of Holy Week.

Nishizawa says his artistic process is a dialogue between his two cultures and their different artistic sensibilities. Although he often uses materials such as large sheets of Japanese paper, Chinese ink with a small hint of color, and Chinese and Japanese techniques of drawing, Nishizawa's subjects are the people and the landscapes of Mexico.

El Penitente (The Penitent), 1955, 66.5 cm × 89.7 cm. Photograph by Javier Hinojosa. Reprinted courtesy of Luis Nishizawa.

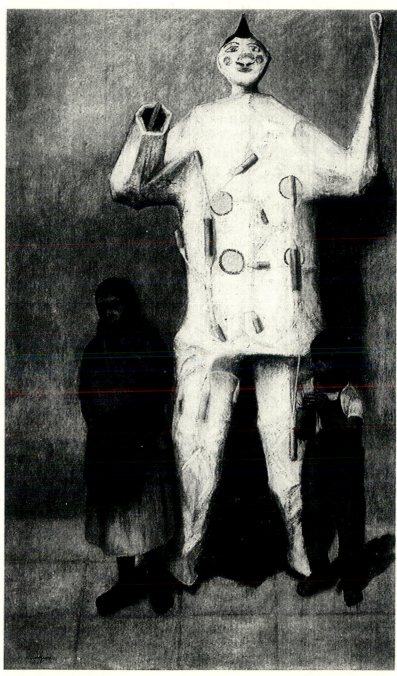

Vendedora de Judas (The Vendors of Judas), 1954, 122 cm by 72 cm. Photograph by Javier Hinojosa. Reprinted courtesy of Luis Nishizawa.

AUTHOR BIOGRAPHY

Ofelia Murrieta received her B.A. from the Universidad del Claustro de Sor Juan. She also studied at the School of Arts, Crafts and Design, National Institute of Fine Arts, Mexico City. She was director of the Museum of Mexican Clothing and Textiles in Mexico City and has been curator for exhibitions of Mexican clothing and textiles in Brussels and Lisbon. She is coordinator of the Bienal de Arte Guadalupano in Mexico City. Murrieta's paintings and silver work have been exhibited at various galleries. Her collection of works, Sculpture in Small Format, *was presented at the International Fair in Lisbon in 1998.*

25

Ethnic Preferences: Positive Minority Status of Japanese Brazilians and Their Ethnic Encounters with Other Minority Groups in Brazil

Takeyuki Tsuda

With an estimated population of over 1.2 million, Japanese Brazilians are not only the predominant Asian minority in Brazil but are the largest community of Japanese descendants outside Japan. Japanese emigration to Brazil began in 1908 and continued in significant numbers until the early 1960s. Many of the emigrants were farmers escaping impoverished conditions in Japan's rural areas who were drawn to Brazil by promises of opportunity and wealth in the expanding and labor-deficient coffee plantations. Although most went to Brazil as temporary migrant workers with dreams of returning to Japan in several years with considerable wealth, reality proved considerably more difficult, and their hopes for eventual repatriation under favorable conditions became impossible to attain. As a result, a vast majority settled permanently in Brazil with their families. Currently, most Japanese Brazilians are second-generation *nisei* (30.9 percent) or third-generation *sansei* (41.0 percent); the original first-generation Japanese immigrants (*issei*) constitute a relatively small proportion (12.5 percent).[1]

The Japanese Brazilians are generally well integrated in Brazilian society—socially, economically, and culturally. Most are urbanized and are concentrated in the most developed southwest and southern regions of Brazil in the states of São Paulo and Paraná; only a few remain in the rural *colônias* (Japanese Brazilian enclaves and agricultural villages).[2] They have experienced substantial social mobility; socioeconomically they are found predominantly in middle-class business and professional occupations, earning salaries well above the Brazilian average.[3] Most are well educated by Brazilian standards, and like Asians in the United States they are overrepresented at top Brazilian universities. In addition to their socioeconomic integration as part of the urban middle class, Japanese Brazilians enjoy almost complete social acceptance among Brazilians. The intermarriage rate is reported to be around 40 percent; as a result, 42 percent of the *sansei* are of mixed blood. Because of this high level of social integration, considerable cultural assimilation has also occurred among the *nisei* and the *sansei*. Except for a minority who are still from the rural *colônias*, few younger Japanese Brazilians maintain Japanese traditions and customs, except at a symbolic level, or speak proficient Japanese.

In contrast to the usual definitions of minorities as social groups that occupy low socio-occupational status and suffer from discrimination, prejudice, and social exclusion (e.g., Castles 1984: 96–100; Giddens 1989: 245; Ogbu 1978: 21–25), Japanese Brazilians can be defined as a "positive minority." Positive minorities are groups that are small numerically and that are not the dominant political power holders in a society but that enjoy a generally higher socioeconomic status than the majority of the populace and whose distinctive cultural qualities and social position are respected if not admired.[4] In general, Japanese Brazilians are well regarded by mainstream Brazilians for what are perceived as their positive "Japanese" cultural attributes, their affiliation with the highly respected First World nation Japan, and their middle-class socioeconomic and educational status—which is considerably higher than the Brazilian average. In turn, Japanese Brazilians feel significant cultural differences with mainstream Brazilians and take pride in their Japanese ethnic qualities, generally distancing themselves from what they perceive negatively as Brazilian.

Therefore, although Japanese Brazilians are well integrated in Brazilian society, they continue to assert and maintain a prominent Japanese ethnic identity that remains considerably stronger than their consciousness as Brazilians because of the sociocultural prestige attached to being a Japanese minority in Brazil. Their positive minority status, in turn, directly influences their ethnic encounters and preferences toward other minority groups, creating a certain reluctance among some to interact actively with other Asian minority groups that are less highly regarded and can potentially damage their favorable ethnic reputation. This stands in contrast to their active engagement with minority groups of European descent.

POSITIVE CULTURAL IMAGES OF JAPANESE BRAZILIANS IN BRAZILIAN SOCIETY

Much of the positive minority status of the Japanese Brazilians is based on favorable perceptions of their Japanese cultural qualities by mainstream Brazilians. Japanese Brazilians are referred to as *japonês* by other Brazilians, not only in unfamiliar contexts when names are not known (such as on the streets) but also when they are discussed by acquaintances. They are hardly ever called Brazilian, Japanese Brazilian, or Asian. Japanese Brazilians are designated "Japanese" not only because of their distinctive Asian phenotype but also because of their perceived cultural differences, which are interpreted favorably as a product of their Japanese cultural heritage and parental upbringing.

The ethnic stereotypes of Japanese Brazilians in Brazilian society are overwhelmingly positive—they are known as hardworking, honest, intelligent, and trustworthy and are thus preferred and liked as "good people" (cf. J. Saito 1986; T. Saito 1986). They are also described as more timid and reserved than other Brazilians, characteristics that again have positive connotations for many (e.g., T. Saito 1986). The only notable remaining negative image of Japanese Brazilians is a sense that they are closed and unreceptive toward outsiders. The perception of Asians in the United States as "geeks" or "nerds" seems much less prominent in Brazil in regard to Japanese Brazilians.

Indeed, many mainstream Brazilians emphasize the positive Japanese cultural qualities of Japanese Brazilians by explaining their behavior ethnically. Many Brazilians tend to interpret the distinctive aspects and behaviors of the Japanese Brazilians they observe (such as high academic achievement, politeness, little inclination to talk and joke, greater social reserve, differences in thinking, and similar factors) as Japanese ethnic characteristics based on a stereotyped notion of Japanese culture. The process at work can be called "ethnic attribution"—the propensity to simplistically explain and interpret the behavior of those from a different ethnic group as a cultural and ethnic characteristic and ignore possible individual or situational explanations for their behavior. The experiences of one Japanese Brazilian woman aptly illustrate this type of ethnic attribution:

> Brazilians always assume that our behavior is a product of our Japaneseness and believe we succeed because of these Japanese qualities. If a Japanese [Brazilian] student does well in school, they say 'of course, it's because he's Japanese.' If a Japanese [Brazilian] works harder than others in his company, his coworkers say 'he works so hard because he is Japanese.' If a Japanese [Brazilian] succeeds in his private business, again the Brazilians say 'it's because he's Japanese.'

Because of their positive minority status based on favorable assessments of their cultural differences, some Japanese Brazilians feel they can do nothing that would embarrass or tarnish the reputation of their ethnic group; some mention that they cannot behave in inappropriate ways as members of the Japanese community.

In addition, virtually all of Japanese Brazilians I interviewed claimed they had never experienced any ethnic derogation or discrimination.[5] Indeed, it can be argued that they experience "positive discrimination" in Brazilian society, in contrast to the "negative discrimination" many minorities suffer. This not only means Japanese Brazilians are favorably treated in the majority society; some employers prefer them over non-Japanese-descent Brazilians because of their supposed greater diligence, honesty, intelligence, and sense of responsibility. As a result, most Japanese Brazilians feel they discriminate more against Brazilians than vice versa; for example, they excluded Brazilians of non-Japanese descent from their ethnic organizations until fairly recently. This situation in which there is more *minority* discrimination than *majority* discrimination may be characteristic of other positive minority groups.

The positive minority status of Japanese Brazilians is also directly connected to Japan's postwar rise to First World economic superpower status. Many Brazilians are aware of Brazil's relatively low and peripheral international status as a Third World country and have a favorable perception of Japan as an economically and technologically advanced First World nation. As a result of Japan's rise to international prominence, Brazil has been saturated with positive—if not idealistic—images of Japan through newspapers, magazines, and television programs, as well as books, Japanese films, and the increased availability of high-quality Japanese products. Although the vast majority of Japanese Brazilians in Brazil were not born in Japan, they are generally seen as closely associated with that country; therefore, most of them agree that their social image and the level of respect they receive in Brazil have increased considerably with Japan's rise in the global hierarchy of nations to First World status.

This has created new reasons and incentives for being *japonês* in Brazil instead of simply assuming a majority Brazilian identity. The reflections of a *nisei* Japanese Brazilian are representative of this experience:

> The Japanese Brazilians have benefited considerably as Japan has become one of the leading nations of the First World. Although we were born and raised in Brazil, the Brazilians associate us closely with Japan—some don't differentiate clearly between the Japanese [Brazilians] living in Brazil and the Japanese of Japan. Many of us feel this prestige because we are associated with Japan. Some even act like we were directly involved in Japan's rise and success, which is obviously a problem.

Therefore, in addition to their relatively high socioeconomic status, their affiliation with a well-regarded First World nation is another factor that contributes to the high social evaluation of Japanese Brazilians as a positive minority.

EXPERIENCE OF POSITIVE MINORITY STATUS AND CONSTRUCTION OF CULTURAL DIFFERENCES

Most Japanese Brazilians are aware of other Brazilians favorable cultural perception of them (cf. Ferreira and Asari 1986) and therefore actively construct and maintain a sense of Japanese cultural distinctiveness. This consciousness of their positive Japanese cultural differences and qualities is also based on a contrast with what are stereotypically considered to be negative and unfavorable Brazilian characteristics.

Although Japanese Brazilians are now dispersed in the cities, their ethnic community remains socially cohesive and consists of active associations and sports clubs that run a multitude of events and activities ranging from large Japanese dinners and performances featuring Japanese karaoke, theater, and dance to various sporting events and Miss *Nikkei* beauty pageants. A large number of Japanese Brazilians actively participate in these ethnically exclusive and generally segregated associations and structure their social lives around them.

Such cohesive ethnic communities create a strong sense of ethnic commonality and identity by maintaining and expressing what are deemed common Japanese ethnic cultural characteristics. Within their communities Japanese Brazilians have opportunities not only to build a sense of solidarity among those in the same ethnic group but also to develop, express, and experience behavior understood to represent a distinctive Japanese culture—especially through activities such as learning Japanese at community schools; cooking, eating, and selling Japanese food; performing Japanese plays, songs, traditional dances, and music; wearing traditional Japanese dress; and conducting Japanese festivals. In addition to such formal activities, many informal social gatherings of Japanese Brazilian families and friends—such as dinners, parties, and other outings—provide opportunities to cook Japanese food, speak Japanese (when possible), and sing Japanese songs.

Japanese Brazilians not only positively regard their cultural qualities and actively maintain them in their communities, but they frequently contrast their own cultural patterns with those of mainstream Brazilians based on unfavorable stereotypes of the typical Brazilian as lazy, easygoing, irresponsible, immature, and dishonest (see also Flores 1975: 95; Reichl 1995: 49, 51, 55; Smith 1979: 58).[6] Therefore, unlike the stereotyped Brazilian, Japanese Brazilians see themselves as possessing better (if not superior) cultural characteristics, which they have inherited through the generations as *japonês*. As is true of ethnic interaction in general, such notions of ethnic cultural distinctiveness are frequently based on negative characterizations and stereotypes of other groups, in contrast to which the ethnic group in question uses positive stereotypes to define and differentiate itself as different and better.[7] Such attributed ethnic traits then become ethnic boundary markers (Barth 1969) clearly indicate who is *japonês* and who is not ("us" versus "them"), as shown by Japanese Brazilians' general habit of calling other Brazilians *gaijin* (foreigners).

Because their understanding of Brazilian society is laden with a certain amount of negative affect, a number of Japanese Brazilians distance and disassociate themselves from majority Brazilians. Even some *sansei* associate and socialize predominantly, if not almost exclusively, with their ethnic fellows in closed social groups and sometimes have few active social relationships with mainstream Brazilians. Such individuals claim they get along better with their fellow Japanese Brazilians than with mainstream Brazilians because of commonly shared cultural values. For example, consider the typical assessment of a Japanese Brazilian:

> It's easier to associate with other Japanese [Brazilians] than with Brazilians because of cultural similarities. With the Japanese Brazilians we can take things for granted and know what to expect because we share similar ways of thinking and behaving, whereas with Brazilians you can't tell. Of course, there are Brazilians who have some of the positive cultural qualities of the Japanese Brazilians, but most of them don't have these favorable characteristics.

Indeed, despite the increasing rate of intermarriage, a number of Japanese Brazilian families (including those in which the parents are *nisei*) still strongly encourage their children to marry another *japonês* instead of a Brazilian for such cultural reasons.

Even among Japanese Brazilians who are culturally assimilated to a considerable degree, there is a continued need to maintain a separate Japanese ethnic identity because they are highly regarded for their Japanese cultural qualities in the dominant society. For positive minorities a loss of ethnic identity and minority status through complete assimilation is equivalent to a decline in their former social prestige and cultural esteem. Since many younger Japanese Brazilians have lost most of their substantial Japanese cultural differences and are completely immersed in mainstream Brazilian society, a Japanese ethnic consciousness is maintained through what has been called "symbolic ethnicity" (Gans 1979)—the assertion of an ethnic identity through purely symbolic means by maintaining a nostalgic allegiance to recreated cultural traditions and symbols expressed through festivals, holidays, food, dress, ethnic media, film, and theater.[8]

In this manner, because of the absence of sufficient cultural differences in their everyday behavior or language, many Japanese Brazilians maintain their Japanese ethnic identity by symbolically reconstructing and reenacting their past cultural heritage and traditions through ethnic activities and gatherings, as described earlier. Therefore, ethnicity becomes "symbolic" in this manner precisely when a positive minority group such as the Japanese Brazilians has become well integrated and assimilated into majority society but continues to find a need to assert a sense of ethnic distinctiveness instead of becoming subsumed by the majority because of the social prestige and cultural respect attached to its ethnic minority status. Since in this case a loss of minority status is concomitant to giving up one's cultural virtue and social standing, individuals continue to emphasize their remaining ethnic differences (even if they are only symbolic) in an attempt to hold on to the last vestiges of a respected minority status.

POSITIVE MINORITY STATUS AND ETHNIC ENCOUNTERS BETWEEN JAPANESE BRAZILIANS AND OTHER BRAZILIAN MINORITY GROUPS

Thus the positive ethnic status of Japanese Brazilians is a source of much pride and self-respect. As a result, they differentiate themselves from the negative aspects of Brazilian society while affiliating themselves with the contrasting positive aspects of Japaneseness. In addition, the minority status of a certain ethnic group can have a direct impact on its ethnic encounters and relationships with other minority groups. The ethnic encounter between Japanese Brazilians and other Asian minority groups (of Korean and Chinese descent), as well as certain minorities of European descent, is structured by the former's favorable, positive minority status in Brazilian society. Because Japanese Brazilians strongly desire to maintain their positive ethnic reputation and image, some of them tend to distance themselves from other Asian minorities that are less favorably perceived. In contrast, no such ethnic reluctance is shown in their relationships with other positively perceived minorities of European descent.[9]

The Japanese Brazilians I knew who spoke about other Asian minority groups were aware that the latter are less well regarded in Brazilian society. Those of Korean and Chinese descent were stereotypically characterized as less trustworthy, dishonest, and even prone to suspicious activities. One Japanese Brazilian described his reactions as follows: "I don't like the Korean [Brazilians] too much. Some of them work hard, like the Japanese [Brazilians], but in general they are not very trustworthy and can tend to be dishonest, especially in business dealings. Sometimes they even cause problems. They aren't always well regarded by other Brazilians, either." This general impression was seemingly confirmed by some Brazilians who spoke about differences between the *Japonês* and the *coreanos*. One of my housemates in Ribeirão Preto, São Paulo, was the most explicit: "The Japanese [Brazilians] are seen [as] much better than the Koreans. We trust the Japanese very much— they are good people. The Koreans—sometimes you can't tell what they're up to or what they're like. They are new immigrants and haven't been around in Brazil too long, whereas the Japanese have been here for many decades."

Japanese Brazilians are especially concerned that the lesser ethnic image of their Korean and Chinese minority counterparts may potentially have a negative ethnic impact on them because of the Brazilian tendency to group the Korean Brazilians and Chinese Brazilians along with Japanese Brazilians because of their shared Asian descent. Perceived racial differences serve as important primordial ethnic emblems and boundary markers differentiate ethnic groups according to perceived cultural differences. In contrast to the clearly defined and mutually exclusive racial distinctions used in the United States (black, white, Asian, Hispanic), Brazilians tend to think in terms of racial gradations and mixtures rather than employing absolute categories, in part because of the greater racial intermixture in Brazil. For instance, instead of the dichotomous racial categories of black and white, Brazilians have a wide array of intermediary racial categories such as *mulatto* and *moreno*.[10]

Even in this world of relative racial distinctions, however, the Japanese Brazilians are immediately recognizable because of their distinctive "oriental" appearance (*traços orientais*), which is seen as markedly different from whites (*brancos*), blacks (*pretos*), and mixed-blood *mestiços* of all types (including *mulattos*, *morenos*, and *pardos*) (cf. Maeyama 1984: 455). Brazilians give much attention to these phenotypic differences, especially because of their high sensitivity to racial characteristics, including slight differences in skin color. Brazilians frequently note the *olhos puxados* (slanted eyes, or literally "pulled eyes") of Japanese Brazilians, sometimes even pulling their eyes upward with their fingers when referring to people or things Japanese.[11]

As mentioned earlier, because of the relative prominence of their perceived racial differences, Japanese Brazilians are called *japonês* by other Brazilians in the streets, stores, and other public areas simply because of their facial features. Since Japanese Brazilians are by far the largest Asian group in Brazil and vastly outnumber others of Asian descent, all people with an Asian appearance (including Korean Brazilians and Chinese Brazilians) are automatically labeled *japonês* because of their similar phenotypic features. This contrasts distinctly with the United States, where there are many more Asian-Americans of non-Japanese descent.

Although Brazilians are aware of distinctions between different Asian ethnic groups, the dominant tendency to group Korean and Chinese descendants together with Japanese Brazilians on racial grounds seems to create some latent concern among Japanese Brazilians that the less well-regarded Koreans and Chinese could tarnish their positive ethnic image. One of my informants even claimed that some members of the international Chinese underworld operate in Brazil by engaging in criminal activities and supporting Brazilian drug trafficking, and the informant worried that they could negatively affect the positive ethnic reputation of Japanese Brazilians. As a result, as mentioned earlier, some Japanese Brazilians tend to disassociate themselves from Korean Brazilians and Chinese Brazilians. Although the maintenance of ethnic distance is not always necessarily a conscious effort (few Japanese Brazilians have contact with their Asian minority counterparts because of the latter's small numbers), one Japanese-Brazilian university student was explicit about his intentions:

> I find this need to differentiate myself from the Koreans. As you know, people with an oriental appearance are always called *Japonês* here in Brazil. In regard to the Koreans, I sometimes feel this urge to point them out to my Brazilian friends, saying "they are Koreans, not Japanese." Some Koreans are not regarded very well or do things that are disapproved, like cheating on exams. So I don't want them to be seen the same as the Japanese.

Another student also noted the relative lack of interaction between Japanese Brazilians and other Asian students at the university and reported that the two groups tend to sit separately in the dining halls.

My close Japanese Brazilian friend in Riberão Preto, Fabio, was the only notable exception I found to this general Japanese Brazilian ethnic reluctance to interact actively with other Asian minority groups. One evening Fabio invited me to a tennis game of doubles with two of his "best friends," who, surprisingly, turned out to be of Korean and Chinese descent, respectively. Fabio reflected later on his rather close friendship with his Chinese Brazilian and Korean Brazilian friends, clearly indicating that he felt unusual among his Japanese Brazilian peers. "I met them at the university," Fabio noted. "They're good fellows, and we do a lot together. But I'm quite rare—most Japanese [Brazilians] don't bother to associate with them too much. Some don't even like them. I just don't have such prejudices. In fact, I associate with them more than I do with the Japanese." Fabio had always prided himself on his openness and receptivity and had characterized himself as an individual *sem preconceitos* (without prejudices) on other occasions as well.

It seems, therefore, that the withdrawn ambivalence some of my Japanese Brazilian informants showed toward the Korean Brazilian and Chinese Brazilian minority was motivated in part by a strong self-consciousness and desire to maintain their positive minority status by distancing themselves from other Asian minorities held in lower ethnic regard. This ethnic separation may also be based on increasing ethnic competition. Korean and Chinese immigrants in Brazil have not only been increasing in number; they have also become socioeconomically successful, entering top Brazilian universities in notable numbers and successfully opening small businesses. As a result, they represent a potential challenge to the prominent and secure educational and occupational status of Japanese Brazilians as positive minorities. In addition, these recent "upstart" Asian immigrants have migrated directly to the cities with a certain amount of capital, unlike earlier European and Japanese immigrants who endured hardships in rural agricultural villages for a considerable time before urbanizing. Again, the ethnic encounter with other Asian minorities, characterized by some ambivalence and antagonistic distance on the part of Japanese Brazilians, is a direct result of the latter's positive minority status and a desire to maintain their position of ethnic privilege.

In contrast, Japanese Brazilians tended to have positive and active relationships with minority groups that, like themselves, are rather favorably regarded. In Rio Grande do Sul, the southernmost state in Brazil, two of the most prominent ethnic minority groups are the Germans and Italians. Historically, white Brazilians of European descent have been at the top of Brazil's hierarchy of racial preference, as shown by the history of Brazilian immigration policy (Lesser 1997), and both the German Brazilians and Italian Brazilians in the region enjoy a relatively high socioeconomic status. Since close relationships with these ethnic minorities do not threaten (and may even promote) the privileged ethnic status of Japanese Brazilians as a positive minority, there was active ethnic engagement with them. One Japanese Brazilian woman commented on the rather favorable relationships between Japanese Brazilians and these two ethnic groups:

> I would say that the Japanese [Brazilians] and the Germans are the ethnic groups in Rio Grande do Sul which are regarded the most favorably. People see both groups as hard-working, honest, and responsible, and they are both associated with advanced First World countries. In contrast, the Italians are liked, too, but are not seen as highly. The Japanese [Brazilians] and Germans get along very well—they respect and like each other. Japanese *colônias* have existed right next to German colonies in the countryside for a long time. There are lots of intermarriages between Japanese and Germans, as well as with the Italians, whereas there are fewer intermarriages between Japanese and other groups.

I also noticed a relatively high number of Japanese-German and Japanese-Italian interethnic marriages among my informants in Rio Grande do Sul.

CONCLUSION

The positive minority status of Japanese Brazilian's in Brazil has undoubtedly served as an "ethnic filter" of sorts that in part has structured their minority relationships with other non-dominant Brazilian ethnic groups. Because Korean Brazilians and Chinese Brazilians are associated with some negative ethnic images and are frequently grouped with Japanese Brazilians because of similar phenotype, they can potentially threaten the positive ethnic reputation of Japanese Brazilians. This has resulted in considerable ambivalence among some Japanese Brazilians in their ethnic encounters with these Asian minorities, in some cases even leading to an active desire to distance themselves from these groups. Meanwhile, Japanese Brazilians show no hesitation in interacting with certain European-descent minorities, who are seen as consistent with their own positive minority status.

Yet at the same time, such ethnic preferences reveal another dimension of positive minority status. Although the currently high socioeconomic and cultural status of Japanese Brazilians in Brazil seems secure, they were not always held in such high ethnic regard in Brazilian society. When the Japanese first began to emigrate to Brazil, they were seen as an "inferior race" (compared with European immigrants) who could not be assimilated and would have negative effects on Brazilian racial composition. During the period of Japanese imperialist expansion and World War II, the unassimilated and enclaved Japanese Brazilians were regarded as a serious threat to Brazilian national security and unity (the "yellow peril") and subject to considerable ethnic repression.

Indeed, the rise of Japanese Brazilians to positive minority status has occurred only in the past few decades as a result of their considerable socioeconomic success, their upward mobility, and Japan's sudden rise to the top of the global order as a respected economic superpower. As a result, some older Japanese Brazilians, who still remember the historical legacy of prejudice and discrimination, are less enthusiastic about their currently positive minority status. Perhaps they are aware that a future negative turn of historical events could as quickly erode the ethnic gains they have recently made, returning them to their former negative minority status. Despite Japanese Brazilians' current favorable ethnic position, they remain a nondominant minority that does not hold power in Brazilian society; thus they are much more subject to historical vicissitudes than majority ethnic groups. Such enduring ethnic unease inherent in minority status undoubtedly makes Japanese Brazilians sensitive about associating closely with negatively perceived minorities who could threaten their fundamentally fragile positive minority status.

NOTES

1. The population statistics presented here are derived mainly from the São Paulo Humanities Research Center (1987–1988) survey on Japanese Brazilians and include both pure Japanese descendants and mixed-blood descendants.

2. Ninety percent of Japanese Brazilians live in cities; only 10 percent remain in rural areas (ibid.).

3. A census of Japanese Brazilians showed that 43.3 percent were professionals, managers, or office workers and another 20.9 percent are in private business. A number were *patrões* (the boss, manager, supervisor, or owner). As a result, their salary levels were much higher than the majority of Brazilians: 30.7 percent of Japanese Brazilians earned less than $400 per month, 48.2 percent earned between $400 and

$1,600, and 21.4 percent earned over $1,600 a month in contrast to wage levels for the general populace where 61.9 percent earned less than $400 a month, 30.0 percent earned between $400 and $800, and only 5.7 percent earned over $1,600 (ibid.).

4. See Liebkind (1982) for a detailed analysis of the Swedish-speaking minority in Finland, another example of a positive minority.

5. Even in the 1970s Hiroshi Saito (1976: 197) observed that Japanese Brazilians no longer encountered resistance or barriers to social mobility in the cities. His informants (even older *issei*) felt they were not subject to ethnic prejudice (1976: 192). Smith (1979: 58), however, suspected that latent ethnic prejudice still existed during this period but was not expressed overtly in the form of discrimination.

6. Despite the dominant image of Brazilians as happy and cheerful, many Japanese Brazilian respondents in the T. Saito (1986) survey also characterized Brazilians as idle, lazy, undisciplined, immature, and irresponsible. Such negative characterizations were less common for Brazilian women, where female stereotypes were more prevalent. Few saw Brazilians as educated, hardworking, intelligent, or responsible. This feeling was also strongly evident in my interviews.

7. As social psychologists Jaspars and Warnaen (1982) have shown in a study of Indonesian ethnic identity, ethnic groups use self-attributed, positive stereotypes to differentiate themselves from other groups.

8. Gans (1979) also described how symbolic ethnicity is maintained by identifying with events and struggles in the ancestral homeland or through remembrance of past historical events. I did not find evidence among Japanese Brazilians that this was occurring.

9. Since I did not systematically collect ethnographic information about this issue during my fieldwork, I will discuss some specific ethnic experiences among my informants as individual illustrations of how positive minority status can structure ethnic encounters without presuming that those experiences are necessarily typical or representative of the group as a whole.

10. Harris and Kottak (1963), in their study of racial categories among Brazilians in a fishing village in coastal Bahia, uncovered forty categories used to describe phenotypic differences.

11. In the United States, such gestures directed toward Asian Americans are considered an affront and an inexcusable insult. In Brazil, however, they are seen not as a nasty insult directed toward Japanese Brazilians but simply as an amusing commentary on their different physiognomy. Undoubtedly, the same "objective" ethnic gesture has different connotations depending on the local cultural order, and an unmitigated insult in one society can be viewed as a good-humored joke in another. Brazilians have a charming way of expressing ethnic prejudice in a jocular manner, thus taking much of the bite out of their "ethnic discrimination."

REFERENCES

Barth, Fredrik. "Introduction." In *Ethnic Groups and Boundaries*, ed. Fredrik Barth. London: George Allen and Unwin, 1969.

Castles, Stephen (with Heather Booth and Tina Wallace). *Here for Good: Western Europe's New Ethnic Minorities.* London: Pluto, 1984.

Ferreira, Yoshiya Nakagawara, and Alice Yatiyo Asari. "Algumas Considerações sobre a Atuação do Imigrante Japonês e seus Descendentes na comunidade Londrinense" (Some Considerations About the Achievements of the Japanese Immigrants and Their Descendants in the Londrina Community). In *O Nikkei e Sua Americanidade* (The *Nikkei* and Their Americanness), ed. Massao Ohno. São Paulo: COPANI, 1986.

Flores, Moacyr. "Japoneses no Rio Grande do Sul" (The Japanese in Rio Grande do Sul). *Veritas* 77 (1975): 65–98.

Gans, Herbert J. "Symbolic Ethnicity: The Future of Ethnic Groups and Cultures in America." *Ethnic and Racial Studies* 2, no. 1 (1979): 1–20.

Giddens, Anthony. *Sociology.* Cambridge: Polity, 1989.

Harris, Marvin, and Conrad Kottak. "The Structural Significance of Brazilian Racial Categories." *Sociologia* 25 (1963): 203–209.

Hewstone, Miles, and J. M. F. Jaspars. "Intergroup Relations and Attribution Processes." In *Social Identity and Intergroup Relations*, ed. Henri Tajfel. Cambridge: Cambridge University Press, 1982.

Jaspars, J. M. F., and Suwarsih Warnaen. "Intergroup Relations, Ethnic Identity, and Self-Evaluation in Indonesia." In *Social Identity and Intergroup Relations*, ed. Henri Tajfel. Cambridge: Cambridge University Press, 1982.

Lesser, Jeffrey. Chapter 4: Hidden Diversity, Open Difference. Unpublished manuscript, 1997.

Liebkind, Karmela. "The Swedish-Speaking Finns: A Case Study of Ethnolinguistic Identity." In *Social Identity and Intergroup Relations*, ed. Henri Tajfel. Cambridge: Cambridge University Press, 1982.

Maeyama, Takashi. "Burajiru Nikkeijin ni Okeru Esunishitei to Aidenteitei: Ishikiteki Seijiteki Genjyo to Shite" (The Ethnicity and Identity of the *Nikkeijin* in Brazil: Politico-Cognitive Phenomena). *Minzokugaku Kenkyu* (Ethnicity Research) 48, 4 (1984): 444–458.

Ogbu, John U. *Minority Education and Caste: The American System in Cross-Cultural Perspective.* New York: Academic Press, 1978.

Reichl, Christopher A. "Stages in the Historical Process of Ethnicity: The Japanese in Brazil, 1908–1988." *Ethnohistory* 42, no. 1 (1995): 31–62.

Saito, Hiroshi. "The Integration and Participation of the Japanese and Their Descendants in Brazilian Society." *International Migration* 14, no. 3 (1976): 183–199.

Saito, Júlia Kubo. "Auto-Estima e Auto-Conceito entre os Jovens Descendentes de Japoneses" (Self-Esteem and Self-Concepts Among Japanese-Descent Youths). In *O Nikkei e Sua Americanidade* (The *Nikkei* and Their Americanness), ed. Massao Ohno. São Paulo: COPANI, 1986.

Saito, Toshiaki. "Brasileiros e Japoneses, Confronto de Identidade" (Brazilians and Japanese: Confrontation of Identity). In *O Nikkei e Sua Americanidade* (The *Nikkei* and their Americanness), ed. Massao Ohno. São Paulo: COPANI, 1986.

São Paulo Humanities Research Center. *Burajiru ni Okeru Nikkeijin Jinko Chosa Hokokusho* (Population Survey Report About *Nikkeijin* in Brazil). São Paulo: Sanpauro Jinbun Kagaku Kenkyujo, 1987–1988.

Smith, Robert J. "The Ethnic Japanese in Brazil." *The Journal of Japanese Studies* 5, 1 (1979): 53–70.

AUTHOR BIOGRAPHY

Takeyuki Tsuda is a Harper-Schmidt instructor in the Social Sciences Collegiate Division at the University of Chicago. He received his Ph.D. in anthropology from the University of California at Berkeley in December 1996 and was a visiting research fellow at the Center for U.S.-Mexican Studies at the University of California at San Diego for two years. For his dissertation research he studied the return migration of Japanese Brazilians to Japan and their ethnic status as the country's newest immigrant minority. Fieldwork and participant observation for this project were conducted in both Brazil and Japan. Articles he has written about this topic will be published soon in Anthropological Quarterly, Ethos, *and the* Journal of Japanese Studies. *His book manuscript is being reviewed by the University of Chicago Press.*

26

Phuri Sherpa: Nepal and Mexico in California

Monica J. Rainwater

Phuri Sherpa and I met twelve years ago in Nepal, the heart of the Himalayas. My mother and I were members of a small organized trek in the Annapurnas, and Phuri was one of our guides. The first night out we camped on a hilltop facing Mount Machhapuchare (Fishtail Mountain). The panoramic views stole my breath away. I was overwhelmed by the beauty of the mountains. Phuri walked over to introduce himself, and when we shook hands our fingers connected like two pieces of a missing puzzle. We have talked about that moment many times over the past twelve years, and we still marvel at the immediate connection we felt at that first meeting. We both felt as if we had met a long-lost friend. Our relationship developed slowly because neither of us spoke a word of the other's language. During the course of our bicontinental "courtship," Phuri took English-language classes and I studied Nepali. We hired people to read our first letters to one another, and we were both frustrated and amused by our situation.

During the six years between our meeting and our wedding, I made three more trips to Nepal, and Phuri came to the United States for a nine-month visit. At first, Phuri did not like what he saw of American culture. The fast-paced daily life in the United States seemed void of the simple daily rituals he was accustomed to. He was surprised by our apparent lack of hospitality. He failed to understand how one couldn't just "drop in" on someone for a visit. When a host failed to offer refreshments, Phuri was appalled. That was unheard of in Nepalese society. When I visited his family in the village where he had been raised, I found myself trying to hide from the daily gauntlet of invitations to more meals than our stomachs could hold. It was then that I finally understood what Phuri felt when he was in my country. And I think that was when I really fell in love with him and his family.

Our marriage remains what I call "our daily, conscious work in progress." At the same time we have a happy ending—our son, Tenzing, who arrived nine months and one day after our wedding in Kathmandu and is the solid, tangible bridge between our two cultures.

One day while our five-year-old son was at the kitchen table sounding out words for his kindergarten assignment, I heard Phuri say, "Muy bueno, Tenzing!" with great enthusiasm. Phuri, a Nepalese Sherpa of Tibetan descent from the Mount Everest region of the Himalayas who had lived in the United States for nearly six years, had started to learn to speak a sixth language, Spanish. He was learning Spanish from his coworkers from Mexico. They work together in Sebastopol, California, at Vacu-Dry, an apple-processing plant. Tenzing had started to learn Spanish in his kindergarten class.

When I asked Phuri what it means for him to make friends with his coworkers from Mexico he says, "Mexican culture seems a lot like Nepalese in the way we are thinking. When my friends and I talk in the lunchroom, we say the same things about Americans [Caucasians] and work. We laugh because it seems American people are a little lazy for hard [physical] work. Why do we not see white people in the fields?"

Phuri also speaks of what he sees as similarities between Mexican and Nepali women: "Some Mexican women can work hard all day in the factory or the fields. Then they go home, cook food, and bring it back to the men in the family who are still on the shift. Nepalese women are that way, too, especially in the village. I think it helps to have a big family sharing one house. Everything gets done easily. Cooking, caring for children. It's a good system, and you don't have to think much about it or talk about it. You just do it."

Interestingly, learning to appreciate different kinds of American food and working in restaurants have been important American experiences for Phuri. One of his first jobs in this country was at an Indian restaurant in San Francisco. Phuri became a *naan* (a kind of bread) chef. Most of his coworkers were also Nepalese. This was of great comfort to him as he set about the daunting task of establishing himself as a new husband in a new country trying to support a pregnant wife. When the first paycheck he received from the restaurant bounced, he was more perplexed than angry. He was unable to understand how someone who had given him a job and whom he had grown to trust could do such a thing. Phuri comes from a culture in which everything, including buying or building a home, is done on a cash-only basis. Credit cards and negotiable checks were an abstract idea to him but he had been willing to trust the system. That changed with the bounced paycheck. He brought home burned *naan* that night.

Phuri sometimes works at a Greek bistro where he has learned a style of cooking he enjoys. According to him, many of the spices are similar to those in Nepal and India and he has devised recipes for our meals at home that combine Greek and Nepali cuisine. He says a well-prepared meal not only

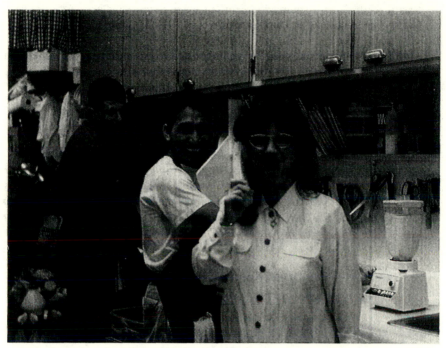

A Nepali Sherpa, a Greek American, and a Mexican working in a restaurant. Reprinted courtesy of Monica J. Rainwater.

fills the hungry spot but is also a measure of one's ability to show hospitality to others—a cornerstone of Sherpa culture. He says, "Food should have a good taste and make your tummy happy. It should be offered to your guests in large quantities. I like all sorts of food, including American; it depends on what it is like. I like a lot of Greek food because of the different spices, which make it interesting. But I also love hamburgers." I know when Phuri has had a good day at work because of the wonderful aromas from the kitchen that greet me when I get home from work.

When I asked him about his two current jobs—at Vacu-Dry and at the Greek bistro—the friends he has made at work, and his life in the United States he said:

I really love Mexican food! The first time I went to the lunchroom at work, I noticed that the men from Mexico ate the same kinds of chilies with their dinner that I did. Same pepper sauce, too. We both like hot food. Western food isn't very spicy. When my work slows down, I think too much. Sometimes I get depressed. Life in America is lonely, too much hard work; I get tired, no friends nearby to talk to. This is not my life. That is when I really miss Nepali and

Sherpa food. When I am making chili sauce and *tsampa* [barley flour] mash in our kitchen, it means that I am homesick.

He looked at our son and said, "It's a little hard to be married to an American sometimes. What we do have is great love together and our wonderful son. We have been together for almost twelve years. That must mean something."

AUTHOR BIOGRAPHY

Monica (Niki) J. Rainwater has a B.A. in journalism from California State University at Sacramento where she was the Campus Scene editor for the student paper, the State Hornet. She has worked as an editor and a proofreader in Sacramento and San Francisco. She, her husband, Phuri Sherpa, and their son, Tenzing, have homes in Solu, Nepal, and in Forestville, California.

Part III

Volcán de Izalco, amén—
Locating the Body and the Land

27

Notes for a Poem on Being Asian American

Dwight Okita

As a child, I was a fussy eater
and I would separate the yolk from the egg white
as I now try to sort out what is Asian
in me from what is American—
the east from the west, the dreamer from the dream.
But countries are not
like eggs—except in the fragileness
of their shells—and eggs resemble countries
only in that when you crack one open and look inside,
you know even less than when you started.

And so I crack open the egg,
and this is what I see:
two moments from my past that strike me
as being uniquely Asian American.

In the first, I'm walking down Michigan Avenue
one day—a man comes up to me out of the blue and says:
"I just wanted to tell you . . . I was on the plane that
bombed Hiroshima. And I just wanted you to know that
what we did was for the good of everyone." And it
seems as if he's asking for my forgiveness. It's 1983,
there's a sale on Marimekko sheets at the Crate &
Barrel, it's a beautiful summer day and I'm talking to
a man I've never seen before and will probably never
see again. His statement has no connection to me—
and has every connection in the world. But it's not
for me to forgive him. He must forgive himself.
"It must have been a very difficult decision to do what

you did," I say and I mention the sale on Marimekko
sheets across the street, comforters, and how the
pillowcases have the pattern of wheat printed on them,
and how some nights if you hold them before an open
window to the breeze, they might seem like flags—
like someone surrendering after a great while, or
celebrating, or simply cooling themselves in the summer
breeze as best they can.

In the second moment—I'm in a taxi and the Iranian
cabdriver looking into the rearview mirror notices my
Asian eyes, those almond shapes, reflected in the glass
and says, "Can you really tell the difference between
a Chinese and a Japanese?"

And I look at his 3rd World face, his photo I.D. pinned
to the dashboard like a medal, and I think of the eggs
we try to separate, the miles from home he is and the
minutes from home I am, and I want to say: "I think
it's more important to find the similarities between
people than the differences." But instead I simply
look into the mirror, into his beautiful 3rd World
eyes, and say, "Mr. Cabdriver, I can barely tell the
difference between you and me."

AUTHOR BIOGRAPHY

*Dwight Okita's poem "Notes for a poem on Being Asian American" was published
in his book of poetry* Crossing with the Light *(Chicago: Tia Chucha Press, 1992)
and is forthcoming in the* Norton Introduction to Literature *and the* Norton
Introduction to Poetry. *Okita's screenplay,* My Last Week on Earth, *was a finalist in the 1998 Sundance Screenwriters Lab competition. His play* The Rainy
Season *was included in the* anthology Asian American Drama: 9 Plays from the
MultiEthnic Landscape, *published by Applause Theater Books in 1997.*

28

Santos y Sombras—Saints and Shadows

Muriel H. Hasbun

I come from peoples in exile.

I became an adult with an extreme sensitivity to the *irreconcilable* . . .

Since 1990 I have committed my creative energy to developing a body of work that explores my family history and sense of identity. *Saints and Shadows* is a refuge against silence and forgetting. The work becomes a personal diary in which I mold the emotional aura surrounding my Palestinian Christian and Polish Jewish family as I was growing up in El Salvador.

With the *Todos los santos* (All the Saints) images, I explore my memories of childhood and delve into the expression of identity of my paternal, Palestinian Christian family. Through finding family photos and documents, collecting oral histories, and re evaluating my own perceptions, I am slowly reconstructing a world that with the process of assimilation and the passage of time had become anonymous.

With the making of the *Sólo una Sombra?* (Only a Shadow?) images, I wander into a world where silence is refuge: Persecuted in both France and Poland during World War II, my maternal family had no alternative but to become invisible. Through my work I begin to unearth the lingering echoes of those previously silenced voices, hoping to regenerate them from burned ash into glimmering light.

My photographic work, then, is a process of re encounter, synthesis, and re creation. Through it, past and present become interlaced in a renewed configuration: The Palestinian desert and Eastern European ash sift, shift, and blend in the volcanic sands of El Salvador to form the texture of the path on which I define and express my experience.

VOLCÁN DE IZALCO, AMÉN (IZALCO VOLCANO, AMEN)

And I was walking. I always knew I would come here one day . . . to my *terruño*—my native soil of volcanic sand, ash, and childhood memories in

231

Volcán de Izalco, amén (Izalco Volcano, amen), 1995–96, from *Todos los santos*. Gelatin silver print, 14″ × 18″. Photo courtesy of Muriel Hasbun.

El Salvador. I photographed the Volcano Izalco, also called the Lighthouse of the Pacific, and I saw it reciting a prayer in Arabic that my great-grandfather Constantino—-Kostas—-had written in his beautiful calligraphy: . . . *in the blissful and eternal happiness of Heaven, in the name of the pure and immaculate Mother of True Light, and all the martyrs and saints, amen.*

LA DOLOROSA (LADY OF SORROWS)

Last year, when I visited El Salvador, I met Aunt Afife for the first time. She is now ninety two. She showed me many photographs her husband Jacobo—Yacoub—had made. When we saw the photo of Jamilleh, aunt Afife told me Jamilleh had suffered a lot; she had lost her husband seven months after they were married, and later she also lost her son. Jamilleh was like a *dolorosa*—a lady of sorrows.

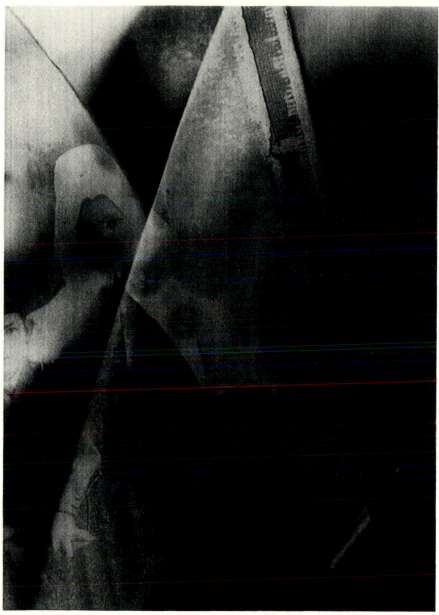

La Dolorosa (Lady of Sorrows), 1995, from *Todos los santos*. Selenium/polytone silver print, 18″ × 13″. Photo courtesy of Muriel Hasbun.

Graecos Schismaticos, 1995–96, from *Todos los santos*. Polytone gelatin silver print, 14″ × 18″. Photo courtesy of Muriel Hasbun.

GRAECOS SCHISMATICOS

I said to my father, Ah so then you were orthodox! What a surprise when I realized that my grandmother Elena had two baptismal certificates, both from the Church of Saint Catherine in Bethlehem The original, from 1907, is from the Greek Orthodox part of the church. The second one was issued fifteen years later by the Latin, or Roman Catholic, part of the church. My great-grandparents must have requested the second certificate so Mama Nena could marry my grandfather Elías in the Catholic Church in El Salvador . . . At that moment they became *graecos schismaticos* . . .

ESTER'S POEMS

When I visited Ester she showed me a little book, made with papers sewn together by a string from Bergen-Belsen. She said, "When I was in concen-

Ester's Poems, 1994, from *¿Sóla una sombra?*, Gelatin silver print, 13.5″ × 17.5″. Photo courtesy of Muriel Hasbun.

tration camp I get from a German a pen, a little pen and a little paper." The book was filled with words in Polish, indescifrable to me, but once it pages had been opened—"Where are you Mommy?"—everything became so clear. . . . Ester's poems were words of sustenance . . .

AUTHOR BIOGRAPHY

Muriel H. Hasbun was born in El Salvador in 1961. While pursuing an M.F.A. in photography at George Washington University (1989), she studied with Ray K. Metzker for a year; she received a B.A. in French Literature from Georgetown University in 1983. She has received numerous awards, including three Individual Artist Fellowships from the D.C. Commission on the Arts (1991, 1994, 1996). Hasbun has held solo and group shows throughout the United States, Europe, and Latin America, including the Rencontres Internationales de la Photographie, Arles, France, in 1998. Her work is exhibited in the collections of the Art Museum of the Americas; the George Washington University; Bert Hartkamp, Amsterdam; Bibliothèque Nationale, Paris; and Galería el laberinto, San Salvador. Hasbun teaches photography at the Corcoran School of Art and at George Washington University and has offered youth and family workshops for the Smithsonian, the Latin American Youth Center, and Arlington County, Virginia. She works and resides in Washington, D.C. Her photographs can be seen at Galería el Laberinto, San Salvador, and on the Internet at www.zonezero.com.

29

never look down in Chinatown

Ann Suni Shin

I refuse to smell the garbage as I walk down Chinatown,
chicken wings and fish skeletons, soft rotting greens.
early morning garbage trucks come and go, leaving
only the smell. you grow used to it
grow blind the way mold spreads quietly
on the underside of fruit.

at Kim Moon there are butter buns, coconut buns,
winter melon, moon cakes, orange tiles, gold lettering
but all I can see is rotting fruit and meat.
how many lifetimes in these backalley kitchens?
women hunch over steel basins piled with bok choy.

and the sidewalks are relentless.
people crowding for morning transactions
we jostle, pressing so close
the refuse, the stains, our own faces
are lost in the movement of all people.

Chinatown. somewhere between old world and new
we slipped from the glinting surface, slipped into disguise
and now these market greens, this wickerware
open crates of fish, these are the national colours.

which part of Asia were you from anyway?
not that it matters, like thronging seagulls
we peck at the sidewalk and fly off, necks outstretched
for elsewhere.

there's fish thawing in some young couple's kitchen
23 stories up in a Bay Street condominium.

their tap water runs over fish scales and bones,
talismans of a history they've not quite outgrown
things simply grow over.

AUTHOR BIOGRAPHY

Born and raised in Canada, Ann Suni Shin is a writer and composer based in Toronto. Her latest publication of poetry, Crossroads Cant, *is about the immigrant experience. She is working on a manuscript titled* Many Words for Home. *Her sound compositions have been heard on CBC Radio, and her writing can be found in magazines and anthologies in Canada and the United States.*

30

Race Markers Transgressors: Mapping a Racial Kaleidoscope within an (Im)migrant Landscape

Naheed Islam

> What is termed "Black", "Hispanic" or "Oriental" by those in power to describe one human being's "racial background" in a particular setting can have little historical or practical meaning within another social formation which is also racially stratified, but in a different manner. Since so many Americans view the world through the prism of permanent racial categories, it is difficult to convey the idea that radically different ethnic groups may have a roughly identical "racial identity" imposed on them.
>
> Manning Marable (1993: 114), Mapping the Landscape

This is a story of transgressions, an (im)migrant exploration into the social constructions of race and the development of racial*ized* consciousness within the landscape of the U.S. I am a dark-brown skinned Bangladeshi woman, and in different spaces and points of time, in the United States I have been classified as black[1], mulatta, African, Indian, Latina, a generic "foreign"/ other, and white. These categories are not a part of my self-identification or historical experiences. But a schemata of racialized ideology[2] informed my viewers of both the categories to place me in and the boundaries of social codes, behavior, and position those categories carry. These categories are considered real, self-evident[3] (Outlaw 1990) and they bear consequences in everyday interactions. Although I was viewed as belonging to different racial categories, I did not claim to fully understand or replicate the historical experience and location of those groups into which I was thrust. I glimpsed some of the consequences of those boundaries, the particular forms of racism faced by middle-class women (of color), and I developed a racialized consciousness and identity. My interpretation of these events was shaped by my social location and the political, historical, and cultural information I had access to at that time. I utilize these narratives of shifts and insights to locate South Asians[4] within the racialized landscape of the United States.

As immigrants we are confronted with a racially stratified system within which we must negotiate our position. Our bodies are a particular marker within its slippery terrain of racial signification. This marker is linked to a historically specific, connected, and shifting labyrinth of ideological and material contexts. Within this racial order South Asians find themselves negotiating multiple racial categories marked by their bodies, what adorns their bodies, what their bodies give off, their nationality or ethnicity, and different histories of encounters with specific groups. The geography and specificity of the underpinnings of contact shape the available racial positioning and its negotiations for South Asians in America.

The first part of this paper describes two such moments of negotiation from my personal history in order to examine our bodies as markers, the racial ideology within which they are read, the particularities of racial categories, and the everyday repercussions of racial categorie. The second part of the paper extends the analysis to a larger context of racial politics and its relationship to South Asian racial identity.

RACIAL MARKERS AND TRANSGRESSIONS

A Small Town in the Midwest

I came from Bangladesh to a Midwestern campus in 1984, a full scholarship and some work-study money in hand (read poor). The small private university had predominantly white, wealthy students, with a small percentage of non-white foreign students (mostly male) and an even smaller percentage of black students. As I walked around campus with other lost students I began to get lessons about my *"foreignness"*, starting with a white roommate's surprise and discomfort on seeing the foreign-alien being she had to share her space with for a year. (We "got along" for a semester, then she moved out.) I began looking for others who felt equally alienated. On the second day of drifting around I ran into an orientation for foreign students. I was not informed of any of the Foreign student activities because I was registered as an American student. I was born in the United States; my birthplace marked my official citizenship. But my meeting with the distinct and segregated foreign community sealed my place[5] within the campus for the next four years.

During my years at the school, the Black Student Center was broken into and portraits of Malcolm X and Martin Luther King were defaced with the word "nigger", a cross was burned in front of a house, and signs to educate about and protest against apartheid in South Africa were ripped up. A few years before my arrival manure had been dumped at the entrance of the Black Student Center. A few meetings were organized, and a forum was created for discussion, but participation was slim, and ultimately students of color, particularly black and African, lived amidst collegiate congeniality with a thinly veiled reminder of a racial order. Segregated communities of black, African, and non-white foreign students—with overlapping friendships—formed enclaves for these students.

I was racialized into the categories of foreign and colored/black in two distinct communities on and off campus. The foreign category was invoked mostly within the small campus community. Foreign students were informants about faraway places, they added color to campus life and were seen as academic high achievers (model-foreign-minority). The campus administration, faculty, and staff shared a friendly and supportive relationship with foreign students. In town, when I walked with the usual diverse group of foreign students, our individual identities were merged into a collective amorphous foreignness. When I walked into stores alone, I faced the cold stares of the store owners. Their eyes monitored my every move around the store and made me invisible when I required assistance or service. In the years to follow I would have brief conversations with some townspeople and they would say, "Oh! You are foreign, I thought you were mulatto/mixed race/a colored girl [variations that were used], you speak English quite well for a foreigner." When I told them I was from Bangladesh most of them did not know where it was and many thought it was in Africa.

Once when I was walking down the small town sidewalk two white men in their thirties or forties, driving by in their big old American car, screamed "get out of town you nigger." I remember a chill went down my spine and I kept walking. The next time it happened I had time to anticipate it. I learned to cringe before it came and to keep walking as the perpetrators drove by jeering. At the time these incidents took place I knew the words were derogatory; I had heard them before, but I never knew their history or what they signified. But it became clear that being categorized as foreign and black carried specific consequences in both the town and campus communities.

Mulatta/black/generic-other/foreign student/Indian/Bangladeshi were used interchangeably to refer to me in different social settings. There appeared to be three main racialized categories in this rural Midwestern town, white, black and non-white foreign. I tried to make sense of this whirlwind of racialized experiences. I started to learn about the historical roots of racial terms and the history of the nation-state and its ideologies. While being called the same epitaphs did not create an instant bond with black students or an understanding of each other's positions, it did facilitate my own initiative to learn more about the racial politics of the U.S. and organize against it. A racialized and feminist analysis became an inextricable element of this politicization. A part of this process was augmented by a shift in subject position created during migration by the loss of class, ethnic, and religious privilege and through the inscription of racial markers in the United States. Migration can open space for re-marking boundaries of self, identity, and community. Deliberate and unanticipated transgressions can produce a transformed consciousness.

URBAN CALIFORNIA

After my four-year initiation in Midwestern racial politics, I moved to graduate school at Berkeley. The first pleasurable sights were the diverse groups, the lack of hypervisibility, and the absence of the open hostilities of rural, all-white middle-American towns. I had arrived with a determination to create the (political) community that I hungered for. I flaunted my ethnic markers through my clothes and makeup, wearing them as war paint to force visibility, yet I enjoyed being invisible as part of a larger community of color. In this urban space people were more aware of the differentiation of categories, they were hyperracialized. The markers of the body were scrutinized for differences and were placed within a more elaborate hierarchy. At Berkeley I became codified as "Indian-South Asian,"[6] a familiar category in this region. For the most part, South Asians in northern California were visible as professionals and were included within the Asian model minority stereotype.

I carved out my space within multiracial and multinational communities. During my second year at Berkeley my closest friend and scholar France Winddance Twine, a black American woman,[7] and I decided that in our struggles to overcome the many barriers to understanding each other's experiences and building coalitions I would share one of her spaces. France usually had her hair braided at Clorenza's apartment in Oakland, and she decided that I would do the same. France explained to Clorenza that she wanted her Asian sister to look like her. Clorenza voiced no questions about my reasons for wanting the braids and welcomed me into the warmth of her home.

France left, and I got comfortable for the lengthy process. Clorenza had lots of videos and food at hand. Amid movie watching, periods of silence, and sharing stories of our families, I discovered that Clorenza's grandmother was part Asian Indian. Upon examining an old black-and-white photograph we realized that I resembled her grandmother. Because of the wide range of phenotypes and color diversity within the U.S. black community, I have been frequently coded as black. But with Clorenza's help I was taking on a marker that would deliberately inscribe me within a black category. The politics of hair[8] is critical to the experience of black women in America, and I was peeking into that space. Skin color, facial features, and hair texture are criteria of beauty that are used to control the images of women and to denigrate them

(Hill-Collins 1990). Black women have been punished for resisting the dominant images. Braiding, relaxing, hot curls, and thick grease are some of the methods used by black women as cultural practices, strategies of accommodation, and resistance against the controlling images.

Initially, I was preoccupied with the feel of seventy tight braids on my head. I spent an uncomfortable night trying to find a position to lay my head and was unprepared for the weeks that followed. Friends and acquaintances would pass by and not recognize me. It was amusing at first, almost like being in disguise. But it slowly sunk in that in the eyes of the viewer I had unambiguously shifted categories. Just the day before I had been classified as Indian-South Asian/Foreign and with the zap of Clorenza's creation, I had become a black-African American. After all, I have black skin color and do not have the racial privilege of Bo Derek, who could wear braids, consume the cultural practice, and exoticize it without consequences. I began to experience what I had intellectually and politically recognized—that in everyday interactions, blacks and South Asians are positioned differently.[9] The most critical reason for and consequences of racial stratification are gendered, political, economic, ideological, and structural positionings. These can translate into perceptible interactional repercussions. I was experiencing some of these differences at the level of individual and interpersonal interactions. When I walked into stores and financial institutions, I noticed immediate surveillance. I had not been subjected to the same degree of surveillance when I was classified as an Indian-South Asian woman in California. In settings where a Bangladeshi woman was expected and I arrived instead as a black woman, much discomfort resulted. Braids themselves were considered a political statement, they flaunted blackness and therefore needed to be censured by the violence of erasure and invisibility. Word spread to a few of my college friends that I now had dreadlocks, and I became a subject of amusement. What is she trying to be? Why is she choosing this particular signifier?

As I wore this marker I began to scrutinize the racialized views of different communities, the appropriateness and consequences of choosing a cultural marker that coded me into the particular political identity and community of black American. For example, when I had braids most blacks thought I was African. They picked up on my body language and verbal cues and coded me outside of an American black identity. I was most often asked if I was Ethiopian. It was unclear what different African or Caribbean American communities thought of me, but whites, Asians, and most other communities coded me as black. As my body traversed the boundaries of socially constructed (racial) categories, Manning Marable's words were taking on an experiential reality. The same markers were interpreted differently or were visible or invisible depending on the viewer's location, the place of encounter, and the sociopolitical context of the interaction. My own experiences could happen because of the particular common sense ideology of race at the time. But if my body can function as a common sense marker for blackness, as well as foreignness, do I then begin to identify myself as black? Wouldn't identifying myself as black inscribe me as an "American"[10] when birth and citizenship cannot? Does this insinuate that the larger Bangladeshi or South Asian groups can "wear" markers of blackness and be absorbed within this category?

I do not identify myself as black in the United States and neither do the Bangladeshi or South Asian communities. As a personal-political stance I recognize that despite experiences of passing for black there are critical differences in the racial location of South Asians and blacks in the United States. An individual's glimpse of difference through one's body is not the same as the larger group being viewed as that category or as having that political identity. South Asians occupy a racialized space between black and white, and they work to maintain it. This non-white space constantly redraws the boundaries of blackness and whiteness and gives racialized meaning to our experiences in the United States. Thus the shifts in racial markers and categories, racial ambiguity, and specificity are related to the location of particular groups within the larger ideological, political, and material context of racial order in the United States.

LOCATING SOUTH ASIANS WITHIN A RACIAL KALEIDOSCOPE

Post-1980 immigrants make up the majority of the Bangladeshi and other South Asian American community. Since the 1965 Immigration Act, Asians have become the fastest-growing minority group in the United States. They are participating in a racial recomposition of major urban centers, making groups like South Asians a part of the majority minority. With increased presence in urban areas, South Asians have also been brought into the arena of national racialized visibility. South Asian immigrants are concentrated mostly in California, New York, and Texas, but growing numbers are dispersed across the United States. Bangladeshis, Indians, Pakistanis, and Sri Lankans are all named South Asian or Indian. Passive "model minority" and "foreigner-with-an-accent" images are becoming prevalent in the media. These images are a method of stratifying growing numbers of non-white groups, a process of racialization and insertion into the national ideology of race. What, then, is the place of South Asians in this racialized landscape?

Viewers' Ambiguity

Bangladeshi scholar Nazli Kibria (1996) discusses her students' reactions to her question, What race are South Asians? Their response amounted to not black, Latino, or white, with some angst over the "not white" category.

One of her students asked, "Aren't Indians Caucasians? . . . . Their features are white; except for their skin color they're basically white." Based on this phenotypical categorization of race, South Asians are marked as foreign and as an ambiguous non-white racial category, says Kibria, but not as Oriental Asian or yellow. Within anthropological literature South Asians have also confounded attempts at neat (pseudo) scientific racial categories. As James Davis (1991) notes, Kroeber's racial criteria became skewed by the "dark-skinned people of India, Pakistan, Bangladesh and some contiguous areas." (Davis 1991: 19). They are both Caucasoid and dark skinned (Davis 1991; Okihiro 1994; Mazumdar 1989; Kibria 1996; Fisher 1980). A National Opinion Research Center survey in 1978 also shows the general ambiguity of the racial categorization of Asian Indians. Eleven percent of respondents said they thought Asian Indians were white, 15 percent said they were brown, 38 percent said they were "other" and 13 percent said they did not know how to classify them.

During discussions in a sociology class about the social construction of race, I informed the students that my Texan birth certificate gave my race as white; I paused for their reaction. One student said, "Well Naheed, I don't understand. If you are really white then why don't you want to accept that you are?" The rest of the class burst into laughter. One student believes indelibly in the scientific categorizations of race, and others look at the markers of race and laugh at the ludicrous idea that I could be classified as white. Yet neither would have mistaken me for white in an encounter on the street or contested that I do not have access to "white" privileges. This "common sense"[10] viewing of race places South Asians within multiple, contested, historically contingent racial categories.

Early History: Confronting Racial Categories

The first Indians were sighted in Salem, Massachussets, in 1790. During this time a few Indians were enslaved; others were indentured servants who married black women and lived within the black community. There are few records of their lives. Later immigrants arrived in New York and California, also in very small numbers. Punjabi Sikhs and Muslims were the largest Indian community in the early years (1880–1930) (Leonard 1992). They were mostly agricultural workers and were viewed as foreign and Hindu outsiders; sometimes they were also viewed as white. A few students were dispersed around the United States with a concentration in New York, Washington, Oregon, and California.

Residential segregation, antimiscegenation laws, and legislated and institutionalized racial discrimination in daily life and employment made up the sociopolitical context within which most early immigrants lived. Indians and other Asians faced exclusion acts that denied them entry into the United

States and U.S. citizenship. Citizenship was defined in 1790 as a right for whites only; by 1870 blacks were granted citizenship with restricted rights.

During the period 1915-1965, Indians—including a few prominent Bengalis—fought the battles for immigration, citizenship, and civil rights. They were trying to gain or retain citizenship based on the "fact" that Indians are Caucasian and are therefore white. Taraknath Das was one of these Bengali Indian political activists who allied themselves with anticolonial struggles, the Irish political movement, and a pan-Aryan organization and fought the courts for U.S. citizenship. Although Indians were assigned to the Caucasian-white category for a period, the courts and Legislature eventually decreed—with pressure from white workers and other political interests—that although South Asians may be Caucasian they were/are not white. Therefore they were denied citizenship until the Luce Cellar Bill of 1946.

Stories from this time point to other alliances and racial consciousness, narratives omitted from history books. Kumar Goshal[12] was one such activist who was also involved in anticolonial struggles. He supported the struggles of minorities and poor people within the United States. Goshal developed relationships with the American left and with black intellectuals such as Paul Robeson and W.E.B. Dubios. He wrote for the *National Guardian* (a leftist journal). During an exchange with the editors of the *Guardian*, Goshal made a poignant point of his affiliations and location in the United States. In 1952, the *Guardian* felt pressure to hire someone "black" so it hired a "black"African American writer. Goshal came to the office of the *Guardian* agitated because as a regular contributor he had been promised the next available paid permanent position. When he was informed that the publication had needed to hire a "black" person, Goshal argued, "Am I not a man of color?" Although this claim needs further examination, the declaration of being a racial minority and nonwhite was a significant public stance by a Bengali-Indian-South Asian activist at a time when black and white were the dominant racial categories.

There are ignored and erased histories that need to be excavated in order to understand the historical shifts of South Asian racial classification, political strategies, alliances, and community building in the United States. At this time there were Indians/Bangladeshis who were married to black, Mexican, and Native American women. Because of the dearth of such narratives, it is unclear what racial identity was being developed by these early South Asian immigrants, but it is apparent that there were diverse groups and affiliations. Bengali men who married black women between 1920–1930 established themselves within the black community. Men who married Mexican women appear to have defined the Indian-Bangladeshi communities until immigrant men were able to return home and bring back wives; these families then slowly defined the communities.

Although there were overlapping relationships among these three types of families and communities, antimiscegenation and immigration laws, as well as racial politics, defined the content of and relationship among these communities. The critical point is that these immigrants had to contend with a racial order; in doing so, they claimed and contested particular racial categories. They were viewed as black, white, and foreign. They were slowly relegated to, and articulated their experiences and location within, a racially marked nonwhite space that is neither black nor white yet informed by both.

Nonwhite (But Not Black)

> The implicit and sometimes explicit devaluing of dark skin is an issue that confronts most South Asians. Internalized racism and cross racial hostility is often expressed by South Asians of varying skin colour, hair types and eye colour. In India, advertisements encourage women and men to use "Fair and Lovely" skin creme, and bleaches, and strong henna in their hair to add an auburn touch. Marriage ads still want Aryan-looking men and women—i.e., fair and sometimes tall (in the case of males). Internationally throughout the diaspora, different degrees of this internalized racism persist. One of my dark skinned uncles (who would probably pass as Black) warned me about the "niggers" in Brooklyn. Some South Asians, of varying class backgrounds, who settle in the United States often don't want to be associated with "those blacks," yet they have a very good chance of physically being mistaken for black folk. (Bhaskaran 1993: 198)

I agree with Bhaskaran and other scholars (Mazumdar, Rajgopal) who point out that South Asians distance themselves from the category black and that we learn and reproduce many of the imageries of blacks through a colonial legacy and the dominant U.S. racial ideology. This negation of blackness is critical to the formation of racial identity, the maintenance of racial order, and an understanding of racial politics in the U.S. Just as loving blackness is a form of resistance (bell hooks), negating blackness can be an act of acceptance of or collusion with a racist order. But this black-white racial paradigm is unable to explain and give meaning to the racial complexities of the U.S. racial order. Although there is explicit distancing from "black" as a category of identification, few immigrant Bangladeshis-South Asians are viewed as black in today's multiethnic urban setting.

South Asians are marked as foreign and as an ambiguous nonwhite racial category (Kibria 1996). The system of differentiation, codes, and markers picks up on their clothing, body language, and language skills and defines these immigrant groups as separate from blacks in the same urban space. During my dissertation research in Los Angeles I have found that in that multiethnic city Bangladeshis are mostly mistaken for Mexicans,[13] Indian, and South or Southeast Asian. South Asians never mentioned the category black, possibly as a strategy of distancing themselves from the category and possibly because the category is rarely imposed on them. South Asians are a visible category of diverse nonwhites.

Hills people from southern Bangladesh described how they are often seen as Southeast or East Asian (read Mongoloid) by other Bangladeshis as well as by different groups in the United States. They may encounter nonhills people from Bangladesh and hear them speak in Bengali or other local dialects, and start a conversation. They are told that one would never have thought that they were Bangladeshi if they had not spoken the same language or claimed or evoked that nationality. Therefore, in the racialized context of the United States, those who in Bangladesh would have been identified as a distinct ethnic group separated by religion, language, and unequal civil rights take on a different racial category. Bangladeshis as well as other South Asians are diverse groups that occupy contradictory and heterogeneous racial categories.

A Bangladeshi woman in Los Angeles spoke to me with consternation about the racialized verbal violence her daughter was facing in her elementary school. She said her daughter was shunned by the other children because they said she was too dark; they called her dirty. I asked her about the background of these children, and she said they were predominantly Korean. During the Gulf crisis and the Oklahoma City bombing, people with Arabic or Persian names (read Muslim), including those of South Asian descent, got harassed by whites and blacks. They were called "Arab" (now used synonymously with) terrorists, and they faced physical and verbal violence.

There are also instances in which the specificity of ethnic origins is racialized. The Dot Busters[14] in New Jersey were particular about their Asian Indian targets. The *bindi* (so called dot) was the gendered marker used to identify Asian Indians. Not all of the perpetrators of racial terrorism against Asian Indians there were white. Today's urban setting provides a much more complex racial battleground. Depending on the demography and geography of groups and interactions in the social, political, and economic arenas, communities face racially marked overlapping, different, and specific relationships.

Growing class differences within Bangladeshi communities create particular racialized interactions with other communities. Professional Bangladeshis live mostly in suburbs and interact with other Bangladeshis, other Asians, and whites; they have little everyday interaction with middle- or working-class blacks and Latinos-Chicanos. Working class Bangladeshis, on the other hand, live in the same or adjacent neighborhoods as working class Latino, Chicano (referred to as Spanish or Hispanic), black, and Asian communities. They work at liquor stores; as gas station attendants, security guards, and taxi drivers; and at other late-night jobs. Their interactions occur within economically depressed minority neighborhoods. Some violent confrontations at the workplace and in the neighborhoods further exacerbates racial tension within all groups. Precarious economic conditions and a racialized discourse of nationality, belonging, social injustice, and rights set the stage for this growing schism between different communities.

Second-generation South Asians are socialized and function within the U.S. racial ideology (Kibria 1996, and Sethi 1994). Although more specific studies on racial identities within this group are needed, I will make some broad generalizations based on my interactions with youth groups. There appears to be a trend among children of middle-class and professional parents to create Indian-South Asian identity-based organizations on college campuses. There is also a move to consolidate the category *South Asian*. Whereas Indians remain the numerical majority and are in control of these organizations, the umbrella category of South Asian subsumes other nationalities and creates a broader base for political representation. An ethnic-regional category is utilized to negotiate racial politics. Although the category is imbued with racial discourse, it attempts to circumvent the black-white racial polarity.

But some children from working-class backgrounds who live in multiracial communities of color seem to blur or transgress these boundaries. For example, many Bangladeshi high school youth in Los Angeles have joined Latino groups. They found themselves without allies in their schools and formed an alliance with Latino youth. They speak fluent Spanish and wear clothing and markers that are shared by Latino youth; and some even function as Latinos within gangs. Although more research needs to be done about how Bangladeshi youth have created this space, how they are viewed by other Latinos, and how they negotiate the cultural messages from within their households, it is clear that interesting transgressions are taking place. Many such moments are occurring within youth music and culture. Of course, one cannot idealize or glorify these transgressions. These deliberate crossings of racial and ethnic categories within new urban settings are used here to deconstruct the essentialist and stable notions of those identities. These transgressions and new racial faultlines show that we need to develop a better understanding of racialized relationships within communities of color than the older simplified frame of "we wanna be white" and "we're not black." We must examine how blackness-whiteness and factors such as class, ethnicity, religion, and gender also give meaning to racialization to develop an analysis of the new racial formation in the U.S.

RE-VIEWING THE MAP

In such nations as the United States and South Africa, in which race is the important calculus of social identity, our interactions with other individuals are influenced, whether we admit it or not, by a racial identity that we attribute to others and ourselves. We perceive this identity as reflected in tangible and easily

recognized biophysical characteristics. Indeed the very existence of physical differences among populations is accepted as concrete evidence of race. We have
been conditioned to respond automatically to the presence of certain varying
physical features as indicators of race and the differences race connotes.
(Smedley 1993, 1)

"Race and racism serve as a structuring principle for national process, in
terms of defining both the boundaries of the nation and the constituents of
national identity"(Cashmore 1992). In the United States race has defined inclusion in and exclusion from entrance, citizenship, civilrights, and political
rights. Race, seen as self-evident categories, maintains boundaries based
on physiology and distinguishes, classifies, justifies, and obscures social
positioning.

South Asian immigrants have been classified as white, their whiteness was
later retracted. They have been viewed as colored, black, Mexican, East
Asian, and nonwhite. These categorizations have had repercussions for their
access to employment, housing, and other civil and political rights. My narratives of transgressing racial boundaries are limited in their ability to explain
and understand these multiple locations and their consequences. But I utilize
them to illustrate the slippery and unstable nature of racial categorization and
to raise questions about the boundaries of nationality, race, and identity.

Bodies can transgress racial boundaries. The viewer and the viewed interact in everyday settings based on the complex and transforming ideology of
common sense and their material context. Categories leak, but their boundaries are constantly surveiled and renegotiated. Transgressors are made aware
of the psychological and economic wages of their crossing. South Asians can
mark multiple racial locations; these locations are inscribed within the history
of their exclusion from entry, citizenship, and rights and their classification
as immigrants, aliens, and racial other. Negotiating their exclusion from
whiteness and rejection of blackness, they attempt to contain themselves
within a nonwhite space. Although the engagement with the bipolarity of
U.S. racial ideology is critical, it can obscure the transformation and emer-
gence of a new racial formation.

Immigrants form new and salient relationships in racially recomposed
urban centers. The racialized identities and alliances of immigrant groups are
a contested terrain. Immigrants (are made to) recognize this salience of race,
of racial politics in U.S. society, and they negotiate and contest their location
within a racialized society. And race is one component of other critical vari-
ables such as immigration status, nationality and citizenship, religion, gender,
and class that shape this negotiation and contestation. Assumptions about
self-evident possibilities of alliances between racial minorities are not based
on an examination of this complexity. A racial order hints at a racial hierarchy
and differences in power within and across relationships. If we hope to under-

stand these new and salient relationships and interactions, we must examine what informs them. We can then locate the possibilities and basis on which alliances between groups could be made in order to organize toward an anti-racist social movement.

NOTES

1. The category black refers to a historically specific and geographically bounded notion that anyone with any African ancestry is black in the United States—the One-Drop Rule.

2. The term *everyday ideology* is used to mean common sense translations of national ideology and racial formations.

3. Outlaw and others have discussed the social construction of race. As he summarizes, "For most of us that there are different races of people is one of the most obvious features of our social worlds. The term 'race' is a vehicle for notions deployed in the organization of these worlds in our encounters with persons who are significantly different from us, particularly in terms of physical features (skin color and other anatomical features). Often combined with these, when they are different with respect to language, behavior, ideas, and other 'cultural' matters . . . we are likewise constantly reinforced in our assumption that 'race' is self-evident" (Outlaw 1990: 58).

4. South Asia is a term that refers to the nation-states of India, Pakistan, Bangladesh, Sri Lanka, Nepal, Bhutan, sometimes Maldives, and Afghanistan. But it is usually used to signify India/n. Bangladesh, Pakistan, and India were "unified" India until 1947, at which point India was divided into Pakistan, (East and West) and India. Pakistan was divided again in 1971 to form the states of Bangladesh and Pakistan. Therefore, Bangladesh, Pakistan, and India are referred to as India before 1947. I specify the national demarcations whenever possible.

5. Although I became active in the foreign community, my location within it was complex. There were multiple communities based on gender and class, ethnic, religious, regional, and national backgrounds, and individual relationships—which formed some of the internal dynamics of the community—overlapped.

6. Indian and South Asian are used interchangeably. The differences between these national identities are not distinguished, and Indian becomes the category for everyone. Therefore I use Indian-South Asian in this section to signify the category one is placed in, not as a category of self-identification.

7. France Winddance Twine self-identifies as a black American and an Indian. Twine is an enrolled member of the Creek (Muscogee) Nation of Oklahoma.

8. Maya Angelou, Paulette Caldwell (1994), Patricia Hill-Collins (1990), and France Winddance Twine (Twine, Warren, and Fernandiz 1991) are some black feminist scholars who deal with the politics of hair within the black community.

9. Here I am referring to everyday interactions only. Further explorations of class and racial stratification are beyond the scope of this paper.

10. The reification of *American* is also racialized. The norm of American is viewed as white-black is included within its boundaries, albeit in a contentious relationship.

11. Here I refer to Gramsci's concept of organic ideology found in common sense.

Gramsci (1971) describes common sense as a constantly transforming folklore that enriches itself with "scientific ideas and philosophic options which have entered everyday life."

12. The biography of Goshal is documented by Leonard A. Gordon (1989).

13. Bangladeshis tend not to distinguish between Latinos and Chicanos. They usually use the terms *Hispanic, Spanish,* and *Mexican* interchangeably. And although Bangladeshis consider themselves to be Indian and have social and political organizations separate from the many Indian communities, it is commonly accepted that they are Indian in the eyes of foreigners (read Americans and all non-Bangladeshis).

14. In early 1986 Asian Indians in New Jersey were faced with varied forms of racial terrorism. Their houses and businesses were vandalized, and covered with graffiti that involved racial slurs, women's saris were pulled, and men and women were struck, harassed, and assaulted. A twenty-eight-year-old man was beaten into a coma, and another was killed. A group calling itself Dot Busters wrote to the *Jersey Journal* and claimed responsibility. The dot was a reference to the adornment women wore on their foreheads.

REFERENCES

Allen, Theodore W. *The Invention of the White Race*. London: Verso, 1994.

Almaguer, Tomas. *Racial Faultlines*. Berkeley: University of California Press, 1995.

Anthias, Floya, and Nira Yuval-Davis. *Racialized Boundaries: Race, Nation, Gender, Colour, Class and the Anti-Racist Struggle*. New York: Routledge, 1992.

Bhaskaran, Suparna. "Physical Subjectivity and the Risk of Essentialism." In *Our Feet Walk the Sky: Women of the South Asian Diaspora*, ed. The Women of South Asian Descent Collective. San Francisco: Aunt Lute Foundation, 1993.

Caldwell, Paulette M. "A Hair Piece." In *Life Notes: Personal Writings by Contemporary Black Women*, ed. Patricia Bell-Scott. New York: W. W. Norton, 1994.

Cashmore, Ellis. "Introductory Comments." In *Racialized Boundaries: Race, Nation, Gender, Colour, Class and the Anti-Racist Struggle*, ed. Floya Anthias and Nira Yuval-Davis. New York: Routledge, 1992.

Davis, James F. *Who Is Black? One Nation's Definition*. University Park: Pennsylvania State University Press, 1991.

Fisher, Maxine. *The Indians of New York City*. New Delhi: India Heritage, 1980.

Frankenberg, Ruth. *White Women, Race Matters: The Social Construction of Whiteness*. Minneapolis: University of Minnesota Press, 1993.

Gordon, Leonard A. "Bridging India and America: The Art and Politics of Kumar Goshal." *Amerasia Journal* 15, 2 (1989): 68-88.

Gramsci, Antonio. *Selections from the Prison Notebooks of Antonio Gramsci*, eds. and translators Quintin Hoare and Geoffrey Nowell Smith. New York: International Publishers, 1971.

Hall, Stuart. "Race: Articulation and Societies Structured in Dominance." In *Sociological Theories: Race and Colonisation*. Paris: UNESCO, 1980.

———. "New Ethnicities." In *Race Culture and Difference*, ed. James Donald and Ali Rattans. London: Sage, 1992.

Hill-Collins, Patricia. *Black Feminist Thought: Knowledge, Consciousness and the Politics of Empowerment*. New York: Routledge, 1990.

hooks, bell. *Black Looks: Race and Representation*. Boston: South End, 1992.

Ignatiev, Noel. *How the Irish Became White*. London: Routledge, 1996.

Jensen, Joan M. *Passage from India: Asian Indian Immigrants in North America*. New Haven: Yale University Press, 1988.

Kibria, Nazli. "Not Asian, Black, or White? Reflections on South Asian American Racial Identity." *Amerasia Journal* 22, 2 (1996): 77–86.

Kroeber, Alfred L. *Anthropology*. New York: Harcourt, Brace and Company, 1948.

Leonard, Karen Isaksen. *Making Ethnic Choices: California's Punjabi Mexican Americans*. Philadelphia: Temple University Press, 1992.

Marable, Manning. "Beyond Racial Identity Politics: Towards a Liberation Theory for Multicultural Democracy." *Race and Class* 35 (July–September 1993): 113–129.

Mazumdar, Sucheta. "Race and Racism: South Asians in the United States." In *Frontiers of Asian American Studies*, ed. Gail M. Nomura, Russell Endo, Stephen H. Sumida, and Russell C. Long. Pullman: Washington State University Press, 1989.

Mohanty, Chandra. "Defining Genealogies: Feminist Reflections on Being South Asian in North America." In *Our Feet Walk the Sky: Women of the South Asian Diaspora*, ed. The Women of South Asian Descent Collective. San Francisco: Aunt Lute Foundation, 1993.

"New Ethnicities." In *Race Culture and Difference*, ed. James Donald and Ali Rattansi. London: Sage, 1992.

Okihiro, Gary Y. *Margins and Mainstreams: Asians in American History and Culture*. Seattle: University of Washington Press, 1994.

Omi, Michael, and Howard Winant. *Racial Formation in the United States*. New York: Routledge, 1986.

Outlaw, Lucius. "Toward a Critical Theory of Race." In *Anatomy of Racism*, ed. David Theo Goldberg. Minneapolis: University of Minnesota Press, 1990.

Roediger, David. *The Wages of Whiteness: Race and the Making of the American Working Class*. London: Verso, 1991.

Sacks, Karen Brodkin. "How Did Jews Become White Folks?" In *Race*, ed. Steven Gregory and Roger Sanjek. New Brunswick: Rutgers University Press, 1994.

Schiller, Nina Glick, Linda Basch, and Cristina Blanc-Szanton. *Towards a Transnational Perspective on Migration: Race, Class, Ethnicity, and Nationalism Reconsidered*. Published by the New York Academy of Sciences, 645, 1992.

Sethi, Rita Chaudhry. "Smells Like Racism: A Plan for Organizing Against Anti-Asian Bias." In *The State of Asian American Activism*, ed. Karin Aguilar-San Juan. Boston: South End, 1994.

Smedley, Audrey. *Race in North America: Origins and Evolution of a Worldview*. Boulder: Westview, 1993.

The State of Asian American Activism and Resistance in the 1990's, ed. Karin Aguilar San-Juan. Boston: South End, 1994.

Stuart, Alan. "Fear of a Black Planet: Race Identity Politics and Common Sense." *Socialist Review* 3 + 4 (1991).

Twine, Frances Winddance, Jonathan Warren, and Francisco Fernandiz. *Just Black? Mult-Racial Identity in the U.S.* New York: Filmmakers Library, 1991.

AUTHOR BIOGRAPHY

Naheed Islam is a Ph.D. candidate in sociology at the University of California at Berkeley. Her works examine the intersections of race, ethnicity, class, gender, and immigration. She is working on the history of Bangladeshi immigration to Los Angeles. Her next project is a comparative study of Bangladeshis in the United States and the United Kingdom.

31

Upon Hearing Beverly Glen Copeland and "Paki Go Home"

Himani Bannerji

LAST NIGHT SHE DRUMMED ME AFRICA

and brought darkness stars
and the wet greenery of the night forest
into this prison of stone
civilization of Greece and Rome
the England of Hawkins and Victoria
fell from us
a heap of soiled clothes
discarded in the new night of history
wind blew from the savannahs
from the clear scent of the waterfalls
southern plantations opened their gates
and the vision of a black mother child in arms
framed by the circle of a dim light
and the furrowed face of a man
intent on fathoming the dark

burst into flames
broke chains
fists fires and fleeting forms
into the night
agitation
cries of victory
yet the centre the still centre
the still torso of the drummer
roosted like a palm tree
into the earth and the drum

the form of the world
calling gathering
reminding

last night she drummed me Africa

"Paki Go Home"

1.
3 pm
sunless
winter sleeping in the womb of the afternoon
wondering how to say this
to reason or scream or cry or whisper
or write on the walls
reduced again
cut at the knees, hands chopped, eyes blinded
mouth stopped, voices lost.

fear anger contempt
thin filaments of ice and fire
wire the bodies
my own, of hers, of his,
the young and the old.

And a grenade explodes
in the sunless afternoon
and words run down
like frothy white spit
down her bent head
down the serene parting of her dark hair
as she stands too visible
from home to bus stop to home
raucous, hyena laughter,
"Paki, Go Home!"
2.
the moon covers her face
Pock-marked and anxious
in the withered fingers of the winter trees.
The light of her sadness runs like tears
down the concrete hills, tarmac rivers
and the gullies of the cities.
The wind still carries the secret chuckle
The rustle of canes
as black brown bodies flee into the night
blanched by the salt waters of the moon.

Strange dark fruits on tropical trees
swing in the breeze gently.
3.
Now, and then again
we must organize.
The woman wiping the slur spit
from her face, the child standing
at the edge of the playground silent, stopped
the man twisted in despair,
disabled at the city gates.
Even the child in the womb
must find a voice
sound in unison
organize.
Like a song, like a roar
like a prophecy that changes the world.

To organize, to fight the slaver's dogs,
to find the hand, the foot, the tongue,
the body dismembered
organ by organ rejoined
organized.
Soul breathed in
until she, he,
the young, the old is whole.
Until the hand acts moved by the mind
and the walls, the prisons, the chains of lead or gold
tear, crumble, wither into dust
and the dead bury the dead
until yesterdays never return.

AUTHOR BIOGRAPHY

Himani Bannerji was born in 1942 in Bangladesh, which was then part of preinde-pendence India. She came to Canada in 1969 and teaches social science at York University, Toronto. Her poems, stories, and essays have appeared in literary and academic journals and in anthologies. She has published two collections of poetry, A Separate Sky (1982) *and* Doing Time (1986). *The poems in this chapter were originally published in* The Geography of Voice: Canadian Literature of the South Asian Diaspora, *ed. Diane McGifford (Toronto: TSAR, 1992).*

32

Soho, Southall, Brixton: Chinatown in New York

Jan Lo Shinebourne

SOHO, LONDON

The waiters at the Canton in London's Soho could not place my accent. It was not Southeast Asian, British, or North American. Instead of listening to my order, they listened to my accent and strained to place it. I used to have to repeat the order twice, even thrice. When I was eating I used to catch them looking at me with intense curiosity. However, in ten years they have not asked if I am from China, Hong Kong, Malaysia, Singapore, or the Philippines. Now they accept that I am a woman who likes to come here to eat. Now the head waiter greets me like an old friend, serves me himself, and gives me his warmest smile.

I go to Soho to meet different friends, to catch up on our various interests. We meet at Crank's Restaurant on Great Newport Street because there is no limit to the time they let us spend there, they do not monitor how much we spend drinking just tea and coffee all day. So Soho in London means many things to me, and it is only one of several places in London that bring back my ancestors.

For example, the quality of the ingredients the Canton uses in its cooking reminds me of my grandmother's cooking in old British Guiana. She was Chinese. Her first husband was a man from Kashmir who had died young, then a man from Delhi became her devoted husband. He spoke Hindi, so did she, and so did we. She wore saris he bought her as tokens of his love. Once a week they went to the cinema to watch romantic Indian films and learn the latest love songs by Latamangeshkar. He taught her to cook Indian dishes— where to buy the spices and how and when to use them, to grow all the vegetables herself, to raise her own ducks and chickens. She made delicious duck

258

curry. So as I sit at my table at the Canton, I am a secure child again in British Guiana. I am with my brothers and sisters. We are chasing ducks around our backyard. I hear my grandmother trying to sing like Latamangeshkar in a Guyanese accent. I enjoy the memory of my Delhi-born step-grandfather who was an affectionate man who always remembered to bring a present for each of his step-children and step-grandchildren when he visited.

When I eat roast duck and Chinese greens at the Canton in London, I taste Indian duck in their Chinese duck, I taste Guyanese *calaloo* in Chinese greens. I am in a Guyanese garden in my memory.

SOUTHALL, LONDON

I have a long journey to the Canton so I don't go as often as I would like. It takes thirty to forty-five minutes on London's Picadilly Line. However, Omi's restaurant is local. It takes me ten minutes from my home in west London to drive there. I have eaten at Omi's for as long as I have eaten at the Canton. There is no better Punjabi food in Southall, especially the curried fish, *pilau* rice, and *bhindi*. Guyanese curries are part of the creole diet I grew up with, and they bear little resemblance to Punjabi cooking.

Kuldip first took me there in the early 1980s. He introduced me to the owners—several brothers and their father whose BMWs were always parked in the forecourt. When Kuldip wanted to treat comrades and journalists from the BBC or the national newspapers, he took them to Omi's. It took a couple of months for the penny to drop—they used to smile at me because they thought I was his girlfriend. When I began to turn up alone, I got the same curious, overprotective looks the waiters at the Canton used to give me.

At teatime students from the tertiary college and secondary schools fill the restaurant. They do all the things they can't do at home or on the streets where their elders can see them. They chat up boyfriends and girlfriends. They smoke, they drink beer. They listen to hip-hop, gangster rap, raggae, and jungle on their ghetto blasters. They live in Southall and environs—Punjabis mainly but also Muslims, Somalians, English, Irish, Africans, Caribbeans, Vietnamese, Chinese. I used to teach at the tertiary college; in those days.

At lunchtime it used to be all English—packed with teachers and local government staff. Those were the days of Ken Livingstone's Greater London Council when Southall attracted the White left. It also used to attract the Black and Asian left because it was once a frontline town like Brixton, where the Caribbean community had also fought racists off the streets. In the weekdays and on weekends, large extended Punjabi families come for early dinner. Between lunch, tea, and dinner it is quieter at Omi's. I take my friends then, and we take as long as we like drinking cups of *massala* tea and mopping the gravy and chutney on our plates with the last piece of *chapati* or *tandoori naan*.

In old British Guiana my father traveled a long way to the town for Chinese cooking, although he ran his own eating place. It was divided in two, the cake shop on the left and grocery on the right. On market days the women monopolized the cake shop when they came to cool their thirst on their way home—then the men had to use the grocery. On Saturday mornings the women came to the grocery—then the men had to use the cake shop. In the cane cutting season the whole place was a refuge of cane cutters. In the mornings it was full of workmen wanting cigarettes and loaves of bread and cheese to take to the factory and fields. Father liked the times when the barriers between these groups came down, the times you would find men and women, children and adults not in an exclusive space but talking to each other.

BRIXTON, LONDON

Mother's menu included *fufu*, *metagee*, peas and rice, plantains, yams, cassavas, *eddoes*, *tanya*, breadfruit, pepperpot made with fermented *casareep*, salt fish, salt beef, *konki*. Her menu weaned me off breast milk. She also used it to teach me to cook for myself. Friends come to my table expecting Chinese food. I have to explain that I prefer to eat Chinese and Indian foods at the Canton and Omi's because cooking them does not come as naturally to me as African Guyanese cooking.

I lived in London for over twenty-five years before I found a restaurant with a menu as evocative of my mother's tastes and lifestyle as the Canton's was of my grandmother's and Omi's of my father's. It took so long because I never looked for one. London was famous for its Indian and Chinese restaurants, not Caribbean ones. I cooked my mother's favorite dishes at home for myself, my family, and my friends. Shopping for the ingredients was as integral to their power to evoke the memory of my mother as was cooking them, although she grew everything in her garden. But growing them involved an intricate communal system—seeds, roots, shoots, and the harvest were exchanged between neighbors. When I travel to Finsbury Park, Shepherd's Bush, or Brixton to find the ingredients for my mother's menu, I relive the journeys she and her friends would make *down the road* in search of a better crop of cassava or *tanya* root to bring back to their gardens, replant, and harvest for cooking.

The first time I went to Cafe Jam in Brixton, the friend who took me there had no idea the chef and the menu were Guyanese. We were hungry and it was the nearest restaurant, so we dropped in and made a snap decision to have lunch there. The waitress told us if we were willing to wait she had to go *down the road* to Brixton market to bring in some of the ingredients. When our meal arrived it was cooked in Guyanese style, down to the black cake dessert. Now I eat at Cafe Jam regularly, and I am happy when I have to wait a long time for the ingredients to be brought in from *down the road*.

CHINATOWN, NEW YORK
OCTOBER 10, 1997

Yesterday I was trying to find my way to Chinatown. I had a need to find the red bean cakes my mother used to make. It was one of the few items of Chinese cuisine she had learned to make after she married my father. I asked a young woman the way. As she gave me directions I heard the unmistakable accent of someone from the Dominican Republic. As soon as she had given me directions she said, "You have an English and a Caribbean accent." She wished me a good day and went on her way, waving as she disappeared into the crowd. It reminded me of how Caribbean people have developed the skills of cultural translation. This was an example of tuning our ears to accents, learning to recognize and use them to map our everyday transactions. Without that skill and others, we would have no maps to negotiate with. So, on my way to Chinatown I was reminded by a woman from the Caribbean that I was from the Caribbean even though I was looking for the home my mother's red bean cake symbolized in Chinatown in New York, which I was visiting for the first time.

I got to Chinatown eventually, and as I walked around it struck me how different New York's Chinatown is from London's. For example, my overriding impression here is of the aggressiveness of the competition for space among the tall buildings, cars and trucks, and people. People are dwarfed like ants by tall buildings and wide roads. I missed London's narrow streets, which seem more people friendly. Here I saw people running for their lives; as they crossed the road the drivers were oblivious to their safety. It made me think of Wild West movies, of wagons and horses stampeding through towns while people run to get out of their path. In the communication style of some of the people of Chinatown I saw the inflections of the Wild West too—the macho John Wayne swagger in the way the owners of jewelry shops guard their trays of jewelry in open view of the pavement, daring anyone to a high noon shootout, if necessary, to protect their gold. I saw the Marlon Brando curl of the lips when they speak. I felt lost, far away from home in a Wild West Chinatown.

But I did not give up on my mother's red bean cake. I asked for them in a cake shop. I was shown red bean cakes I had never seen before, but the proprietor and I ended up having a conversation about the differences between the cakes I buy in London's Soho and the cakes on display in his shop. I explained that in London I always got my mother's red bean cakes from Soho.

We were translating to each other the specificities of our different locations by talking about Chinese cakes. Cakes had become a metaphor of home for us both. This gave me the confidence to explore a bit more, to get beyond the John Wayne and Marlon Brando macho barrier guarding the border to New York. And I came home with a bag of food much better for my diet than red bean cakes—beautifully fresh pak choy, string beans, and spring onions—and I was amazed at how much cheaper they are here and how much you get for a dollar. I paid three dollars for a bag of vegetables that would have set me back about eight pounds in London, that is, eleven dollars. New York wasn't so bad.

Later that night I found red bean cakes, exactly like my mother's, in a Guyanese restaurant in Brooklyn. In London I get red bean cakes in Chinatown but not in Guyanese restaurants. In New York I do not find them in Chinatown but in a Guyanese restaurant in Brooklyn. As I ate the cake I felt I had arrived in New York but the journey I took to get here was one in which I had to negotiate a chain of cultural translations to get "home"—and home in New York could only be symbolized by finding my mother's red bean cake.

AUTHOR BIOGRAPHY

Jan Lo Shinebourne was born in and grew up in Guyana. She has lived in London since 1970 and works there as a freelance writer, lecturer, editor, and critic. She holds a master's degree in Contemporary English Studies from the University of London and is completing a doctorate in creative writing at the University of East Anglia in the United Kingdom. She is also completing her third novel, Water Table. *Her first novel,* Timepiece *(Peepal Tree Press, Leeds, 1986), won the Guyana Prize for a first novel. Her second novel is* The Last English Plantation *(Peepal Tree Press, 1988). She is also a short story writer; her stories have appeared in several journals and anthologies including* Best West Indian Stories *(Longmans, 1982),* Her True True Name *(Heinemann, 1989),* Caribbean New Wave *(Heinemann, 1990),* Leave to Stay *(Virago, 1996),* Trinidad and Tobago Review *(Port of Spain, Trinidad),* Wasafiri *(London), and* Everywoman *(London). She has also written reviews of fiction, drama, and academic works and has published academic essays in* Kyk-Over-Al *(Georgetown, Guyana),* SpareRib *(London),* Race Today *(London),* Southall Review *(London),* New Beacon Review *(London),* Saturday Times Review *(London), and* Macomere *(U.S.). She is European associate editor of* Macomere, *the journal of the Association of Caribbean Women Writers and Scholars.*

33

Archipelago

Raissa Nina Burns

I/me as location
Here
i am happening

In Portland Japanese Gardens.
I am three.
I am the color of old paper.
Inuit eyes in the American Northwest.
In Mama's dark arms,
in a red-yellow-blue padded jacket.

I am mixed Indo bones
in Leonie's *kabaya*.
My name is carved in Dutch letters
in a Chinese graveyard.
I am my great-great-grandmother.
I served a thousand cups of coffee on my dwarf's head.
Come, drink with me a while.
Let the black drops fall
blood again on this old stone.

I/me as location
Here
i am happening

I wear purple cotton pants.
I dance
in Marken Square
in a bonnet over braids. I
slide my brown little hand into a Dutch white one.

I am my great-grandmother Jeanne's fingers,
dusty knots of pins in a lame lap.
I knit,
under over under over,
in a camp in Java for whites and half-whites.
So many bras are made in wartime,
when your daughter's face turns army keys,
when she has slipped out to sell opals
from behind a high, high wall.

I/me as location
Here
i am happening

I am my grandmother, Jeanne Eugenie,
meat in a Japanese oven,
the kind they use,
the metal box.
They put women in.
They bake us in the yard under noonday sun.
Keep small. I can't
hold all my body parts.
Don't touch the sides.

I/me as location
Here
i am happening

On a third-grade playground, obsessed
with my dark knees.
I kill their color by peeling the bark back,
by looking
straight ahead.

In London, last October.
I grow darker,
darker, darker
on a street
bathed in oil,
reflecting my face.
It is of a pygmy with a plated lip.
It is of a Bedouin with her feet in water,
a chain of islands touching under salt.
I ask an Englishman:

WHAT DO I LOOK LIKE?
WHERE DOES THIS BROWN CHEEK TELL YOU I'M FROM?

and a man with an umbrella says Italy and He says Greece and He says Algeria, Iran,
    Spain, Afghanistan and
even the Asians don't say Asia.

I am my mother, Irana,
my freckles
little scars of mixed race which teachers thought were dirt.
I came to the States at fourteen.
I was called "nigger."
I use my/oppressor's language
to comfort my three-quarter white American child.

I/me as location
Here
i am happening

I am blond rejection.
I sit on haunches and not on chairs.
IamsoawareofthebumponmynoseIamsoashamed.
I am the Portland Chink, who,
after driving down to California through the Cascades at age four,
became a Dirty Mexican.
I cry into all my dark arms.
I stay indoors at three P.M.,
when the streets flood with white schoolboys,
who still terrify me,
who might call me by my name.

AUTHOR BIOGRAPHY

Raissa Nina Burns was born in 1977 in Spokane, Washington, to an Indonesian European mother and a Jewish American father. She wrote "Archipelago" at age nineteen in the workshop of Los Angeles-area poet Cathy Colman. Also a visual artist, Raissa savors the materiality of text and is currently enrolled in the Creative Writing Program at University of California, Santa Cruz. She dedicates "Archipelago" to her foremothers.

34

De Oro

Bill Woo

Margrita,
you give me life
with your silky black hair
flowing like an ample river
and your brown skin
smooth and tender.

lava flow through my veins
when we touch
under the black pearl sky
my heart fluttering in the wind
your smell
hypnotizing.

We are immigrants,
you and I,
from Peru
by way of the Spanish galleon,
from the Middle Kingdom
on the wayward junk.

Why is it I love *Lomo Saltado*,
Ceviche,
and *Camaron Frito*?
And you Mongolian Beef,
cod in garlic sauce,
and brazed shrimp?

Dígame, ¿cuál es mejor?
Un menú especial
todos los platos esquisitos

de las comidas
y las vidas
el único Chifa Cantones Peruano

Catholicism, Buddhism
prayer candles, prayer wheels
the Pope, the Dalai Lama
the Virgin Mary, the Reclining Buddha
Heaven, Nirvana
does it matter?

We are the same
you and I
and the great universe
everything around us
rush on by
in the ebb of time.

AUTHOR BIOGRAPHY

Bill Woo is a first-generation Chinese American living in California. Born on the island of Taiwan, he grew up in Austria and in the former West Germany. He says, "Moving is a constant in my life, and writing is no different." Woo received a B.A. in economics from UCLA and an M.B.A. in marketing from Pepperdine University. He is working on a collection of poems and short stories.

35

Queen Mariachi

Gabriela Kinuyo Torres

I can be anything I want to be is what my papi tells me. And I believe him because I am a lot already. I am Japanese American, I am Mexican, and I live here in Los Angeles. I'm thinking that I want to be lots of other things too, though, like maybe a ballet dancer, a veterinarian, and maybe an astronaut. But now I'm thinking of two of my favorite things I want to be when I grow up.

I go to Nisei Week in Little Tokyo almost every year and dream of being the Nisei Week queen. I love going to the Nisei Week parade because it is so much fun. I get to eat California rolls—my mami's and my favorite kind of sushi—and I get to dance *ondo* with all the *ondo* dancers who wear long, bright-colored kimonos. We usually go with my grandma, who loves to listen to the taiko drummers and their huge loud drums that make my heart beat to their rhythm. I like to sit on Grandma's lap so that I can put her hand on my heart to make her see that I'm telling the truth. Grandma always buys *mochi* balls, which I like to chew slowly, feeling their sticky doughiness in my mouth.

But mostly I just go to see the Nisei Week queen. The Nisei Week queen always wears a big pink ribbon and a crown, and gets to ride on a big white float with other princesses. I got to meet the Nisei Week queen one year because Grandpa Funakoshi won some award and got a fancy dinner at a big fancy hotel for being a "good man in the community," Mami said. She was really beautiful and looked like a real queen with her crown, which had a million shiny diamonds on it. I wondered how she kept it balanced on her perfect head and long, graceful neck. After the award ceremony I went up to her and gave her a picture I drew of her while I was supposed to be eating my fancy dinner—and she loved it. She even took a picture with me. She told me I was very pretty and that I must be Japa 'cause all Japa kids were pretty. I couldn't believe it. She said I was pretty. She said when I grow up I can be a Nisei Week queen, too.

When I go stay with *abuelita* and *abuelito* in Guadalajara I become a singing star. Not just any kind of singing star, either. I want to be a mariachi and bolero singer. I love mariachi songs 'cause you gotta have a lot of feeling. "You gotta sing like your heart hurts," my papi says. My favorite song is "Volver." Whenever I hear it, on the radio or at a mariachi concert or even at a Cinco de Mayo celebration in Los Angeles—my papi and I sing it at the top of our lungs as we sway side to side.

Whenever I go to Mexico for Christmas there is always a great performance. All my *tía abuelas*, my *abuelita's* four sisters, come over to *tía* Coty's house the night before Christmas day with their families. All of my eight cousins become now more like eighteen with the extra cousins, and so we run around chasing each other and hiding. There's lots of talking and loud laughing, mostly by *abuelito* who sits at the head of the table. He laughs in loud explosions as he jokes with his sons-in-law, nephews, and brothers-in-law and bounces a grandkid he's caught and plopped onto his lap. In the kitchen you hear high-pitched laughter and smell such delicious smells—the kind that make your stomach talk. My *abuelita's* specialty is *posole*, and my *tía* Nena has brought her famous sweet tamales from home. After the huge and delicious dinner, my *abuelita* and her sisters get ready to sing. *Tía* Laura brings out her guitar, and they all begin to sing in high sweet voices. They start with Christmas songs and end with boleros. My favorite is "Sabor a Mi," which is also my *abuelita's* favorite. She pulls me onto her big cushiony lap, and I sing it with her.

Mariana with her gelled-back braids and pink frilly dress, who is always whining, once pulled her eyes back at me after I had finished singing. She called me a *gringa mugrosa* and stomped away. When I told Papi about it, he said that I was special and that Mariana was just jealous. I felt better after that and gave Mariana the dirtiest look I could until she finally had to say she was sorry. She said I sang prettily, and would I like to play with her kitty, Casia? We were friends again until she saw the baby doll I got from Papi that could shut its eyes, and she tried to steal it from me. That's when I decided she was just plain mean. When I'm not in Mexico I sing all the songs I can remember while I'm in the bathtub and think of my *abuelita* and her wide smile.

So right now I'm confused about what I want to be. Should I be the Nisei Week queen and wear a big crown of diamonds, or should I be a famous mariachi singer and get to wear those tight long skirts with studs on the side and a big sombrero? Maybe I'll be both and sing "Sabor a Mi" as I ride down the street on the big white float. Yeah, that's just what I'll do. I'll even let Mariana be one of my princesses.

MY HOMES

"This is our new house?," I ask as I glare at the brick-red, crooked, tired wooden house. My papi smiles funny, making his beard spread across his face.

"It's not that bad," he answers, crossing the jungle of tall dead grass and candy wrappers that's supposed to be our front lawn. Ericka, my step-mother, brushes the back of her hand over her sweaty brown eyebrow and says, "All we need to do is decorate the house, and you'll feel right at home." Home. I'd always been happy living the way I did—with my mami one day and with Papi and Ericka the next. That was until Eddie Spaghetti, my next-door neighbor from Mami's house, the one who had a heart-shaped birthmark on his stomach, said that it was "weird" that my mami and papi got along the way that they did. He said that I should be living with my mami all the time and only get to see my papi on the weekends, like he did. He said he was going to call the cops on us. I would scrunch down in my papi's "green machine" every time I saw a cop car after that. They never caught us, but I still thought that something was wrong with our little family, that everyone got along so well. And here I am moving into another house with Papi and Ericka.

The house is so small that I can walk from the front of the house to the back, passing through all of the rooms, in twenty-three regular steps. The brown living room carpet is lighter in some places and darker in other places, like a really old teddy bear might look. The knobs on the kitchen sink both say "C." "Cold and *caliente*," my papi jokes. I smile, trying to feel good about our new home. While reluctantly helping to unload the few things that we have out of the green machine, I check out our street for any bikes, handballs, or scooters, but there are no signs of any kids. I'm sitting in one of our ancient wood-and-straw chairs whose seat has such a big hole that my tiny *nalgas* are peeking out the bottom when Ericka says "Gabi, the next-door neighbor girls want to know if you want to play handball with them." Butterflies get loose in my stomach. Ericka must have spotted some kids and told them which I was the new kid on the block, the one without any friends. I run and look in the dirty bathroom mirror to see a dark-skinned Asian looking girl with baby fat that never seems to leave. Ericka lets me borrow her long black skirt that I love because of the way it blows out when I turn, and off I go to make friends.

A tall girl with big rosy cheeks and pretty brown eyes smiles at me from her snow-white front porch. "My name's Beverly. Do you like handball?" We were already playing for a while, with my skirt constantly sneaking off my thin hips, when another girl comes out of the back door of their much bigger house. It's Cindy, Beverly's sister. She giggles behind an open hand at my tripping over my skirt. We take a break to drink Kool-Aid, and the sisters ask me questions, Cindy in her quiet way and Beverly in her loud, funny way. What is my step-mother, Jewish? What is that weird mole-looking thing growing from under her nose with all the hair sticking out of it? Did all step-moms have them? You're Japanese and Mexican! That's soooo cool! What kind of Hello Kitty stuff did I have? That much! (giggle giggle). Daddy's home.

Beverly stands up to go into their big white house, and Cindy wipes her lipstick-stained mouth with the sleeve of her shirt. I get nervous and follow them into their house. "Hi Daddy," they say in unison. I smile nervously at him and am going to say what a nice house he has when, without a glance at me, he barks "Where's your mother?" He walks, all red and sweaty, toward the bathroom. We stand in the kitchen like statues in a museum as the loud, angry voice of their father's yells at their mother behind a closed door. I see their mother come into the kitchen, a scared mouse, and immediately start to cook some meat from their big, perfectly white refrigerator. The man growls "Beverly, Cindy!" Then they are the scared mice. I hear the bathroom door slam, then I hear their father's voice booming through the huge house. "Did you brush your teeth this morning! You didn't, did you." Then I hear the slaps and the high-pitched cries. I look at their mother to see her calmly cutting some bright red tomatoes, totally ignoring what is going on around her. I run out of the immense, clean white house, tripping on my skirt and unnoticed by the mother, to my home. My papi greets me at the door of our lazy falling home, kisses me, and asks how my handball game went. I hug my papi's familiar belly with its comforting baby fat tires, and tell him everything. He listens, smiling at the funny parts, frowning at the scary parts, then he hugs me without saying a word. Ericka comes into the room warmly smiling at us, saying that dinner is ready. Suddenly, I am happy in my old tiny house and all its problems. It is my home.

DESPEINADOS

I have distinct memories about the different types of hair in my family. My mami's hair is midnight black and is tough and prickly when you rub it against your face. When I was little I would crawl into her bed on cold nights and cuddle up against her, playing with her hair with one hand and sucking the thumb of the other hand. I liked the sleek feel of her hair as it coiled about my fingers. Ericka has short, thin, flat coffee-brown hair that never curls. Even on hers and Papi's wedding day, she could not get her hair to conform to the hot curlers. My uncle Jerry had a mass jungle of wild snake curls. Mami told me of how once he had dyed his hair to such an extreme color of orange that everyone had to put sunglasses on just to look at him. Mami said that another friend of theirs looked like Desi Arnez, so they'd call that friend and my uncle Jerry Lucy and Desi. I remember the lightness of his hair as it rested on my tear-streaked face when my papi lost consciousness of the world. My uncle Jerry had hugged me then as if he would never let me go, as if I was the only person in the world, as though he could feel the terrible pain inside. Then I remember the way his hair had turned totally white and perfectly straight when we went to take care of him, almost exactly a year later. This time it was Jerry who was leaving us, but not like Papi had, this time it was another hateful disease called AIDS.

Then there's my papi's hair. I remember seeing pictures of my papi as a boy in his Mexican school army uniform. I couldn't believe he had once been absolutely bleach blond because his hair was such a dark dirty-brown at the time. Papi's hair was crazy like he was. He never liked to brush his shoulder-length hair, so he would hide its craziness under a wild-colored beret, only usually a tangled mass would escape and peek out at you from underneath. My mami would complain, Ericka would complain, but he would not cut his hair. I remember when my papi had decided that he could probably fly if he carried a sheet with its bottom tied to his sneakers on a windy day. I had dared him to do it. I can still see him, and his messy hair following him, as he ran down our street with one of our sheets.

That's why I cried when he asked me to shave it all off for him. He said it was either that or his hair would be coming off in clumps because of the chemotherapy he was getting for his cancer. I had shaved his head, and he had rewarded me by making me laugh with his impersonation of Sinead O'Connor. Sometimes between chemotherapies his hair would grow back, but it never would fully grow back because of the treatments. So I would kiss him on his bald head when I left his house to go to mami's, leaving a kiss mark on him. The last memory I have of my papi is of his hair, about how I buried my face in what little hair he had in disbelief of what the doctor said: that my papi was dead. I remember feeling the softness of his thin hair and smelling the rich smell of the last shampoo he had used. And then I kissed him good-bye.

My hair is a good mixture of my parents' hair. It's black like my mami's but thin and soft like my papi's. It used to be a lot weaker. I was bald for a long time as a baby, my mami has told me. Now it is stronger and thicker. I know my papi's watching me with his hair all wild again. I know my uncle Jerry is up there, too, with his hair a big curly mass of orange. That's why I don't comb my hair sometimes. That way they know that I know that they are there.

AUTHOR BIOGRAPHY

Gabriela Kinuyo Torres is a Japanese Mexican American woman majoring in American Studies at the University of California, Santa Cruz. Her loves include going salsa clubbing with her beautiful and normal pero un poquito acelerada salsera mami and spending time dancing and talking with her best friends, Corey, Sharlene, and Zoreisha. Her dreams for the future include, but are not limited to, winning the lottery, ridding herself of her many inhibitions, traveling around the world several times, having many fun and passionate love affairs (she can't help it, she's a Scorpio), finally settling down with a strong and gentle man to raise children in Hawaii, and spending all her time with loved ones doing things she loves. She'd like to thank her mami, Kay, for giving her the strength and confidence to be truly happy; her step-mami Ericka, for the laughter and helpful advice; her lovely tap dancing grandma for her love and tuna noodle casseroles; her "sistas" Beverly and Cindy; Rechele, Michi, and Cuba for showing Gabi her spirituality and sensuality; and her princely papi, Cesar, for his silliness and love and who she dreams of seeing again one day.

36

The Valley of the Dead Air

Gary Pak

The day after Jacob Hookano died, that old hermit who had lived at the very end of Waiola Valley, a bad air from the ocean came in and lingered over the land. The residents of the valley thought a that Kona wind had brought in that rotten smell from the mangroves and mudflats of the coastal area, and they waited impatiently for another wind to take the smell away.

As Leimomi Vargas said succinctly, "Jus' like old Jacob wen fut and dah fut jus' stayin' around."

And stay around it did, for weeks. There seemed no end. The residents prayed for that new wind to blow the obstinate smell away, but no wind came, and the air became stagnant and more foul as if the valley were next to an ancient cesspool that had suddenly ruptured after centuries of accumulations. The malodor permeated the wood of the houses, it tainted the fresh clothes hung to dry, and it entered the pores of everyone, making young and old smell bad even after a good scrubbing. The love lives of the residents became nonexistent.

"We gotta do somet'ing 'bout dis *hauna*," Joseph Correa complained. The retired sewers worker from the city and county sat on a chair under the eaves of an old abandoned store that fronted the main road.

"Yeah, but what?" said Bobby Ignacio. He turned his gaunt, expressionless face toward Correa, then returned to his meditation of birds eating the ripened fruits of a lichee tree across the road.

"You know, Bobby," Correa said in a voice shaded ominously, "I betchu dah gov'ment is behind all dis. Look how long dis *hauna* stay heah. Long time already. If was jus' one nat'ral t'ing, dah wind already blow 'em away."

Ignacio, a truck farmer up the road in the valley, spat disconsolately into the wild grass growing on the side of the store.

"But I tell you dis, Bobby. I betchu one day dah gov'ment goin' come down heah and dey goin' brag how dey can take dis *hauna* away. And den they goin' take 'em away. But I betchu little while aftah dat, dey goin' come back and try ask us for do dem one favor. You watch." Correa nodded his head. "No miss."

The farmer shrugged his narrow shoulders. "But you know what everybody saying?"

"Who everybody?"

"Everybody."

"So what everybody saying?"

"Dey saying old Jacob dah one doing all dis."

The old retiree nervously stretched out his tired legs, his head twitched a few times, then he looked out languidly toward the mango trees across the road.

"I nevah had no problems with old Jacob," Correa said weakly. "I was always good to him. I nevah talk stink 'bout him or anything li' dat."

The smell persisted, and somehow it infected the rich, famous soil of the valley. The earth began to emit a terrible odor of rotten fish. While plowing one corner of his sweet potato field, Tats Sugimura uncovered a hole full of fish scales and fish bones. He didn't think anything of it until his wife complained to him later how fishy everything smelled. The bad smell of the valley had numbed his nose so Tats couldn't smell anything worth shit now. His wife, on the other hand, had a super-sensitive nose and she often would sniff the air in her kitchen and know exactly what the Rodriguez family was cooking a quarter of a mile down the road.

"Tats, you wen' dump some rotten fish around here or what?" she said. Sugimura shook his head. He wasn't the talking type, even with his wife. "Den whas dat stink smell?"

He thought of telling her about the fish scales and bones, then he thought that perhaps a bunch of stray cats had had a feast in that corner of his field. The fish were probably tilapia or catfish the cats had caught in the nearby stream. But he was tired from working all day under the hot sun and in the stifling humid air, and he didn't have the energy to describe to his wife what he had seen. The fish scales and fish bones were unimportant, and he shrugged his thin, wiry shoulders and said nothing.

But something bad was in the soil. When Tats and the other sweet potato farmers began harvesting their produce a few days later, they found abnormally small sweet potatoes, some having the peculiar shape of a penis.

"How dah hell we goin' sell dis kine produce?" complained Earl Fritzhugh, a part-Hawaiian sweet potato farmer. "Dey goin' laugh at us. So small. And look at dis one. Look like one prick!"

"Somet'ing strange goin' on in dis valley," said Darryl Mineda, another farmer. "Get dah story goin' around dat old Jacob doin' all dis to get back."

"Get back at who?" Fritzhugh asked irately.

"At us."

Fritzhugh looked at Mineda incredulously. "At us? Why dat old Hawaiian like get back at us fo'? He wen live by himself. Nobody wen bother him."

Mineda shook his head. "Somebody tol' me all dah land in dis valley used to be his family's land, long time ago. Den dah Cox family wen come in and take dah land away from his family. Somet'ing 'bout Jacob's family not paying dah land tax or water tax or somet'ing li' dat, and dah haole wen pay instead."

"But what got to do with us? I not responsible. Dah haole wen do it. Not me."

Mineda shrugged his shoulders.

"Eh, I was good to dah old man," Fritzhugh said. "I nevah bother him. When he used to go up and down dis road, he nevah said not'ing to me, so I never say not'ing to him." He paused. "But I wonder who goin' get his land now he *ma-ke*. He no mo' children, eh?"

Mineda shrugged his shoulders again. "Maybe das why," Mineda said.

"Maybe das why what?"

"Maybe das why he got all salty. Nobody pay attention to him. Nobody talk story with him. Nobody go bother him."

"So what you goin' do? Dah buggah dead already."

"What . . . you no believe in dah spirits?"

"Eh, no fut around."

"No. I asking you one simple question. You believe in dah kine Hawaiian spirits or what?"

"Yeah, I believe in dat kine," Fritzhugh said, looking warily across his sweet potato field then back to Mineda's furrowed face. "But so what? Why . . . you think he wen curse dah valley or what?"

Mineda looked at his feet. He was silent for a while. "Crazy," he said finally. "All of dis. And how we going sell our produce to dah markets?"

A white car with the state emblem on the doors came by the store one day. Correa sat up and stared into the car curiously. Then he nodded his head. "You see, Bobby, you see," he said. "What I tol' you. Dah gov'ment goin' come down heah and try get somet'ing from us. I tol' you all along, dis *hauna* was from dah gov'ment. What I tol' you?"

Ignacio leaned forward, squinting his eyes to read the emblem. "Department of Agriculture," he muttered. He slouched back into his seat.

"What I tol' you, eh, Bobby? Look, dah Japanee going come out and he goin' try smooth talk us. You watch."

"Fritzhugh wen call dem fo' come down and try figure out whas wrong with dah dirt."

"Look dah buggah, nice clean cah, air conditionah and everyt'ing," Correa said sardonically, pretending he had not heard what his friend had said.

The man got out of the car and went up to the two men.

"Yes, sir," Correa said officiously. "What can I do fo' you today?"

The man crimped his nose at the fetid air. "You know where I can find Earl Fritzhugh?"

"Yeah-yeah. He live up dah valley. Whas dis fo'?" Correa asked.

"He called me about some problems you farmers having over here. Something about the soil."

"Not dah soil," Correa said. "Dah air. You cannot smell how *hauna* dah air is?"

The man nodded his head. "Yes . . . yes, the air kind of stink. Smell like rotten fish."

"Smell like somebody wen unload one big pile shit in dah middle of dah valley."

The man from the state grinned.

"So why you come," Correa asked pointedly, "and not one guy from dah Department of Air?"

The man from the state looked at Correa with dying interest. "You can tell me where Earl Fritzhugh lives?" he asked Ignacio.

"Yeah, brah," Ignacio said, pointing up the valley road. "You go up this road, maybe one mile into the valley. You goin' pass one big grove bamboo on the right side. The farm right after that going be the Fritzhugh farm. No can miss 'em."

The man thanked him, then got back into the car and left.

"You better call up Fritzhugh and tell him dah Japanee comin' up question him," Correa said.

Ignacio waved the flies away from his face, then spat into the grass.

There was nothing wrong with the soil, the state worker told them a few days after he had come up and taken samples to the downtown laboratory. Nothing was wrong. The farmers left that meeting with remorse. Then what was wrong with the crops?

A day later heavy rains came, and for three days the whole valley was inundated with torrents and flash floods. The residents welcomed the storm, for they believed that the rains would wash the soil of the inscrutable poison and cleanse the air of the bad smell. But came the fourth day and a bright sun, and when the residents smelled the air again the odor was still there, now more pronounced than ever and denser. It was as if the storm had nurtured the smell like water nourishes plants.

"You did anyt'ing to old Jacob?" people were now asking each other. And the answer was always, "No . . . but did you?" And when the informal polling was completed, it was determined that everybody in the valley had left old Jacob alone. But they all cast accusing looks at one another, as if everyone else but themselves was responsible for the curse that old Jacob seemed to have thrown over the once peaceful and productive valley.

One morning a haole salesman came to the doorsteps of one of the houses.

"Heard you folks here were having problems with fires," he said in a jovial voice, a Midwestern accent.

"No," Tats Sugimura's wife said sourly. "Not fires. The smell. You cannot smell dah stink smell?"

The haole laughed. "Well, you know what they say," he said.

"No, what dey say?" Harriet said.

"They say that if you can't see it, then you can surely smell it." He laughed again. Harriet was about to ask who had said that when the salesman segued quickly into a sales pitch about a new fire prevention system his company was now offering in the area. And for a limited time, he concluded, they would install the entire system without charge.

"We not interested," Harriet Sugimura said. "Go away. Go talk to somebody else."

"But you don't understand," the salesman said. "Along with this fire prevention system comes our new, revolutionary, home odors maintenance system. And for a limited time, we will give it to you free if you purchase our fire prevention system. Here . . . smell this."

The salesman took out a small aerosol can and sprayed it inside the Sugimuras' house from the front door. Instantly, the spray cleared the air of the ugly smell that Harriet had almost gotten used and the whole living room smelled fresh like roses.

"Your system can do this?" she gasped with delight.

"Yes, and more. Why, because our system is computer controlled, you don't have to lift a finger. Everything will be done automatically."

Harriet's face beamed with promise. It had been so long since she smelled the scent of flowers. "So how much is it?"

"Retail, it sells for eight hundred and fifty dollars. But for this limited offer, we will sell it to you for two hundred and fifty dollars."

"Two hundred fifty!"

"Well, if you know of a friend or neighbor or family who would want this system, too, I can give it to you for two twenty-five."

"Hmm. Wait, let me call my neighbor."

Soon the entire valley was buzzing on the telephone lines, talking about that new machine that would wipe out the bad smell in the homes. If the valley was going to stay bad smelling, that didn't mean the homes had to have that smell, too. So almost every other household bought one of those systems, and the salesman, being a nice guy, even reduced the price by another twenty-five dollars, prepayment, stating emphatically that the company was now making only a twenty dollar profit from each unit sold. The residents waited impatiently for that big brown truck that the haole promised would bring the fire-prevention-home-odor-maintenance system, and they waited past the promised three-day delivery period, but the truck never came.

The smell worsened to the point that every other person in the valley was getting a constant headache.

"Somet'ing has to be done about the smell," Ignacio said. "If we cannot do anyt'ing about it, den we gotta take dis to the state."

"Nah, how you can do dat?" Correa asked. "Dah state already wen say dey cannot do not'ing about it."

"But something gotta be done," Ignacio said.

"Something gotta be done," Harriet Sugimura said to her husband sheepishly, a few days after her husband, for the first time in seven years, had lost his temper when she told him how she had spent their tax refunds.

"If this smell continue on, I'm getting the hell out of this valley," Pat Fritzhugh said to her husband.

"Me, too," Fritzhugh replied.

"You know what the problem is?" Leimomi Vargas said to her neighbor, Elizabeth Kauhale. "The problem is nobody honest wit' everybody else. I betchu somebody wen get the old man real angry. Really angry. And das why he wen curse the valley wit' dis stink fut smell before he *ma-ke*."

"I think you right, Lei," Elizabeth said sadly. "We gotta be honest wit' each other. Das dah only way."

"Then maybe the old man going take back the curse," Lei said.

"Maybe we should go get one kahuna bless dah friggin', stinkin' place," Elizabeth said.

"You nevah know the old man was one kahuna?"

"I know, but he dead."

"Still yet."

"But I t'ink you right. We gotta get to the bottom of this. Find all the persons responsible for him cursing the valley. Then make them offer somet'ing to the old man's spirit. Or somet'ing like that. Whachu t'ink?"

So from that conversation the two women went door-to-door, struggling with the others to be honest. For starts, Lei told about the time when she was a small girl and she went up to the old man's place and stole an egg from one of his hens. And Elizabeth said one time she saw her brother throw a rock at the old man as he was climbing the road to his hermitage, and because her brother was now living on the Big Island she would take responsibility for his wrong action. Then slowly, the others began to unfold their stories of wrongdoings against the old man, even Joseph Correa, who admitted that he wronged old Jacob when they were young men growing up in the valley and wooing the same girl and he had told her parents that Jacob didn't have a prick and that he was a *mahu*. About the only person who hadn't sinned against Jacob was Tats Sugimura, who lived the next lot down from Jacob's. In fact, he had been kind to Jacob, giving him sweet potatoes and letting him use his water at the far end of the field (where Tats had found the fish scales and bones, 'though Tats couldn't figure out that that was where Jacob used to clean his fish).

So they organized representatives from each household of the valley to go up the road and pay their homage to Jacob's vindictive soul. They went to his place one late Saturday afternoon when the sun was beginning to set behind the mountains, parking their cars and trucks at the end of the dirt road where the road turned into a trail that led into Jacob's forbidden plot of land. They brought taro, sweet potatoes, corn, watermelons, yams, several 'awa roots, a dozen cans of meat, a basket of freshly laid eggs, a tub of fish and another tub of crawling crabs, loads of ti leaves, bunches of green bananas, and a fifth of good bourbon so that Jacob could wash all of the offerings down. They silently climbed the narrow path that the valley road turned into, winding up through dense brush and trees towards old Jacob's place. Lei was the only one in the contingent who had been up to Jacob's place before, but that was years and years ago and all she had seen were the dilapidated chicken coops, and everyone's senses were suspended in fear, not knowing what they might expect or see at the end of the trail.

Finally, they reached a flat clearing where they saw a sweeping view of the precipitous mountain range. They searched anxiously for his house until finally Elizabeth Kauhale found it hanging a few feet above the ground, with vines attaching it to a giant *kukui* tree. It was made out of scrap wood and looked like a big crate with a small opening on the side where a tattered rope ladder hung down. The box house began to swing and there was heard hollow laughter coming from within. The entourage retreated a few steps, their faces blanched with the expectation that Jacob's ghost might leap out after them. The laughing stopped, and they quickly dropped their offerings in an untidy heap under Jacob's pendular house, not daring to glance up the rope ladder. Then, hurriedly, they filed down the trail.

When they reached the bottom they stopped, looked back, and made sure everyone who had gone up was back down. After they finished counting heads they ambled off to their cars, murmuring among themselves how they hoped things would come out all right and the smell would leave the valley. Then, suddenly, there came loud, crackling laughter from deep in the valley that made the plants and trees shake. Everyone crammed into whosesoever's car was nearest. They raced down the road and did not stop until, breathless and terrified and worried for their very lives, they were down at the old abandoned store, and here they sat speechless until Leimomi Vargas shouted at the top of her lungs, "I think dis is all silly—us guys getting our pants scared off our 'okoles!'"

Embarrassed smiles came upon everyone's face and there was heard some nervous laughter. Someone suggested that they celebrate in the memory of old Jacob, and without further ado they voted unanimously to go back to their homes and get what they had to eat and bring it all back down to the abandoned store where they would party for the rest of the night. So the people who were in the wrong cars got out and into the cars they had originally gone up the road with, and they all went back home and took boxes of chicken or beef or squid or whatever they had out of the freezers and thawed them under warm running water. The Ignacios brought down a pig Bobby had slaughtered that morning; the Fritzhughs brought a big barrel of fish their oldest son had caught that day; and Tats Sugimura trucked down a load of his miniature, mutant sweet potatoes; and the others went into backyards and lopped off hands of bananas and picked ears of corn and mangoes and carried off watermelons from the fields; and they brought all that food and all the beer and whiskey they had in their homes down to the store. Earl Fritzhugh and his two sons chopped up a large *kiawe* tree and made a roaring fire in the empty lot next to the store, and everyone pitched in and cooked the copious amounts of food in that sweet-smelling charcoal inferno. Bobby Ignacio and friends—Earl Fritzhugh, Fritzhugh's youngest son, Sonny Pico's two boys and his daughter, Tats Sugimura's brother, and Joseph Correa—brought down their ukes and guitars and a washtub bass and provided the entertainment that lasted exactly three nights and two days. And when the festivities finally ended—the smoke from the *kiawe* fire was still smoldering strongly— everyone at the old store began hugging each other and then meandered off to their homes.

But before they fell into deep sleep, Earl Fritzhugh and his wife made love for the first time since the smell began putrefying the air of the valley. And so did Tats and Harriet Sugimura. And there were at least a dozen or so illegitimate liaisons committed at that festive time—for one, Elizabeth Kauhale saw her teenage son go in to the bush with Bobby Ignacio's willowy daughter—which was probably the reason why in weeks ahead there would be more festivities when three of those liaisons would be legitimized and why months later, on the same day, there would be added three new members to the community.

And before he slept old Joseph Correa dragged his feet to the old cemetery next to the clapboard Catholic Church, and there he laid a bunch of wild orchids on the grave of his beloved wife, Martha, and he sat down on the soft, wet ground, 'though it was a struggle for his brittle old legs to do so, and he sang that song that was a favorite of his wife—"Pua Lilia"—because his wife's middle name was Lilia, and he had often sung that song to her when she was alive and he had sung that song to her when she was dying. And after that song he gazed up the valley and apologized once again to his former friend, Jacob Hookano, for saying those damaging things about him in the past. "But she was worth fighting for," he said with a choke in his voice. "And you can see, my friend," he added with a touch of jealousy, "that you with her right now."

When the people of the valley finally woke up the next morning or the next afternoon or whenever, the first thing they noticed was the smell: the fresh clean smell of the ocean. It was the smell of salt, and the warm winds that carried it over the valley swept up to the highest ridges of the mountains, and there the warm air married with the cold dampness and thick clouds formed, and soon, with the shift in the trades, rain began to fall over the silent, peaceful valley.

AUTHOR BIOGRAPHY

Gary Pak is on the writing faculty at Kapi-olani Community College, Honolulu. His book-length collection of short stories, The Watcher of Waipuna, *from which "The Valley of the Dead Air" is taken, won the 1993 Association for Asian American Studies National Book Award for Literature. He has also published a novel,* A Ricepaper Airplane *(University of Hawaii Press, 1998).*

37

Self-portrait Dressed in a Mexican Costume

Tomoyo Hiroishi

I painted this self-portrait of myself dressed as a Mexican in 1994. I had just arrived in the United States to attend college, and it was the first time I had been away from Mexico. I was questioning my roots in both Japan and Mexico, but I realized that I missed Mexico most of all. I longed to be a Mexican. Even though I was raised by Japanese parents who had introduced me to one of the most beautiful cultures in the world, I missed the scenery and smells of the country I grew up in. Coming to the United States allowed me to realize the richness of Mexican culture. When I closed my eyes I saw the mountains and bright colors that illuminate us, the people of Mexico. I was inspired to draw and paint the memories of my home country and of my childhood. The reflection I saw in the mirror was that of an Asian girl in Mexican clothes.

I am wearing an off-white indigenous traditional dress I brought from home. The stripes in the center, composed of different primary colors, suggest a typical Mexican color palette—mainly red, blue, and yellow. The red scarf draped around my arms is worn by many Indian women as a shawl, a decoration for their hair, or a belt to tie around their waist. I am holding a Mexican ceramic coffee cup. A cup and a plate from Puebla appear in the foreground.

Self-portrait Dressed in a Mexican Costume, color, 24″ × 35″. Reprinted courtesy of Tomoyo Hiroishi.

38

La Niña del Rebozo— The Young Girl in a Shawl

Luis Nishizawa

La Niña del Rebozo, 1949, 96 cm × 72 cm. Photograph by Javier Hinojosa. Reprinted courtesy of Luis Nishizawa.

285

39

Her Body: A Stage, An Altar
The Performance Art of Astrid Hadad

Astrid Hadad

Edited and translated by Roshni Rustomji-Kerns

AUTHOR BIOGRAPHY

Astrid Hadad was born in Chetumal, Quintana Roo, Mexico, and is a graduate of the Centro Universitario de Teatro. She has participated in several theatrical productions including director Jesusa Rodriguez's very successful adaptation of Mozart's *Don Giovanni*. Ms. Hadad has produced shows such as *Nostalgia Arrabalera y Del Rancho a la Ciudad* (Suburban Nostalgia and From the Rancho to the City) in which she performed her own versions of traditional rancheras and boleros. She also produced and acted in the musical tragicomedy *La Occisa o Luz* (The Victim or the Light), based on the life of Mexican singer Lucha Reyes. She has formed a musical group, Los Tarzanes, which performs her works including *La Mujer Ladrina* (The Barking Woman) and *La Mujer del Golfo* (The Woman from the Gulf). Her best-known work is *Heavy Nopal*.

Astrid Hadad has acted in telenovelas and in a film. Her first CD of the popular music of Mexico was titled *AY*, and her second CD, *Corazon Sangrante* (Bleeding Heart), was made into a video under the direction of Ximena Cuevas.

Ms. Hadad has performed her works and participated in theatrical and cultural festivals throughout Mexico, Europe, Canada, the United States of America, South America, Australia, and New Zealand. In 1995 she participated in the Second Festival of One Hundred Artists Against AIDS held in Mexico City.

The photographs included in this anthology exemplify Ms. Hadad's use of the multiple cultures and mythologies of Mexico in her theatrical art. In her

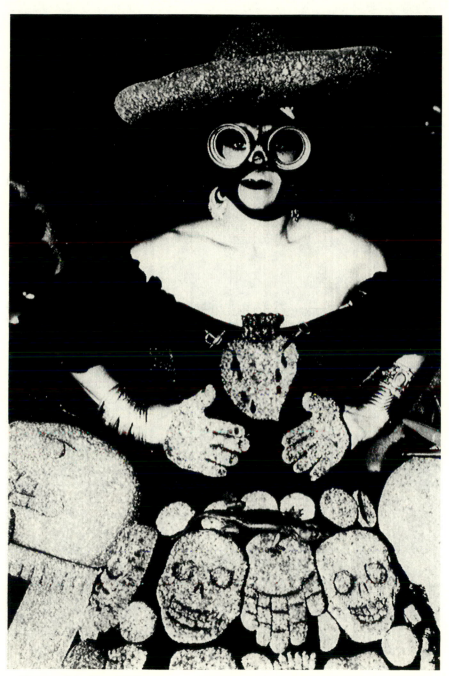

Photograph by Cheryl Bellows.

Photograph by Maritza López.

performances she takes traditional and contemporary musical themes—
mainly from the music of Mexico—and reconstructs them to highlight issues
such as the role of women in Mexican society and art. Besides using the lyrics
of songs, Astrid Hadad constructs scenery and wears multiple "costumes"
and masks, such as skirts depicting the ancient Goddess Cuatlique or the leg-
end of the birth of the cactus depicted with contemporary gas masks and outrageous "hats" with replicas of national monuments, in her sociopolitically
charged performace art. Olivier Debroise in a review of Astrid Hadad's works
wrote that Astrid Hadad's body becomes "not only the stage but also an altar.
On her shoulders she carries a baggage of myths, rites and images of the Mexican people. Somebody once described Astrid as a 'walking museum of popular cultures.' " In the notes to one of her CDs, Astrid Hadad expresses her
gratitude to the Virgin for giving her the power to present her own contradictions—a Mexicana, a Mayan, a Lebanese—in her work.

40

Hotel Room (Mayaro, Trinidad)

Rienzi Crusz

The third day of Genesis,
the waters—
and this shabby white room foretold.
With veins once salted by the Indian Sea,
the Sun-Man returns to himself,
to another sea presence.

Here, sepulchered,
two wooded stores resist the wind;
a room's slit louvered eyes
hesitate towards the sea,
but the sea glares in, rage anxious
for its breathing archives.

I am caught in ocean bestiary:
the polyp sounds its growing,
the coral chiseling,
twisting its white limbs;
a sudden confusion of water,
the flat-headed shark laughing,
thrashing in its water bed?
The shell in my palm screams,
I am on the lap of Mayaro's sea;

A kingfish grazes my elbows,
something jellied blows bubbles
under my nose; a sand crab is praying
on my bed, my feet tickle
to the five slits
on the sun dollar's face,

the mirror on the wall beckons:
my hair is seaweed,
I am wearing the marble eyes of the sail fish,
cheeks boasted with saltwater,
sea-palm leaves thick about my ears.

I retire, ghosted,
a fisherman in my skin,
my tired body netted, stretched
on a bed smelling of ocean, wet.
I am claimed.
Two ghosts now breathe heavily
in each other's arms
as the room drones in peace,
in its own sea ears.

MAYARO SEA SCULPTURE

4 July, 1972: from a rock
on Mayaro Beach, Trinidad,
I watch the waves break, rush
the yellow-grey shore;
how they froth to crocheted embroidery,
nibble at a beached boulder, dissolve
in quiet retreat.

Something must happen in time, I thought,
to this lone hunk of stone.
What will the sculptor make
of its black anonymity,
its bleached loneliness,
the juttings angular
like a freakish jaw?

I visit the spot daily
for two weeks
anxious to see the boulder diminish
to the salty caress of the sea.
Nothing, but a slippery wetness
on its skin, its shape
still squat as a lump.

July 4, 1982:
from the same rock, same Mayaro Beach,
I see a wave collapse, gush to shore,
spread a white foaming arm
'round a Buddha shape, smooth, squatting,
carved to deep comtemplation:
the nothingness of time, of space, of form?
The Enlightened One
with eyes still closed waiting
for my curious return.

THE INTERVIEW

Two TV cameras trained like guns,
   I, the Sun-Man,
your caressing eyes,
   and the countdown . . .

You coax me into beginnings,
   past inventions in the snow,
then deftly persuade deeper fires,
   my thin Canadian ice
to thaw in my throat,
   the maple leaf smudge in my passport.

I am in the mouth of the sun,
   the Immigrant Song,
how I hear the elephant in my sleep;
   white landscape in ruins,
I find my own, green forest, island sea;
   the ocelot's eye, the jambu bleeds,
my childhood dream
   in the claws of the sand crab.

And what shaped your book
   Flesh and Thorn?
Blood on the sun,
   the Scarlet Ibis blurred in the swamp,
how deceit crouched in the crotch,
   "love with his gift of pain".

Suddenly, I split the act in two,
   juggle two red balls,
the poem made, the poem becoming:
   I swim in your saucer eyes,
fingers search the curved fruit
   under your shirt,
I nose ebony configurations,
   dream the almond under the husk . . .

AUTHOR BIOGRAPHY

Rienzi Crusz was born in Sri Lanka and moved to Canada in 1965. He was edu-cated at the Universities of Ceylon, Sri Lanka; London, England; and Toronto and

Waterloo, Canada. His works have appeared in several Canadian and international journals and anthologies. He has published eight volumes of verse. His latest book is Insurgent Rain: Selected Poems 1976–1996 *(Toronto: Toronto South Asia Review, 1997).*

41

Ganesh

Feroza Jussawalla

I don't like to camp.
But I like to come up here,
To the top of the world,
On the high mesa,
Where every rock has an animal face,
Revered, replicated, resurrected.

There I saw Ganesh
In the sandstone
Among the Ostrich
And the Eagle
And the Dead Horse
The Native Americans wouldn't have recognized him
So, he remains unfaceted,
embedded in the shape of the rock.

But, I, saw him distinctly,
With his trunk going down
And turning upwards.
Could I have carved him out?
Should I have carved him out?

To carve him I must offer
The spirit of the rock
Tobacco
According to the Indians

At home they would have balked at tobacco,
Offering
Flowers and fragrant sandalwood.
But neither tobacco nor sandalwood being available,

Among the high desert scrub oak,
I leave him uncarved—
Near the Virgin of Chimayo,
Where he was already
In the spirit of that rock.

42

When Nana Died

Eileen Tabios

She was old enough to be my grandmother. She even looked like Nana: wrinkled cheeks, a permanent furrow on her brow, thinning white hair, a slightly stooped back, black polyester pants, an acrylic sweater whose sleeves ended too soon, and a smile indicating an eagerness to please. Her hands shook under my glare, pleading and raised defensively as I screamed at the top of my lungs "Starch! Starch! Starch!"

She had forgotten to starch the collars of my husband's shirts. In the back of the laundry, by a curtain thrust aside when I first started screaming, her son stood as still as a statue except for his eyes, which kept twitching between me and his mother. He knew I was attacking the old woman trembling in front of me. But like his mother he could not speak English well enough to discuss my problems, let alone calm me down—calm down a most important customer who unfailingly dropped off shirts to be hand laundered and ironed, six shirts a week, fifty two weeks a year for a pricey $3.75 a shirt. He could only stand there red faced, a tic pulsing under his left eye and breathing quickly through an open mouth.

As I continued to yell at his mother, my spirit rose and hovered over the scene. I had not seen my shimmering twin sister since I berated my father for once insisting that my husband, a lawyer, advise a distant cousin who had arrived illegally in the United States. "Immigration is not his specialty," I said truthfully. But when I added, "And I'm sick of these people we barely know trying to cadge free legal services," I felt my ears pop and my spirit float away. My spirit had a habit of leaving my body whenever she thought I was committing a shameful act; she would waft off into the air with, depending on the situation, an expression of sadness, disgust, or anger rippling on her translucent face.

As I screamed about the importance of stiff collars on my husband's 100 percent cotton shirts, my spirit again departed. Floating above the wall dryers, she pursed her lips and inclined her head at the son—a young teenager with hair cut raggedly across his forehead, a large pimple on the left side of his nose, and eyes so wide I could have counted the veins surrounding his pupils. The furrow in the middle of his brow seemed to deepen, as if he were aging visibly in front of my eyes.

I was not a bully. Indeed, I had always considered myself to be rather nice, polite, and especially respectful of people who were of my grandmother's age. But there I was, purple faced, shaking, hands clenched, and on the verge of saying *it* to the elderly Chinese woman. *It*. It—"Why don't you go back where you came from?"

I stopped my tirade only when, looking away from the boy whose chest began heaving behind his thin T-shirt, my eyes stumbled on a bare patch of pink and seemingly paper-thin skin at the center of his mother's scalp. It made my tongue rear, silenced me abruptly. The patch of flesh reminded me of my grandmother's funeral the previous day. After kissing Nana's forehead as she laly in her coffin, I had touched her hair. I remembered my disconcertment at feeling how her hair had become so sparse that my fingers could differentiate individual strands against the flesh of her scalp. They had felt like scars.

I turned from the laundry woman's bowed face—her quivering chin—and walked toward the exit. I halted once to say without turning around, "My husband will be back." As I opened the door, I sensed my words hanging in the air as if I had meant them as a threat, which only made me walk faster from their silence.

But I knew as I left the laundry that I would be the one to return. As soon as I could regain self-control, I would return to apologize. My grief at my grandmother's death was not the burden of the Chinese family, who I knew worked long hours to meet their rent. I knew they worked hard because we had spoken many times of the burdens of immigration and assimilation in slow, broken English punctuated with smiles and empathetic sighs. We had shared such a conversation just the previous week when I had dropped off the batch of shirts they had forgotten to starch. As for my grandmother, she had been the only person who had managed to soothe her American-born but distinctly Asian-looking granddaughter when I had raged at how the bullies of my childhood made me suffer. The bullies always yelled at me, "Ching. Chong. Chinee. Why don't you go back where you came from?" I was not Chinese, but to them all Asians looked alike.

Halting on a street corner, I sensed my tears attracting attention from the crowds enjoying the unseasonal warmth and cloudless sky of a winter day. But I continued to watch the sidewalk dampen at my feet. My grief over Nana's death needed more time to abate. And I also had to begin mourning the fact that last week had become part of quite a distant past.

AUTHOR BIOGRAPHY

Eileen Tabios is the author of a poetry collection, Beyond Life Sentences *(Anvil, 1998)* and Black Lightning: Poetry-in-Progress, *a collection of essays about Asian American poets (Asian American Writers Workshop [AAWW], 1998). She is editing* Dovelglion: The Selected Works Of Jose Garcia Villa *(Kaya Production, 1999). Editor of* the Asian Pacific American Journal, *she received a 1997 poetry grant from the Witter Bynner Poetry Foundation, as well as fellowships from the Virginia Center for the Creative Arts, Fundacion Valparaiso of Spain, and the Helene Wurlitzer Foundation in New Mexico. Her poetry, fiction, and essays have been published in the United States, the Philippines, Guam, and Canada, including in anthologies;* Flippin': Filipinos Writing on America *(AAWW, 1996);* Contemporary Fiction by Filipinos in America *(Anvil, 1998);* Poetry Nation *(Vehicule, 1998);* The Nuyorasian Anthology *(AAWW, 1998); and* Writers of the Information Age *(CrossConnect, 1996 and 1998).*

About the Editors

Roshni Rustomji-Kerns is the co-editor of *Blood into Ink: South Asian and Middle Eastern Women Write War* and the editor of *Living in America: Poetry and Fiction by South Asian American Writers*. She is Professor Emerita, Sonoma State University, California, and visiting scholar at the Center for Latin American Studies, Stanford University.

Rajini Srikanth teaches in the English department at University of Massachusetts Boston. She has published in the fields of Asian American studies, South Asian literature, literature of the American south, and diaspora studies. Her research interests lie in examining the political participation in South Asian Americans, the literature of diasporic Asian communities—particularly South Asian—and the relationship between arts and activism. She is co-editor of two anthologies, the award-winning *Contours of the Heart: South Asians Map North America* and *A Part yet Apart: South Asian Americans in Asian America*.

Leny Mendoza Strobel currently teaches at the Hutchins School of Liberal Studies and American Multicultural Studies Department at Sonoma State University, California. Her writings have appeared in *Filipino Americans: Transformation and Identity*, *Amerasia Journal*, *Paterson Literary Review*, *Pleaides*, *Toronto South Asia Review*, *The Other Side*, *Beyond White Noise*, and *Filipina Magazine*.